Cultivating Cultures of Thinking in Australian Schools

This book is a call to action for educators who seek to move beyond superficial learning and engage students in deeper, more meaningful thinking. At a time when education is dominated by standardisation and a crowded curriculum, this book champions a different path, prioritising student agency, curiosity, and thinking.

Grounded in the influential Cultures of Thinking™ approach developed by Dr. Ron Ritchhart from Project Zero at the Harvard Graduate School of Education, this book showcases real-life case studies from Australian classrooms where these principles have been successfully applied. It explores how teachers can develop students' thinking dispositions, make thinking visible, and shape classroom cultures that foster engagement and intellectual growth. Editors Cameron Paterson and Simon Brooks, who have worked extensively with the Cultures of Thinking approach, bring together voices from across Australia, offering a rich tapestry of insights, strategies, and experiences. Through practical examples and compelling analysis, *Cultivating Cultures of Thinking in Australian Schools* provides educators with a concrete blueprint for transformative teaching.

This book is an essential read for teachers, school leaders, and education professionals who want to create vibrant learning environments that prepare students for the complexities of the modern world. It is a powerful resource for those seeking to move beyond traditional assessment-driven teaching and cultivate a culture where thinking and learning flourish.

Cameron Paterson is the Director of Learning at Wesley College, Melbourne. He also works for Harvard's Project Zero. His accomplishments have been recognized with awards for teaching, leadership, and innovation. He is the co-editor of *Flip the System Australia*.

Simon Brooks is an educational consultant working with schools around the world interested in transforming learning and teaching by promoting thinking, understanding, and engagement for all learners. He has held senior educational roles in the UK, Australia, and Malaysia, most recently as Principal of the Australian International School Malaysia.

EDITED BY
CAMERON PATERSON
AND SIMON BROOKS

Cultivating Cultures of Thinking in Australian Schools
From Control to Curiosity

LONDON AND NEW YORK

Designed cover image: Getty

First published 2026
by Routledge
4 Park Square, Milton Park, Abingdon, Oxon OX14 4RN

and by Routledge
605 Third Avenue, New York, NY 10158

Routledge is an imprint of the Taylor & Francis Group, an informa business

© 2026 selection and editorial matter, Cameron Paterson and Simon Brooks; individual chapters, the contributors

The right of Cameron Paterson and Simon Brooks to be identified as the authors of the editorial material, and of the authors for their individual chapters, has been asserted in accordance with sections 77 and 78 of the Copyright, Designs and Patents Act 1988.

All rights reserved. No part of this book may be reprinted or reproduced or utilised in any form or by any electronic, mechanical, or other means, now known or hereafter invented, including photocopying and recording, or in any information storage or retrieval system, without permission in writing from the publishers.

Trademark notice: Product or corporate names may be trademarks or registered trademarks, and are used only for identification and explanation without intent to infringe.

British Library Cataloguing-in-Publication Data
A catalogue record for this book is available from the British Library

ISBN: 9781032892061 (hbk)
ISBN: 9781032892030 (pbk)
ISBN: 9781003541745 (ebk)

DOI: 10.4324/9781003541745

Typeset in Joanna
by KnowledgeWorks Global Ltd.

Cameron dedicates this book to Mum for patiently reading *What Do People Do All Day?* so many times and to Dad for making me swim across the lake – the best teachers anyone could want.

Simon dedicates this book to Sally, for taking a gamble on a lanky backpacker and for years of love and laughter ever since.

Table of Contents

Foreword – Ron Ritchhart   x
List of Contributors   xx

Introduction: From Control to Curiosity   1
Cameron Paterson and Simon Brooks

Empowering Learners   Section I   13

Unlearning Control   **One**   15
Cameron Paterson

Stoking the Fires: How Cultivating Curiosity Leads to Enhanced Engagement and Deeper Understanding   **Two**   24
Simon Brooks

Shifting Paradigms   Section II   41

Restructuring Schools for Relationships, Play, and Time to Think   **Three**   43
Pasi Sahlberg

Indigenous Knowledges – Valuing Different Thinking Paradigms   **Four**   58
Melitta Hogarth, Justin Wilkey and John Doolah

Transforming Classrooms   Section III   71

"Will This Be on the Test?": How Teachers in Australian Schools Help Students Focus More on Learning and Less on Work   **Five**   73
Simon Brooks

Six Exploring Collaborative Learning *Milica Savic*		88
Seven Encouraging Learners to Do the Heavy Lifting *Lana Fleiszig*		100
Eight Creating a Culture of Self-Directed Learning: Risk-Taking, Feedback, Goals, *Repeat* *April Taylor*		111

Section IV Leading Professional Growth — 123

Nine Pathways to Cultures of Thinking in Troubled Times *Nicole Mockler*		125
Ten Cultivating a Culture of Thinking at Masada College: Something We Are, Rather Than Something We Do *Ryan Gill and Carla Gagliano*		136
Eleven Principles of Adult Learning in Cultures of Thinking: Challenges, Calls to Action and Triumphs *Samantha Gooch*		145
Twelve Empowering Educators: Using Professional Learning Communities to Embed Cultures of Thinking *Kara Baxter*		159
Thirteen Why Are School Meetings So Bad? Some Reflections on Improving Collaboration in Schools *Doug Broadbent*		170

Section V Navigating Change — 179

Fourteen Pitfalls and Pathways: Transforming Culture and Sustaining Change in a Culture of Thinking *Mark Church*		181
Fifteen Breakfast, Phonics and Cultures of Thinking: Modern Tools for An Education Renaissance *Lani Brockwell*		192

Seeping Upwards and Across: Embedding Cultures of Thinking at Brisbane Girls Grammar School **Sixteen** 204
Bruce Addison and Susan Garson

Thinking at the Forefront: Immanuel College's Cultures of Thinking Journey **Seventeen** 216
Martyn Anderson

Conclusion: The Best Teachers Are Subversive 229
Cameron Paterson and Simon Brooks

Index 235

Foreword

There is an admonition teachers of English often give to their young writers: Show don't tell. This advice is grounded in the idea that good writing brings readers into events and helps them to experience what the characters are feeling. So, rather than merely telling us a character is excited about an upcoming event, good writers will take us into their preparations, thoughts, internal dialogue, and the conversations they have with others as the event approaches. As readers we desire that vicarious thrill of being scared, disappointed, excited, frustrated, upset, and so on even as we sit comfortably reading in our easy chair. Showing what a character is experiencing allows us to not only develop empathy for the characters but also to live through them even as we become more in touch with our own feelings and experiences. Reading then becomes an immersive, engaging experience that transports us into new states of being, unique possibilities, alternative realities, and future possibilities.

In psychology, the idea of *social proof* builds on this idea of showing rather than telling to guide individuals into potentially new ways of acting. This term was coined by Robert Cialdini (1984) in his book *Influence: The Psychology of Persuasion*. His thesis is that as humans we are easily overwhelmed by all the information we are bombarded with in the modern world. Consequently, we find a plethora of facts not all that useful in making decisions on how to act. Instead, we rely on the actions of those like us for cues about how to behave and what to do. We trust the decisions made by others – usually others we respect or feel are like us. We assume our peers have done the hard work of sorting through the information and come to valid conclusions. Therefore, we read reviews, watch video testimonials, listen to stories told by users, or make use of case studies to guide our actions more than we rely on digging into the data of effect sizes and statistically meaningful results. Sure, we may have heard of and be generally aware of the effects of healthy eating, but we will be more influenced by a peer group or spouse that takes on and models these practices. This is particularly true if we can see changes and results in them as a consequence of their actions. These peers can show us how to act versus the scientific studies that merely tell us.

It will come as no surprise that advertisers and those in the business of persuasion often rely on social proof as a tool of influence. For instance, the marketing firm CXL advises clients that their website landing pages need to include some kind of social proof to engage and persuade potential clients (Mullin, 2024). Just look for the endorsements, testimonials, or pre-selected reviews displayed prominently on the sites you visit. Likewise, pay attention to which reviews you give the most credence to before making a purchase. Likely, it will be those that mirror either your own background or needs in some way.

Social proof is important in the world of education as well. Schools are constantly in a process of implementing some form of change. Leaders are often keen to get those in their charge to implement some new approach, program, or policy that represents at least some departure from past practice. According to Simon Breakspear (2024), one mistake school leaders often make is trying to sell these new practices by building a case and citing the evidence behind them, thinking that the telling itself will be persuasive. However, the reality is that people need to be shown. Thus, investing in a group of champions who can provide social proof to other teachers in the school is often much more effective than leaders giving an impassioned speech. These people are not just early adopters or the first wave, but a way of making the practices real to the larger group. Leaders strategically select champions who will be representative of the school as a whole. A group made up solely of secondary teachers will easily be rejected by primary teachers and vice versa, causing the initiative to be siloed. When teachers can see how colleagues like them have implemented things, see the effect in classrooms just like theirs, and with a group of students that they themselves teach; they are more likely to adopt the actions themselves. The risk of the innovation has been diminished and the unknown demystified based on the actions of others. This is the kind of social proof that lays the foundation for growth and change.

In my own work over the last 25 years, I have certainly seen the power of social proof to move teachers into action. My research and writing have relied on case studies, and I have produced over 50 video pictures-of-practice. As a teacher myself, I am acutely aware of how important it is to see ideas, frameworks, theories, and practices contextualized. While the evidence of effects and outcomes is certainly important, and my research has documented these, it is not what actually creates change. Dylan Wiliam, though a strong advocate for evidence-based practice in education, says that "In education, 'what works?' is not the right question because everything works somewhere and nothing works everywhere." Instead, he insists that we need to understand the nuances of teaching practices: What works where? Under what condition? With what kinds of support? For whom? For Wiliam, "Teaching is all about knowing the conditions under which a particular technique is likely to work. That is why I say that you can't tell teachers what to do...because the nature of expertise in teaching is not the kind of expertise you can communicate [simply] by telling people" (Wiliam, 2006, p. 11).

In one school with whom I worked, the idea of social proof was pivotal in moving the school forward. The school was a new start up that grew by one grade level each year. Thus, there were always new staff being added and not much of a common set of teaching practices on which to draw. What is more, the school had adopted the International Baccalaureate program and was working toward certification, which meant teachers were focused on doing and documenting their IB curriculum more than examining their teaching. By year three of our work together, I was still struggling to get the ideas and practices of building a culture of thinking to take hold in any serious way. There was some dabbling by a few individuals, but things were not taking off the way that I had seen elsewhere. This was a school in a small community and the opportunity to have conversations with other teachers was somewhat limited. I felt that progress was not being made because teachers at this school still needed to see and feel a culture of thinking for themselves. My simply telling them was not enough. I needed to really show them a culture of thinking.

I planned a series of inter-state trips in which I took small groups of teachers to visit schools who had been immersed in growing cultures of thinking for many years. We spent two days on each of these trips visiting classrooms, watching real teaching in action, and talking with teachers, students, and school leaders. On our first trip, a very senior history teacher who had not previously engaged with Cultures of Thinking™ ideas in any way, was blown away by the discussion he witnessed in a history class we sat in on. Students were not only engaged, but they exhibited a high degree of agency. The teachers, the class was team taught, had put in place protocols for discussion in which the students had become well versed. With minimal effort, the teachers were able to launch the class and let the students step forward to guide the discussion. The students themselves moved their desks into a circle and assigned a facilitator. There was eye contact, accountable talk in which students acknowledged and built on the contributions of their peers, questioning, listening, and generally positive interactions amongst the group. Every so often the teachers would interject a question that required students to dig a bit deeper. However, they were quite careful to do this without derailing or hijacking the community the students had established. That evening over dinner the history teacher, who was already well past retirement age, said that if he could get his class to be like that, then he could teach another 10 years. He had seen how the teachers leveraged the cultural forces (Ritchhart, 2015) and used thinking routines (Ritchhart et al., 2011; Ritchhart and Church, 2020) that made the power of a culture of thinking come alive for him, and he was ready to take his own actions to move forward.

This book, *Cultivating Cultures of Thinking in Australian Schools: From Control to Curiosity*, is all about showing and not telling. Its value, importance, and timeliness reside precisely in its provision of the kinds of social proof that can create excitement, build buy-in, and inspire action amongst its readers. It is about contextualizing the frameworks, practices, and mindsets of the Cultures of Thinking™ initiative, of which I have written extensively elsewhere, in a way that helps readers better understand what works where, when, in what context, and with what support. Australian readers will have the opportunity to learn from teachers, leaders, and researchers who are grappling with the same constraints, issues, and problems they are. Non-Australian readers will recognize many common issues of teaching with which all educators grapple. Readers will learn not "the answer" in how to overcome these challenges but be shown various ways educators working in their own unique context have sought to address them. So, what exactly can readers expect to be shown here? I highlight five key takeaways I have had as a reader. No doubt you will find others.

What a culture of thinking looks, feels, and sounds like. Throughout this book, the various authors take us into classrooms and staff rooms to provide a firsthand glimpse of what a culture of thinking can be. Seeing what a culture of thinking might look like in secondary classrooms, middle years programs, and primary spaces across different schools in different states provides an invaluable opportunity for readers to connect to and find resonance in the journey of others. This is exactly the kind of social proof we seek as we embark on a new adventure. What have others done? How did they start? How did they navigate their journey? How did they personalize Cultures of Thinking practices? What you will find in these stories is that none of the authors simply rolled out a program or implemented a script. Instead, they connected the frameworks, practices, mindsets, and tools of Cultures of Thinking to their own goals and beliefs as teachers. In some cases, Cultures of Thinking ideas allowed them to lean in and enhance key values, in other instances the ideas challenged established practices and precipitated a rethinking of teaching as usual. For instance, Lana Fleiszig began to question her reliance on direct instruction to merely get students to replicate answers and skills she had shown them. Gradually, she began to trust her students to think through problems and issues as a crucial first step in learning that deepened rather than merely covered the learning she was trying to promote.

As you read these accounts of transformation and growth, I encourage you to pay special attention to the pivotal moments that move teachers forward in shifting their practice. You'll find a great deal of honesty as teachers recount lessons that didn't work, student uprisings, or frustrations with the status quo. You can almost see Simon Brooks (Chapters 2 and 5) rolling his eyes or falling into a shoulder squeezing cringe posture as he recounts those teaching moments that pulled him up short, made him take a step back, and precipitated some deep rethinking of his teaching. For Cameron Paterson (Chapter 1), pivotal moments often emerged from discussions with his students that he used to gain a better insight into the needs of his learners. Listening to their voices and taking their advice seriously was a catalyst for change.

The power of reflection to keep our stories moving. You will find in all the various personal journeys shared here that there is a common theme that keeps them progressing. Each educator was and continues to be guided by ongoing reflection on their practice as an educator to continually move their practice forward. No one is waiting for phase 2, my next book, a new set of routines, or their upcoming training. Instead, each educator is continually asking themselves: What's working? For whom? How can I extend that, so it happens more often and for more students? What's not working? What feels off? The authors represented here share a common trait I have seen in all the great teachers I have studied, that is, they are never satisfied. They are always questioning and interrogating their practice to improve. Pay mind to the questions that these teachers are asking themselves as well. Perhaps you are asking yourself these same types of questions. Seeing how others have grappled with them can provide that important social proof for helping you to move forward.

It turns out that continual improvement and growth that the educators here are demonstrating, rather than meeting some marker of success, is one of the keys to personal happiness (Brooks, 2022). Success too often comes with a post-accomplishment let down (Dawson, 2024). More beneficial is to keep the focus on our ongoing growth trajectory. I encourage you to take this lesson from these authors onboard yourself. This is what keeps us moving and allows us to find ourselves in that all-important, dopamine-inducing cycle of growth. In the following chapters, you will see that these authors focus on what Sullivan and Hardy (2021) refer to as "the gain," or the difference between where one started and where one is currently, versus on "the gap," or how far one is from an identified goal. Though it sounds cliche, it truly is the journey not the destination that matters. Too often in education we want to quicky measure a new initiative to see if it is "meeting our goals." This focuses on the *gap*. Instead, celebrate the small and large successes you have that center you in the *gain*. While I am at it, I'll share another key to happiness from Brooks that is particularly important for mid-career folks, and that is sharing one's knowledge and insights with others, something all these authors do both here and on their home turf. Let their voices speak to you as a trusted colleague.

The effects and results of building a culture of thinking for teachers and students. I and my co-authors Mark Church (2020) and Karin Morrison (2011) have written about the difference building a culture of thinking makes to students and teachers alike. Chief among these is the idea of engagement. As you read the classroom and staff room accounts here, make note of how teachers show us the engagement of their students and teachers as they begin to question more, engage with each other in dialogue, and collaborate authentically. Of course, these are not merely emergent characteristics of a culture of thinking, teachers must make room for these things to happen in the first place and then celebrate and reinforce these behaviors as they appear if they are to be sustained over time. Pay attention to how the authors accomplish this. Another important outcome is depth, in almost every chapter you will encounter a reference to either *deeper* learning, *deeper* thinking, or *deeper* understanding. Such references reflect that not only are the teachers here focused on depth as a natural goal of a quality education but also are looking for it as a yardstick by which to measure their success as teachers. For those wondering about that traditional measure, test results, Simon Brooks (Chapters 2 and 5) shares some of those too from his work in various schools.

The tension between what is and what can be. Throughout this book, you will find that the authors do not shy away from calling out the tensions, challenges, and conflicts that exist between efforts to create cultures of thinking more broadly across Australian schools and some of the current issues facing teachers. Pasi Sahlberg (Chapter 3) argues that our focus on standardization of schooling and accountability has created schools that fail to prioritize the cultural force of interactions and the mindset of creating spaces where students feel known, valued, and respected. He offers a new vision forward that prioritizes belonging, well-being, and play as central to developing healthy, well-educated children. Another conflict that many teachers will recognize is the tendency of schools to highlight, market, advertise, and promote the performance of a school's top ATAR achievers (often through a prominent display at Reception) as if learning was a competition that must have winners – and thus, losers. Mark Church (Chapter 14) rightly calls out this limiting focus for the potential damage it can do to learning and learners. This narrow goal of producing top scorers, which are a fixed number that can never be increased, not only negates the achievement of the vast majority of students but also misses an important opportunity to help students learn from one another and develop the dispositions needed for life. Mark presents ways we can positively rethink this all too common practice.

A cornerstone of creating cultures of thinking is seeing all students as capable learners and thinkers who bring a wealth of experience and innate abilities to every learning task. Melitta Hogarth, Justin Wilkey, and John Doolah (Chapter 4) identify the longstanding issue of approaching the education of Indigenous Peoples from a deficit standpoint, focusing on what they have yet to achieve rather than the richness they bring to the learning moment. This belief in all students as thinkers is key to any successful endeavor to promote a culture of thinking. Too many times, I have seen teachers view their students as lacking, as empty vessels to be filled, rather than curious minds to engage. So too, we hear policymakers advocating for explicit instruction to fill the gaps rather than encouraging teachers to nurture students' innate curiosities and intelligence. Hogarth, Wilkes and Doolah call on all of us to "flip the deficit logics."

Yet, another tension teachers all over the world are facing is the pressure from policy makers to make direct explicit instruction the default method in schools. As is all too common in education, policymakers look for easy answers to achieving quick gains on tests and the standardization of teaching rather than embracing its natural nuisance and complexity. Of course, we as teachers have expertise and information to be shared, but we want our students to engage in that information deeply and retain it for the long haul. Consequently, in this collection, you won't find a vilification or outright rejection of explicit instruction, but rather a recognition of where, when, and how it fits. For instance, Lani Brockwell (Chapter 15) shares how she sees no conflict between her roles as both an advocate for systematic synthetic phonics instruction and Cultures of Thinking. Importantly, recognizing the role phonetics plays for readers doesn't require us to teach as if phonetics is all there is to reading. Getting students to actively think about information makes it "sticky" because it engages their cognitive processes, forcing them to connect new knowledge with existing understanding, thereby creating a deeper and more meaningful memory trace in the brain, leading to better retention and application of the information learned. Essentially, when students actively process information by analyzing, evaluating, and applying it, they are more likely to remember it long-term. Put simply, learning doesn't occur through the delivery of information, only when learners do something with that information. As Nicole Mockler (Chapter 9) points out in her chapter, good education is about "encounter." She identifies the encounter between students and teachers, and students and students as being key. Drawing inspiration from David Hawkins' (1974) seminal 1974 essay on teaching, "I, Thou, and It," I would add a third element to this encounter: content.

The potency of cultivating teacher agency. In addition to being shown how a culture of thinking looks in the classroom, numerous authors in this volume show us what a culture of thinking can look like in the staff room as well. One of our guiding principles in the Worldwide Cultures of Thinking™ project is that for classrooms to be cultures of thinking for students, schools must be cultures of thinking for teachers. This, of course, means more than just using thinking routines in staff meetings or protocols when discussing a text. At its core, we need to respect the thinking, questions, and wealth of experience teachers bring to their work with students. At the same time, our professional dialogue must be centered on building a shared understanding of the enterprise of teaching and learning even as we recognize its complexity. Rather than running away from or being scared by this complexity, our acknowledgement of it should spark curiosity and allow us to enter a state of grace in which risk-taking and learning from mistakes are the norm rather than the exception. Nicole Mockler highlights these features, along with teacher creativity, as keys to nurturing a *democratic*, versus *managerial*, professionalism in our schools (Sachs, 2001). Extending on Nicole's chapter, Ryan Gill and Carla Gagliano (Chapter 10), Samantha Gooch (Chapter 11), and Kara Baxter (Chapter 12) take us into their schools to show how they encourage teacher agency through inquiry that is guided, supported, self-directed, and collaborative in nature.

I've tried to highlight a few important ways in which the collection of authors represented here have not merely told us about what they are doing in their schools and classrooms to build cultures of thinking but have shown us the process, tensions, results, and the joys of their journey. No doubt you will see additional forms of social proof that will resonate for you personally and connect either directly or tangentially to your own professional circumstances. My hope is that you use these stories not as a blueprint for replication but as sources of inspiration. No doubt you will, as I did, encounter many gems, insights, and key actions you will want to take on board yourself. I encourage you to make these practices your own and incorporate them into your journey in a way that feels authentic. As you embark on or continue your expedition into Cultures of Thinking, keep your focus on the gains you are making, the small triumphs, the joyous moments, and the increased engagement and reinvigoration both you and your students are finding in learning rather than the gap between where you hope to be one day and where you are now. Remember our happiness lies not in achieving some arbitrary marker of success but in continual growth and improvement. Finally, I encourage you to share your stories, for there will be many, in whatever forums are available to you. This might be with a trusted colleague, in staff meetings, or larger professional settings. As we articulate our growth, identifying how it happened and why, our pedagogical understanding is deepened. As a result, you will experience something else all of these authors have shown us, and that is that engaging in the process of creating cultures of thinking changes people not just in the short-term but for the long haul.

Dr. Ron Ritchhart
Director, Worldwide Cultures of Thinking Project

REFERENCES

Breakspear, S. 2024. Show, don't just tell: the benefits of creating social proof. *Breakspear's Blog*. [Accessed 15 November 2024]. Available from: https://simonbreakspear.com/social-proof/

Brooks, A.C. (2022) *From strength to strength: finding success, happiness and deep purpose in the second half of life.* Bloomsbury Publishing.

Cialdini, R. 1984. *Influence: The Psychology of Persuasion.* Business Library.

Dawson, A. 2024. *Finishing First: What It Really Means to Win.* [Accessed 24 September 2024]. Available from: https://www.templeton.org/news/finishing-first-what-it-really-means-to-win

Hawkins, D. 1974. I, thou, and it. In *The informed vision: essays on learning and human nature.* New York: Agathon Press, pp.48–62.

Mullin, S. 2024. *Social proof: definition, types, examples and how to work with it.* [Accessed January 2025]. Available from: https://cxl.com/blog/is-social-proof-really-that-important/

Ritchhart, R. (2015) *Creating cultures of thinking: the 8 forces we must master to truly transform our classrooms.* San Francisco: Jossey-Bass.

Ritchhart, R. and Church, M. (2020) *The power of making thinking visible: practices to engage and empower all learners.* New Jersey: Jossey-Bass.

Ritchhart, R., Church, M. and Morrison, K. (2011) *Making thinking visible: how to promote engagement, understanding, and independence for all learners.* Jossey-Bass.

Sachs, J. (2001) 'Teacher professional identity: competing discourses, competing outcomes', *Journal of Educational Policy*, 16, pp. 149–161.

Sullivan, D. and Hardy, B. (2021) *the gap and the gain: the high Achievers' guide to happiness, confidence, and success.* Hay House, Inc.

Wiliam, D. 2006. *Assessment for Learning: Why, What and How?* Cambridge Assessment Network Conference, Faculty of Education, University of Cambridge. Cambridge UK.

List of Contributors

Dr Bruce Addison is Deputy Principal (Academic) at Brisbane Girls Grammar School where he is responsible for the creation and advocacy of school wide pedagogy as everyday practice. He has much experience in educational leadership as a scholar, leader, and practitioner and is currently Queensland President of the Australian Council of Educational leadership.

Martyn Anderson is the Head of Senior School and Director of Teaching and Learning at Immanuel College in Adelaide, South Australia. He is an experienced leader and teacher who is also the South Australian Branch President of the Australian Council of Educational Leaders. He values innovative, thinking-focused cultures for staff and students.

Kara Baxter is the Deputy Principal Learning and Teaching at Strathcona Girls Grammar and is an educator dedicated to innovation in pedagogy, professional learning, and student-centered excellence. She has held leadership roles in both the Independent and Catholic sectors, including Deputy Principal at John Paul College and Head of Teaching and Learning at Mentone Grammar.

Doug Broadbent has served in several leadership positions in Australian schools. He is currently the Head of Teaching and Learning at Shore. Fascinated by collaboration, he is currently working on a doctorate exploring conceptions of collaboration.

Lani Brockwell is a coach in both literacy and Cultures of Thinking, living in Adelaide, South Australia. She has taught in both the independent and public sectors, developing her practice in a range of mainstream, trauma informed and special needs settings. She is currently working for the South Australian Department for Education's Literacy Guarantee Unit.

Simon Brooks is an educational consultant working with schools around the world interested in transforming learning and teaching by promoting thinking, understanding, and engagement for all learners. He has held senior educational roles in the UK, Australia, and Malaysia, most recently as Principal of the Australian International School Malaysia.

Mark Church has been an educator for over thirty years and has particular interest in helping teachers and school leaders think deeply about their efforts to cultivate thinking and learning opportunities for students. With Ron Ritchhart, he is the co-author of *Making Thinking Visible* and *The Power of Making Thinking Visible*.

Dr John Doolah is a Torres Strait Islander of Erubam le (Erub person) and Meriam le (Mer person) heritage. He belongs to the sager people of Mer. My Mer nosik (clan) division, is Samsep-Meriam. His teaching background is in course development, course coordination and lecturing local, national, and international students in Aboriginal and Torres Strait Islander Studies courses. In his current position at the University of the Faculty of Education, he lectures and coordinates Indigenous Education undergraduate and the Master of Teaching First Nations Education courses. His overall research interest is in the impact of colonization on Indigenous Australians.

Lana Fleiszig is an Education Consultant who specializes in teaching and learning Mathematics through inquiry. She has spent the last 30 years supporting teachers to build a culture of thinking in the maths classroom, give students agency over their learning, and provide powerful opportunities for learners to enjoy constructing meaning.

Susan Garson is the Director of the Centre of Cultures of Thinking at Brisbane Girls Grammar School, a steering committee member for PZ Australia, and is completing a PhD in middle leader agency.

Ryan Gill and Carla Gagliano are passionate about collaboratively cultivating and promoting rich cultures of thinking. Working side-by-side with students and teachers at Masada College, Sydney, and educators from across the region, their central goal has been to actively promote a learning environment in which collective and individual thinking is valued, visible, and actively promoted.

Samantha Gooch is an experienced educator and school leader with a passion for nurturing cultures of thinking. She took a lead role in developing the Kambala Institute of Teaching Excellence (KITE) and is currently serving as Deputy Principal Pastoral Care at Kambala.

Professor Melitta Hogarth is a Kamilaroi woman and is the Director of Ngarrngga, as well as the Associate Dean (Indigenous) and Principal Research Fellow in the Faculty of Education. Her research interests revolve around the intersection of education, equity, and social justice for Indigenous peoples, which draws on her years of experience as a teacher and a researcher.

Nicole Mockler is Professor of Education at the University of Sydney and Honorary Research Fellow at the University of Oxford. She researches and writes on education policy and teachers' work and learning. In 2022, she was awarded the Australian Council for Educational Leadership Dr Paul Brock Memorial Medal.

Cameron Paterson is Director of Learning at Wesley College, Melbourne. He also works for Harvard's Project Zero. His accomplishments have been recognized with awards for teaching, leadership, and innovation. He is the co-editor of *Flip the System Australia*.

Pasi Sahlberg is a Professor of Educational Leadership at the University of Melbourne. His contributions to the field have been widely recognized, as evidenced by his receipt of numerous prestigious awards, including the 2012 Education Award in Finland, the 2013 Grawemeyer Award in the U.S., the 2014 Robert Owen Award in Scotland, the 2016 Lego Prize in Denmark, and the 2021 Hedley Beare Award in Australia.

Milica Savic has taught French, Design, and Media in the middle years and works as the Coordinator of Learning and Teaching and as a Professional Learning Coach at Wesley College. She is passionate about promoting agency, deep thinking, and collaborative learning for both staff and students.

April Taylor is an educator with over 20 years' experience teaching History in the United States and NSW, Australia, and is a 2019 graduate of the Gandel Holocaust Studies Program for Australian Educators. She has 10 years' experience in educational leadership in Australia as a Head of Department, Director of Teaching and Learning, and Principal.

Mr Justin Wilkey is a Ngarrindjeri man and a Research Assistant at Ngarrngga, as well as a doctoral candidate within the Faculty of Education. His research examines the experience of Indigenous students attending boarding school and the impact this has on their social and emotional well-being. He is dedicated to working with Indigenous peoples to provide meaningful educational opportunities that reflect their values and meet their needs.

Introduction: From Control to Curiosity
Cameron Paterson and Simon Brooks

Welcome to *Cultivating Cultures of Thinking in Australian Schools: From Control to Curiosity*. This book is the culmination of a deeply rewarding journey for both of us, spanning many years working with schools and educators across Australia. As editors, we bring together over 60 years of teaching experience and more than 40 years in school leadership. However, this work is so much more than the sum of our professional backgrounds. It is our passion project.

At the heart of this book is a commitment to transforming education by cultivating environments where thinking is encouraged and nurtured. We are privileged to amplify the voices of a wide range of Australian educators who share this vision. They are teachers and leaders who, day by day, put thinking and understanding at the forefront of their classrooms and schools. Through their accounts and stories, we explore how they foster a culture where curiosity thrives, thinking is deepened, and students are empowered to become independent learners.

This work is inspired by Cultures of Thinking™, an approach to learning and teaching grounded in the pioneering work of Dr. Ron Ritchhart from Project Zero at the Harvard Graduate School of Education. Cultures of Thinking challenges educators to move beyond rote learning and surface-level engagement, instead creating learning communities where thinking is valued, visible, and actively promoted (Ritchhart, 2015). While these ideas have gained traction worldwide, Australia's educators have embraced and adapted this approach in innovative ways. We are excited to share their insights and experiences with you in this book.

STORY OF SELF

As a young English teacher, I (Simon) always looked forward to the time of year when I taught Shakespeare's *Hamlet*. What a wonderfully rich and evocative play it is. I particularly looked forward to reaching Act 3 and diving headfirst into the famous 'To be or not to be' soliloquy, Mount Everest for all teachers of English Literature!

Thinking back, I remember one particular year early in my career when *Hamlet* came around again. I was excited. I had learnt the entire speech by heart, ready to recite to my students. I had even sourced a jet-black cloak to wear to class, hoping it would capture something of Hamlet's grief and despair.

I entered the classroom, stage right. On reflection, my goal was to bludgeon my students into loving Shakespeare through the force of my own personality. I performed the soliloquy with panache, even receiving a round of applause at the end. If I was enthusiastic enough about the play, I reasoned, then something about my love of Literature would rub off onto them.

Once the dust had settled, I launched into a round of tried-and-tested Chalk and Talk. Taking up my copy of the play, I proceeded to walk them through my analysis of the soliloquy, line by line. They were to follow along in their own copies, annotating as they went. In fairness to my younger self, I tried to make it engaging. There was something in the way of whole class Q&A as we went along. But fundamentally, my goal was to have them note down in their books the same annotations I had made in my own.

The lesson moved towards a close. In a moment of great hubris, I remember thinking to myself, "Wow, what an amazing lesson this is. Aren't they lucky to have me?" I swooshed my cloak with a self-satisfied flourish.

At the end of the lesson, I gave them an essay to write on 'To be or not to be'. I was eager to see what they would make of it. A week later, the deadline arrived, and they submitted their offerings.

I was horrified. The essays were pedestrian at best. They demonstrated little depth of understanding about the soliloquy. There was no sense of a personal, critical voice. It was almost as if none of them had attended the amazing lesson I had bestowed upon them a week earlier…

It was then that I experienced a profound moment of realisation that has shaped the rest of my career to date. Here's what I worked out. In that lesson, I had done a fabulous job of teaching myself the 'To be or not to be' speech from Shakespeare's *Hamlet*, and my students were in the room while I was learning. In order to communicate key ideas about the speech, there is no doubt that I was actively immersed in a rich process of thinking, including describing, explaining, reasoning with evidence, making connections, considering different perspectives, making conclusions, posing questions and uncovering complexity. In short, I was engaged in the type of thinking identified in the Understanding Map (Ritchhart, Church and Morrison, 2011), a framework of powerful thinking moves that support the development of understanding. Crucially, I was the one doing the thinking, not my students.

Learning is not something we can do for someone else, however much we want to, and however hard we try. A foundational mindset in a culture of thinking is that 'Learning is a consequence of thinking' (Perkins, 1992, p. 8). It is only when we provide opportunities for students to think about content in a myriad of different ways that they develop meaningful and lasting understandings (Ritchhart, Church and Morrison, 2011).

This story from Simon's classroom highlights some of the core beliefs and values we both share, which run like threads through the various chapters and accounts in this volume:

- We believe that educators should foster student thinking dispositions that not only promote deep understanding of content in the present but also lay the foundations for lifelong learning beyond the classroom (Perkins, Jay and Tishman, 1993; Ritchhart, 2023)
- We believe that coverage is the enemy of understanding (Gardner, 1993, cited in Brandt, 1993)
- We believe that 'learning is a consequence of thinking' (Perkins, 1992, p. 8)
- We believe that curiosity is 'the engine of learning' (Engel, 2006, p. 6)
- We believe in fostering authentic collaboration that allows students to learn from and with one another (Ritchhart, 2023)
- We believe that thinking and learning are processes that are deepened when we make them visible (Ritchhart, Church and Morrison, 2011).

Although these six principles represent our shared pedagogical destination, the paths we each took to arrive here were, naturally, a little different.

For Cameron, teaching felt like a natural pathway, and from the beginning he was intrigued by the gap between learning and schooling. As a young History teacher, Cameron was drawn to the Harvard Project Zero focus on thinking, understanding, and creativity, completing online courses, attending conferences, and then moving to the United States to complete a Master's degree at Harvard University, which led to opportunities teaching online and serving on the faculty at the annual Project Zero Classroom. Cameron's approach to teaching and education leadership has been profoundly influenced by David Perkins, Tina Blythe, Daniel Wilson, and Ron Ritchhart, and the mantras that "learning is a consequence of thinking" (Perkins, 1992, p. 8) and "for schools to be cultures of thinking for students, schools must be cultures of thinking for teachers" (Ritchhart, 2023, p. 1).

From an early age, Simon developed a passion for both English Literature and learning. After training as a teacher in the UK, he moved to Australia with his young family and became Director of Learning and Teaching at Masada College in Sydney, connecting for the first time with Project Zero and Ron Ritchhart. For Simon, discovering Cultures of Thinking felt like a homecoming, since the ideas and practices resonated so deeply with him. His journey with these ideas saw him transforming Masada into a lighthouse school for Cultures of Thinking pedagogy and practice, before going on to support other schools around the world keen to build cultures of thinking for themselves. Simon continues to be inspired by the work of Ron Ritchhart, Mark Church, Shari Tishman, and David Perkins, and firmly believes that going to school should be so much more than simply preparing for an exam.

STORY OF US

It is late afternoon on a Saturday in February 2017, and Cameron and Simon are seated in an auditorium in Sydney for the first Project Zero Sydney Network conference for K-12 educators.

Inspired by Project Zero ideas, Cameron, Simon, and a small-group of Sydney-based educators had founded the Project Zero Sydney Network (now the Project Zero Australia Network) the year before. Our mission was simple: to share our passion for Project Zero ideas by providing free professional learning opportunities for Australian educators across all sectors, fostering professional collaboration, collegiality and shared growth.

As we look around the auditorium, we are amazed by what we see. Over 300 teachers and educators have given up their Saturday to come and learn about creating Cultures of Thinking. After an inspiring keynote by Ron Ritchhart, participants then attended two workshops chosen from a selection of over thirty, all designed and facilitated by Australian educators. Workshop topics included themes such as, 'How can I push for depth in my students' thinking?', 'Thought-provoking-questions', 'Putting students in the driving seat', and 'The heart of collaboration'.

Cameron and Simon turn to one another and can't stop smiling. There is palpable sense of joy and excitement in the ether. It is clear we have struck a chord. Nobody sitting in this room is required to be here. Something about Cultures of Thinking pedagogy and practice is resonating with these educators. And it is resonating strongly enough that they are prepared to invest their entire Saturday to join this community and find out more.

Countless educators across Australia have a similar story to tell. For many of us, the discovery of Cultures of Thinking has been the single most transformative experience of our entire professional lives. It is something that has helped us make sense of what we do every moment of every day. It has reminded us why we became teachers in the first place.

There are several possible reasons for this. For instance, Cultures of Thinking provides a wealth of practical tools and strategies that teachers can put to immediate us in their classrooms, allowing them to experience quick success.

However, there is much more to it than this. At its heart, Cultures of Thinking is underpinned by a visionary and altruistic question: 'What do we want the students we teach to be like as adults?' (Ritchhart, 2023, p. 31). Over the years, Cameron and Simon have asked this question of thousands of teachers, parents, and students, and the answers are always fascinating. As adults, we want our children to be curious, to be thoughtful, to be able to tell right from wrong. We want them to be innovative, to be solutions-focused, to be analytical and to be good listeners. We want them to be empathetic, to be receptive to feedback, to be open-minded yet healthily sceptical.

These are grand and noble ambitions. They encourage us to remember that we don't arrive at school every day 'just' to get through Act 4 of 'Macbeth', or tell them about topographic maps, or teach them what a surd is. We are here to help them become more creative, more collaborative and more metacognitive, all in the process of learning about 'Macbeth', topographic maps or surds.

Ritchhart envisages schooling as an enculturative process that cultivates dispositions of thinking (2002). He contends that what stays with us from education are enduring patterns: patterns of behaviour, patterns of thinking, and patterns of interaction. In his words, 'What stays with us, what sticks from our education, are the patterns of behaviour and thinking that have been engrained and enculturated over time' (Ritchhart, 2002, p. 229). These 'dispositions' describe our patterns of interaction with the world. They cannot be directly taught or tested. They can only be enculturated. Lev Vygotsky's (1978, p. 88) assertion, "Children grow into the intellectual life of those around them," captures the essence of enculturation. It highlights how individuals internalise the ideas and beliefs that they regularly engage with, shaping their intellectual development.

This is a goal we can get out of bed for. This is something that excites us, that has the power to effect meaningful societal change. Perhaps this is part of the reason that our passion for Cultures of Thinking is shared by so many other educators in Australia.

So why Australia? Over the past twenty years, awareness of Project Zero and Cultures of Thinking has grown exponentially in Australian schools. Even a decade ago, when Cameron and Simon gave talks or facilitated workshops, they would ask, "How many people have heard of Cultures of Thinking or thinking routines?" and quite often nobody would raise their hand. These days, most Australian educators have encountered these ideas in one form or another.

To some degree, this has been supported via widespread advocacy of Cultures of Thinking through many channels and networks in Australia. Ritchhart's first book on the topic, 'Intellectual Character', was published in 2002, followed by four subsequent books in 2011, 2015, 2020, and 2023, which expanded and refined the ideas. From 2005, Bialik College in Melbourne began a research collaboration with Ron Ritchhart and the team at Project Zero which led to the publication of 'Making Thinking Visible' in 2011. Bialik College then went on to host biennial Cultures of Thinking conferences.

Under the leadership of Cameron and Simon, respectively, Shore School and Masada College in New South Wales were also early adopters of Cultures of Thinking pedagogy. Mirroring Bialik College, Masada hosted three biennial conferences with Ron Ritchhart as a keynote speaker in 2010, 2012 and 2014. Soon after the publication of Ritchhart's 'Creating Cultures of Thinking' in 2015, the Project Zero Australia Network was founded in November 2016. Beginning with the 2017 conference at Shore, the Project Zero Australia Network has gone on to host six free conferences from 2017 to 2024 along with numerous other events and workshops, all of which have served to raise awareness of Cultures of Thinking pedagogy and practice.

While Project Zero ideas have spread and taken root around the globe, it is interesting to note that they have found a particularly fertile home in Australia. The reasons for this are likely multifaceted and might include: a healthy focus on innovative educational practices, a priority on professional learning, a culture of collaboration and openness, global connectedness, and an emphasis on critical thinking and creativity. These factors combine to create a robust environment where Project Zero ideas can thrive and make a significant impact on teaching and learning in Australia.

STORY OF NOW

So what is the story of learning being told right now across Australia?

According to Ron Ritchhart, 'A culture lives in the messages it sends… These messages taken together constitute the story of learning we enact with and for our students… To change a culture, we must change the messages we are sending to write a new story of learning' (2023, p. 53). In this book, we highlight the many ways in which Australian educators are writing a new story of learning: a story of thinking, curiosity, empowerment, complexity, and collaboration. This book serves to make these stories visible and amplify the initiative for ongoing change.

As we move forward, however, we remain mindful of the counter-story, an old story that sometimes masquerades as new, a parallel narrative that threatens the story we truly wish to tell.

As education systems grapple with the demands of a rapidly changing world, teachers are often made scapegoats for deeper systemic shortcomings. In Australia, politicians and bureaucrats seek quick solutions to wicked school challenges (Hunter and Carter, 2024). Government-mandated changes undermine teacher professionalism and one-size-fits-all approaches exacerbate the growing exodus of experienced educators (Mahoney, 2024). Mistrust in teachers' knowledge and professional judgement is widespread, sometimes amounting to gaslighting, an underhand attempt to undermine teachers' confidence in their capacity to make informed decisions (Poulton, 2024).

Perhaps the most insidious issue is the oversimplification of inherently complex teaching practices (Brunker, 2024). Teaching is not a commodity that can be packaged and sold, and learning is not an algorithm. Teachers are constrained by corporate jargon and bureaucracy; pressured to prioritise standardised testing over authentic learning experiences (Netolicky et al., 2019). As a result, student thinking often goes unnoticed, overshadowed by the emphasis on exam results as the sole measure of success. Education systems focus on covering vast curricula, which at their very worst devolve into teaching by mentioning. This can lead to superficial understanding, where students recall facts in the short-term for examinations, but struggle to apply knowledge in more meaningful ways.

In Susan Blum's recent book *Schoolishness* (2024), she explains how the grammar of contemporary schools has inadvertently become institutionalised. Despite our inherent propensity for learning and curiosity, much like the persistence of foot-binding in China for over a thousand years, harmful institutions can endure. Yong Zhao (2018) highlights this in his discussion of education systems, emphasising that what works may also harm, producing unintended side effects. He uses the example of direct instruction, which, while efficiently boosting achievement on standardised measures, can stifle curiosity and creativity.

Schoolishness is a pressing problem: schools can feel alienating, making authentic learning difficult to achieve. How do we shed this inhumane, foot-binding version of school and create spaces that nurture genuine curiosity and human potential? History shows that change to entrenched systems is possible – smoking on airplanes, once the norm, is now unthinkable. Schools, too, can evolve. The rising willingness of young people to challenge systems, particularly in areas like sustainability, demonstrates a readiness to contest long-standing norms.

The premise of this book is for a curiosity-driven approach which shifts the focus from controlling young people to deeply engaging with ideas. It encourages students to ask questions, explore interests, and make connections. By fostering an environment where curiosity is valued and nurtured, educators can create learning experiences that are more engaging, relevant, and impactful. This shift not only enhances student engagement but also cultivates learners who are motivated by an intrinsic desire to understand the world around them. Moving from control to curiosity requires educators to rethink their roles, nudging classrooms towards being dynamic spaces of inquiry and discovery, and away from being more static repositories of bits of information.

At the 2024 Australian Council for Educational Leaders' annual conference, neuroscientist Alan Finkel (2024) declared, 'Comprehensive teaching of critical thinking is the revolution we need to have'. While the call to prioritise the teaching of thinking is not new, it has become more urgent. But can we truly teach students how to think, or is it more about fostering a culture where thinking can thrive? This book argues for the latter, illustrating how this shift is taking place in Australian schools today.

The book is divided into five sections:

- 'Empowering Learners': In this section, we introduce the key themes that set the foundation for the rest of the book: empowering students to take ownership of their learning and nurturing their curiosity. We highlight innovative classroom practices that engage students as active creators, initiators, and problem solvers.
- 'Shifting Paradigms': This section offers a broad contextual overview of the challenges facing Australian education, advocating for the reform of outdated systems and critiquing the predominance of mono-cultural teaching. It argues that education systems are failing to prepare students for an unpredictable future, with an overemphasis on standardised testing and rigid accountability stifling creativity and neglecting diverse student needs.
- 'Transforming Classrooms': This section offers practical insights for educators to create active learning, deep thinking, and student agency. Drawing on Project Zero research, these chapters explore innovative teaching methods that empower students to take ownership of their learning. Key themes include cultivating dispositions such as curiosity, persistence, and intellectual growth, reimagining traditional teaching approaches, and encouraging learners to "do the heavy lifting."
- 'Leading Professional Growth': This section emphasises the importance of cultivating school cultures that prioritise thinking and inquiry, not just for students but for educators as well. It advocates for a shift from traditional one-off workshops to ongoing, embedded professional learning that promotes reflective practice, courageous leadership, and meaningful collaboration.
- 'Navigating Change': Insights and strategies are offered for fostering a Culture of Thinking in Australian education. We address common challenges, propose alternative pathways for lasting change, and provide case studies to illustrate key concepts.

Cultivating Cultures of Thinking in Australian Schools amplifies the voices of some of Australia's most exceptional teachers, all of whom have been inspired by Cultures of Thinking ideas. Teacher voices are especially significant here, as educators are often hesitant to share publicly or are constrained by the systems they work within. These narratives are enriched by insights from leading education scholars, who provide valuable context and broaden the lens through which these contributions are understood. We are immensely grateful to our contributors for dedicating their time and energy, despite their busy schedules, to share their passion for transforming teaching and learning.

Through practical examples and experiences, this book serves as both a roadmap and a call to action for Australian teachers, urging them to foster environments where deep thinking, collaboration, and meaningful learning flourish. This is a rallying cry for a paradigm shift, empowering educators to become agents of change in their classrooms and schools, and empowering learners to take ownership of their educational journey.

REFERENCES

Blum, S. (2024) *Schoolishness: alienated education and the quest for authentic, joyful learning*. New York: Cornell University Press.

Brandt, R. (1993) 'On teaching for understanding: a conversation with Howard Gardner', *ASCD*, 50(7). [Accessed 15 October 2024]. Available from: https://ascd.org/el/articles/on-teaching-for-understanding-a-conversation-with-howard-gardner

Brunker, N. 2024. Escape oppression now: disrupt the dominance of evidence-based practice. 13 June. *EduResearch Matters*. [Accessed 15 Oct 2024]. Available from: https://blog.aare.edu.au/escape-oppression-now-disrupt-the-dominance-of-evidence-based-practice/

Engel, S. 2006. Open Pandora's box: curiosity and imagination in the classroom. *Child Development Institute*. Occasional Paper Series. [Accessed 25 September 2024]. Available from: https://www.sarahlawrence.edu/media/cdi/pdf/Occasional%20Papers/CDI_Occasional_Paper_2006_Engel.pdf

Finkel, A. 2024. *Reimagining our future planet*. ACEL National Conference, 2 October, Adelaide.

Hunter, J.L. and Carter, D. 2024. Is there a 'right way' to teach? Recent debates suggest yes, but students and schools are much more complex. *The Conversation*. [Accessed 15 October 2024]. Available from: https://theconversation.com/is-there-a-right-way-to-teach-recent-debates-suggest-yes-but-students-and-schools-are-much-more-complex-235421

Mahoney, T. 2024. What mandated phonics means for Victoria's haemorrhaging teacher numbers. *The Age*. 18 June. [Accessed 15 October 2024]. Available from: https://www.theage.com.au/politics/victoria/what-mandated-phonics-means-for-victorias-haemorrhaging-teacher-numbers-20240618-p5jmn8.html

Netolicky, D., Andrews, J. and Paterson, C.(eds.) (2019) *Flip the system Australia: what matters in education*. New York: Routledge.

Perkins, D.N. (1992) *Smart schools: from training memories to educating minds*. New York: The Free Press.

Perkins, D.N., Jay, E. and Tishman, S. (1993) 'Beyond abilities: a dispositional theory of thinking', *Merrill-Palmer Quarterly*, 39(1), pp. 1–21. [Accessed 15 October 2024]. Available from: http://www.jstor.org/stable/23087298

Poulton, P. 2024. Are we now gaslighting teacher expertise? 27 September. *EduResearch Matters*. [Accessed 15 Oct 2024]. Available from: https://blog.aare.edu.au/are-we-now-gaslighting-teacher-expertise/

Ritchhart, R. (2002) *Intellectual character: what is it, why it matters, and how to get it*. San Francisco: Jossey-Bass.

Ritchhart, R. (2015) *Creating cultures of thinking: the 8 forces we must master to truly transform our classrooms*. San Francisco: Jossey-Bass.

Ritchhart, R. (2023) *Cultures of thinking in action: 10 mindsets to transform our teaching and students' learning*. New Jersey: Jossey-Bass.

Ritchhart, R., Church, M. and Morrison, K. (2011) *Making thinking visible*. San Francisco: Jossey-Bass.

Vygotsky, L.S. (1978) *Mind in society*. Cambridge, MA: Harvard University Press.

Zhao, Y. (2018) *What works may hurt: Side Effects in education*. New York: Teachers College Press.

Empowering Learners
Section I

"If we support students in becoming active creators, initiators, problem finders and community members while we as teachers focus on coaching, mentoring and being community navigators, then students' understanding, engagement, curiosity, and self-direction will increase" (Ritchhart, 2023, p. 73).

We believe that most educators want more for their students than mere compliance, conformity, risk aversion, and unquestioning receptiveness. However, it is all too easy for teachers to fall into roles that inadvertently lead to these outcomes. The pressures of curriculum coverage and examination preparation can transform us almost unwittingly into information deliverers, rescuers, and authoritative sources of wisdom (Ritchhart, 2023).

In this section, we introduce the foundational themes at the heart of this book. We argue that by releasing control and cultivating curiosity we can help students develop a sense of agency, becoming responsible and self-directed learners. We present a variety of strategies and innovative approaches designed to empower and energise the students we teach.

Cameron Paterson argues that to genuinely empower our learners, we must unlearn our desire to control them. This process begins with teachers nurturing a genuine interest in uncovering and understanding their students' thinking, followed by efforts designed to stretch and challenge that thinking. Cameron suggests that teachers can easily fall into the habit of doing most of the thinking and learning for their learners. He challenges us to position them as co-constructors of their learning experiences, involving them in processes that are typically under our control. In doing so, we create curious and empowered students with greater agency and a strong desire to learn.

Simon Brooks argues that cultivating curiosity leads to enhanced engagement, deeper understanding, and improved well-being. He proposes three common expressions of students' curiosity – looking closely, asking

DOI: 10.4324/9781003541745-2

questions, and engaging in authentic inquiry — and describes transformational practices for educators who wish to foster curiosity in their classrooms. Simon challenges teachers to cultivate students' curiosity despite the pressures of time and content coverage. Highly effective teachers understand that how they choose to allocate time reflects their pedagogical values. If we want our students to be curious, we must intentionally create opportunities for that curiosity to flourish.

REFERENCES

Ritchhart, R. (2023) *Cultures of thinking in action: 10 mindsets to transform our teaching and students' learning.* New Jersey: Jossey-Bass.

Unlearning Control
Cameron Paterson

One

Teaching is the best job in the world, a daily adventure into student thinking. It is a profoundly creative act, an art that brings learning to life. Throughout my career, I've relied on student feedback to refine my teaching practices. One year, during a mid-year survey, I posed a question designed to spark reflection: "What advice would you give teachers to bring out the best in students?" Among the many insightful responses from my Year-9 class, two stood out and have stayed with me ever since:

- *"Don't always plan really far ahead. Ask the kids what they want to do and see if you can make it happen. Don't always do what you want."*
- *"Let them grow into themselves instead of making them be something else."*

I remember feeling pride in my students for their thoughtful comments, even as I felt an unexpected sting, like a sucker punch, at the same time. Their responses were not only entertaining and eloquent but also deeply challenging, compelling me to confront my own assumptions about teaching and learning.

In response to their challenges, I have shifted my teaching practices to make thinking more visible, allow students to be confused, work hard to build relational connections, and ask deeper questions than 'guess what's in my head'. I have concluded that if I really do want my young learners to 'grow into themselves', then I need to relinquish the desire for control.

MAKING THINKING VISIBLE

Teacher-centred instruction is deeply ingrained in schools; teachers as authorities at the front of the room delivering information. Despite calls for more child-centred approaches echoing through the teachings of Socrates, Montessori, Freire, Vygotsky, Piaget, Bruner, Malaguzzi, Dewey, and Foucault, the traditional view of teacher and student roles has proven remarkably resistant to change.

DOI: 10.4324/9781003541745-3

In contrast, I have gradually learned to trust the minds of learners by really listening for, valuing, and trying to understand their thoughts, experiences, and insights, and then using them as a starting point. It is only by thinking that people get better at thinking, and everything that I do either supports or diminishes my students' reliance on their ability to think.

How do I know when my students are thinking well? Active listening and thoughtful questioning are the foundation of constructive classroom interactions, and the heart of these practices is respect for and interest in students' thinking. I need to be genuinely curious about what sense a learner is making and how a learner understands something. This requires asking questions without steering them towards a predetermined response. Duckworth (2006, p. 162) warns, "We cannot learn anything about what children think if we signal to them what we hope they will say." Too often the conversations in my class revolve around students attempting to guess what's in my head.

By observing closely and listening carefully to the thoughts of my students, I gain the information necessary to ask them good questions in the first place. It is my role to pose questions, to push learners to see where their answers hold up and where they do not hold up, to ask the right question at the right time in order to press a learner's thinking. When we make thinking visible in our classrooms, we ask less factual recall questions and more constructive questions: What do you notice? What puzzles you? What are you wondering? How does this connect to what you already know? Can you show me? Where do you see that? What do you mean? Why do you think that? How did you get that? What makes you say that? What else?

When I make students' thinking visible, the balance of power shifts, transforming the dynamic between my students and me, and fostering a relationship built more on trust and respect. I become a student of my students, driven by curiosity about their learning and the desire to make my teaching responsive to them (Ritchhart, 2020). When students realise my genuine interest in their thoughts, they become more inclined to willingly share them.

NAVIGATING CONFUSION

Confusion and conflict are needed in order to learn, and failure is a necessary building block for ultimate success. Thinking is difficult and doubt is the basis of all good thinking.

Exploring wrong ideas is always productive. A wrong idea corrected not only corrects the error but also enriches understanding more profoundly than if the misconception had never arisen in the first place. By considering alternatives and working through them, learners come to master ideas more thoroughly. I have learned to be less impatient for my students to develop clear ideas, because putting ideas in relation to each other is confusing; and I need to give that confusion time. We all need time to dwell in our confusion if we are to build a solid base of breadth and depth that provides significance to our knowledge (Duckworth, 2006).

Perhaps one of our most constructive approaches is to build the capacity of young people to embrace discomfort. I vividly remember teaching a Year-12 class about the Pol Pot regime in Cambodia. Following a discussion about the atrocities that occurred after the Khmer Rouge victory, I introduced the perspective of a left-wing historian who posited a counter-narrative. He argued that the Khmer Rouge's decision to evacuate Phnom Penh in 1975 might have been driven by genuine fear of US bombing and the inability to feed the population. One student furrowed her eyebrows and grasped her head in her hands, exclaiming, "Now I don't know what to think!" And I recall thinking to myself, "Perfect, now she is exactly where she needs to be." Placing the student right at the heart of the muddle resulted in deeper and more meaningful learning.

RELATIONAL CONNECTIONS

My foremost job is to connect. Students learn best when they feel known, valued, and respected by both the adults in the school and their peers (Ritchhart, 2023). Classrooms that build community cultures where students are intrinsically motivated and committed to supporting one another are at a significant advantage.

The most important thing I do to build relational connections is to commit to knowing all student names by the end of the first class. This effort signals genuine interest and lays a strong foundation for fostering meaningful rapport. I set the tone for each class by welcoming students with a relevant thematic song (such as Split Enz's 'History Never Repeats') when they enter the room. Lessons can also be started with quick team-building activities like Rock, Paper, Scissors, or Crazy Handshakes. Short role plays and simulations to start a class serve a similar purpose. A two-minute role play depicting factory work during the Industrial Revolution adds an interactive element and sets an engaging and constructive tone for the lesson.

One of the profound realisations that slowly dawned on me is that problem children are not problem children. Rather, the system produces exactly what it is designed to produce. Young people often struggle to focus on tasks they consider irrelevant, they become bored with the sterility of standardisation, and now they have less patience than previous generations. This is not a medical condition.

Something fundamental has shifted in modern childhood and the culture of school. The relationship with school has become more optional, and young people are voting with their minds. Attendance rates in schools are on a downward trend, accompanied by a rise in disruptive behaviour and disturbingly high levels of mental health issues among students. Over three-quarters of Australian students have reported they didn't fully try in the latest Pisa tests (Cassidy, 2023). ATAR is now not used by more than 75% of our young people (Learning Creates, 2023). Australian parents are now homeschooling more than 43,000 children (Bita, 2024).

Many young people seem to intuitively sense, even if they cannot explicitly express it, that the current educational offerings fall short in adequately preparing them for the challenges of the future. Instead of recognising these signals as indicators of a systemic issue, the default response tends to blame young people. What if we interpreted their behaviour as a form of feedback, signalling that something is wrong? Rather than assigning blame, we might introspectively ask: What are they telling us?

We can learn to become intentionally curious about resistant young people in an effort to understand them. After all, should we not teach young people that sometimes there is a need to break the rules, to challenge authority, for disobedience? In her brilliant book *Troublemakers*, Carla Shalaby (2017, p. 168) writes, "If adults were better at bearing their responsibility to see and hear children, the need for children to rely on disruption as a strategy for visibility might decrease."

While there are countless strategies teachers have developed to connect with young people, an easy and effective one is the Two-by-Ten (McKibben, 2014). The premise is simple yet powerful: dedicating two minutes daily for ten consecutive days to engage with a disruptive student. The intentional investment fosters a connection, breaking barriers, and building rapport.

THE ART OF QUESTIONING

In Seymour Sarason's (1971, pp. 105–106) seminal work, he observed:

1. Teachers ask between 45 and 120 questions per half-hour.
2. The same teachers estimate that they ask between 12 and 20 questions per half-hour.
3. Between 67% and 95% of all teacher questions require a straight recall from the student.
4. Every half an hour, two questions are typically asked by children in the class.
5. The greater the tendency for a teacher to ask straight recall questions, the fewer the questions initiated by children.
6. The more a teacher asks personally relevant questions, the more questions students ask in class.
7. These results do not vary across IQ level or social class.

What if the culture of the classroom was question-centred? Inviting questions in class is not the same as intentionally teaching the skill of designing good questions. Teaching students the art of asking powerful questions might be one of the greatest gifts we can bestow.

When students generate their own questions, a thought-provoking query on the ill-fated Gallipoli campaign: "What were they hoping to achieve?" can become a recurring focal point throughout a unit. Students can come to understand that questions are more important than answers and that it is OK to ask questions that we might not know the answers to. It's about fostering the disposition of curiosity and acknowledging that different people bring different questions to the table.

Questions are one of the pivotal ways we engage with students. According to Ritchhart, "Our questioning helps to define our classrooms, to give it its feel and energy, or lack thereof. Questions are culture-builders, linking students, teachers, and content together" (2015, p. 221). When teachers focus on developing a culture of thinking, their questioning tends to swing away from procedural and review questions towards more constructive and facilitative questions that push student thinking and make thinking visible. I have long felt that the best focus for any classroom observation is questioning: What sort of questions are being asked, and, more importantly, who is asking them?

Too much classroom questioning is the conventional Question-Response "ping-pong" style of questioning. Much more valuable is collective basketball questioning (McIntosh, 2012), where teachers pose a question, pause, ask another student to evaluate the initial answer response, and then ask a different student for an explanation of how and why it is right or wrong – more like a basketball game where "we have lots of players taking turns with the ball, rather than a simple back-and-forth with the teacher" (Ritchhart, 2015, p. 104) and "the ball (question) is passed around and ideas are bounced off one another, as the ball is moved down the court" (2015, p. 213). Empowering students to share thoughts and insights sparks a shift towards collaborative inquiry, distributing power across the class instead of centring it within the teacher.

Engaging students in discussions about this research can transform the way that they talk and learn as a group. Several years ago, one of my classes coined the metaphor of building on each other's ideas like "ice-cream scoops," instead of individually "pop-corning" their own individual thoughts. They even went as far as self-assessing themselves at the end of a class, with comments like, "We did too much pop-corning today and not enough ice-creaming."

EMPOWERING LEARNERS

I often find myself doing lots of the thinking for my students, raising questions about what tasks I might be withholding from them and what valuable learning experiences they may be missing out on. The biggest change to my teaching practice is that I now bring students into processes that teachers typically control, like assessment, leading discussions, and the choice of topics. When students are empowered as co-constructors, a sense of ownership and engagement is fostered in their learning experiences (Ritchhart, 2023).

Integrating peer feedback and self-assessment into the learning process yields significant benefits. Listen to Year-9 student Hamish, "I have learned how to provide better feedback to my peers. When I read their work, I learn how I could improve my own writing, and this helps me take more responsibility for my own learning" (Paterson, 2022). If you ever believe that children are too young to provide each other with effective feedback, watch the inspiring video "Austin's Butterfly" (EL Education, 2016).

Assessment is usually something that is done to students, so an empowering shift is to co-construct assessments with them. This involves them in the evaluation process and puts assessment criteria into student-friendly language rather than cryptic teacher-speak. By involving students in the 'secret teacher business' of forming assessments, we empower them to better understand expectations and take a proactive role in their own learning. Year-9 student Spencer articulates the impact of this, "We designed the marking guide as a class. It helped us know what was needed before we did the task, instead of being told what we did wrong when it was too late" (Paterson, 2022).

Additionally, empowering students to set their own classroom norms can be a transformative practice, and the use of restorative practices offers effective solutions for behaviour management and discipline. A concluding class at the end of the year represents an opportunity to distribute lesson planning documentation for students to leave warm and cool Post-it note feedback to collaboratively co-create a curriculum vision for the upcoming year. In fact, almost anything that a teacher can think to complain about can be solved by empowering young people.

Many of the workload concerns voiced by teachers are missed learning opportunities for students, often because educators underestimate the capabilities of young people. However, young people possess a remarkable capacity to teach, assess, offer feedback, facilitate discussions, plan curriculum, and even handle disciplinary issues. Yet, most teachers insist on shouldering all these responsibilities themselves. At a subconscious level, teachers may find a certain satisfaction in their workload, as it boosts their professional identity. However, research suggests that the most successful learning environments are those in which leadership roles are shared between the teacher and the students (Schmuck and Schmuck, 1992).

Teachers do too much of the learning and thinking for students. It does not have to be this way. When we work harder than students, young people become inculcated into coming to school to watch us work, but genuine learning and thinking cannot be outsourced. While the instinct to rescue students in the face of challenges is common, teachers who prioritise autonomy actively seek opportunities to step back, encouraging students to take the lead.

When given some independence, young people tend to become more independent. They live up or down to expectations. If we want them to take responsibility for the culture and feel of the classroom and school, we need to invite them into the conversation, and even step away and let them take the lead.

FOSTERING CULTURES OF THINKING

Reflecting on the student responses at the start of this chapter, I've come to realise that not every decision has to be mine to make. I'm also getting better at allowing students to grow into their authentic selves, rather than shaping them into something else; always an ongoing process.

Teaching isn't about following a medicalised 'evidence-based' Science of Learning script or wielding judgemental performative measures; it is a creative art that thrives on curiosity, listening, and relational connections. The transformative approach presented in this book represents a profound shift in mindset; an intentional transfer of agency to students by actively listening to their voices and genuinely valuing their thinking.

Elise Heil, a Principal, aptly captures the transformation teachers undergo – from content delivery to skilfully facilitating thinking – through a less controlling approach. "Teachers now listen more than they speak. It's made teaching more interesting and more enjoyable. Teachers don't feel like they constantly have to perform. They don't have to plan every minute detail. Teachers are more relaxed and happier. We have to unlearn the desire for control" (Paterson, 2019, p. 20).

REFERENCES

Bita, N. (2024, March 11) Tutors cash in on homeschooling. *The Australian*.

Cassidy, C. (2023, January 12) Nearly 80% of Australian students say they 'didn't fully try' in latest Pisa tests. *The Guardian*. Available at: https://www.theguardian.com/australia-news/2024/jan/12/nearly-80-australian-students-say-they-didnt-fully-try-in-latest-pisa-tests [Accessed 14 November 2024].

Duckworth, E. (2006) *The having of wonderful ideas and other essays on teaching and learning*. New York: Teachers College Press.

EL Education. (2016) *Austin's butterfly: models, critique, and descriptive feedback*. Available at: https://www.youtube.com/watch?v=E_6PskE3zfQ&t=5s [Accessed 14 November 2024].

Learning Creates. (2023) *Learning beyond limits: insights and learnings from visionary schools and communities working toward a fit-for-purpose learning system*. Available at: https://www.learningcreates.org.au/media/attachments/2023/12/17/learningbeyondlimits-report-dec2023.pdf [Accessed 14 November 2024].

McIntosh, E. (2012) *Stop ping pong questioning. Try basketball instead*. Available at: https://edu.blogs.com/edublogs/2012/02/stop-ping-pong-questioning-try-basketball-instead.html [Accessed 14 November 2024].

McKibben, S. (2014) The two-minute relationship builder. *ASCD*. Available at: https://www.ascd.org/el/articles/the-two-minute-relationship-builder [Accessed 14 November 2024].

Paterson, C. (2019) Churchill fellowship report. Available at: https://www.churchilltrust.com.au/fellow/cameron-paterson-nsw-2019/ [Accessed 14 November 2024].

Paterson, C. (2022, August 15) What can students do? Getting Smart. Available at: https://www.gettingsmart.com/2022/08/15/what-can-students-do/ [Accessed 14 November 2024].

Ritchhart, R. (2015) *Creating cultures of thinking: the 8 forces we must master to truly transform our classrooms.* San Francisco: Jossey-Bass.

Ritchhart, R. (2020) *The power of making thinking visible: practices to engage and empower all learners.* New Jersey: Jossey-Bass.

Ritchhart, R. (2023) *Cultures of thinking in action: 10 mindsets to transform our teaching and students' learning.* New Jersey: Jossey-Bass.

Sarason, S. (1971) *The culture of the school and the problem of change.* Boston: Allyn & Bacon.

Schmuck, R.A. and Schmuck, P.A. (1992) 'Leadership', in *Group processes in the classroom.* 6th ed. Dubuque: Wm. C. Brown Publishers, pp. 108–153.

Shalaby, C. (2017) *Troublemakers: lessons in freedom from young children at school.* New York: The New Press.

Stoking the Fires: How Cultivating Curiosity Leads to Enhanced Engagement and Deeper Understanding

Simon Brooks

Two

Sitting at the back of Jenny Stephens' Year 10 Science classroom in rural New South Wales, I am surprised to find myself becoming increasingly curious about the topic of Mendelian inheritance. This was something I knew nothing about before arriving today but, as Jenny's lesson unfolds, I am all in.

Jenny begins by sharing a little background information about Gregor Mendel, the nineteenth-century biologist known as the Father of Genetics.

"I'm going to put a diagram on the board," she says, "and I'd like you to take a couple of moments to look at it very closely. What do you notice? What do you think might be going on here?"

The students are silent for a little while, paying close attention to the image. I am struck by the fact that nobody calls out. This is a place for quiet, attentive, interruption-free observation.

"Tell me what you see," says Jenny in due course.

"A first generation and a second generation," says one child.

"An arrow connecting them," says another.

"Cucumbers," says a third.

"Not cucumbers, beans!" laughs someone else.

Another pause.

"What else do you see?" asks Jenny.

"The beans outside the squares are slightly larger than the ones inside," offers a student.

"I see a large yellow bean outside the grid at the top, and a smaller yellow bean inside the grid at the bottom, both with the same coding, 'yy'," says another.

Jenny allows them to share their noticings, occasionally prompting them to look again or look more closely. This continues for five minutes or so.

When the moment feels right, she moves them on. "Now that you've looked closely, I'd like you to start trying to explain what's going on here,"

DOI: 10.4324/9781003541745-4

she says. "Have you got any ideas or hypotheses about what this is all about? And what evidence have you got to support that?"

It strikes me that Jenny is using the 'See Think Wonder' thinking routine (Ritchhart, Church and Morrison, 2011), a routine for close observation and interpretation. However, at no point does Jenny announce, "now we're going to do See Think Wonder." This is See Think Wonder by stealth. It is less about 'doing' the routine, and more about drawing on its steps as a scaffold for student thinking.

Now, the lesson really starts to come alive.

"It's got something to do with recessive genes," reasons a student. "Recessive genes," repeats Jenny, "what makes you say that?" "Well…." says the student, "in the second generation there are two green bean parents with three green offspring and one that is yellow. That yellow one wouldn't exist if not for recessive genes."

Another student joins in. "I agree," she says, "and connected to that, I think the capital Y is code for green, whilst the lower-case y is code for yellow."

Quick as lightning, a third student joins the fray. "What makes you say that?" he says, "surely it would make more sense to use G for green and Y for yellow." The second student pauses for thought. "No, I think it's that capitals indicate the dominant colour in the gene, with lowercase letters for the recessive… like if we were talking about curly hair, it might be a capital C for straight hair, and a lowercase c for curly."

I look around the classroom. Students are relaxed, but attentive. They are leaning in. They are not afraid to share their thinking with Jenny and each other. They are enjoying the conversation. For them, their time together seems to carry with it a sense of 'perceived worth' (Ritchhart, 2015, p. 164), a feeling that the lesson has value in-and-of itself.

In the final phase of the lesson, Jenny asks them what questions they still have and what they are wondering. Questions lead to tentative explanations, and tentative explanations to more wonderings. As their thinking deepens, Jenny introduces discipline-specific terminology when appropriate, including words such as Punnett squares, dominant and recessive genes, genotypes, phenotypes and alleles. As she does so, she takes care to get the balance just right: not too much input, not too little.

Ultimately, when the bell rings and Jenny's students are free to go to lunch, none of them go. Instead, they stay behind and pepper Jenny with questions and theories. One thing is very clear. Jenny does not believe that good teaching is about transmitting what she knows straight into the minds of her learners. For Jenny, teaching is about stoking the fires of curiosity and creating the optimum conditions for learning.

As Jenny herself told me later, 'I've found that students grasp the complex concepts of my subject area much faster and far more meaningfully in a single lesson of "See Think Wondering" than in two solid weeks of old-fashioned content delivery' (Stephens, 2016).

WHAT DOES CURIOSITY LOOK LIKE?

Curiosity is notoriously difficult to define. However, as Susan Engel argues, most of us know it when we feel it (2015). Spend a few moments in the classrooms of teachers like Jenny who make it their mission to cultivate curiosity, and the reasons for doing so become very clear. As research indicates, curiosity is among the most powerful mechanisms of high-impact learning, leading to enhanced memory (Gruber, Gelman and Ranganath, 2014), deeper understanding (Kashdan and Silvia, 2009) and improved wellbeing (Zainal and Newman, 2023).

Metaphorical descriptions for curiosity abound: for Ward (Cited in Kang *et al.*, 2009, p. 1), curiosity is 'the wick in the candle of learning'; for Engel (2006), it is the 'engine for learning' (p. 6). American psychologist George Loewenstein defines curiosity as 'a form of cognitively induced deprivation that arises from the perception of a gap in knowledge or understanding' (Loewenstein, 1994, p. 75). In other words, curiosity is an itch we need to scratch. We are curious when we are aware there is something within our reach that we don't yet understand, and are motivated to close that gap in understanding.

Drawing on Berlyne's contention that curiosity is aroused by the incongruity of external stimuli (1966), I propose a working definition as follows: curiosity is a strong desire to learn more, typically sparked by ambiguity, incongruity or complexity.

But how can we tell if our students are feeling curious? What behaviours might they exhibit when acting on their curiosity? Reflecting on Jenny's lesson and others like it, at least three common expressions of curiosity emerge:

Looking Closely (Studying Something Intently, Tinkering, Taking Apart)

Looking closely means taking the time to lean in and observe in forensic detail. When we look closely, we explore each and every facet of a visual stimulus, taking the time to observe 'more than meets the eye at first glance' (Tishman, 2018, p. 2). Close looking may involve more than just the sense of sight, as in the case of slow listening, or noticing with all our senses. Sometimes, it involves opportunities for students to tinker and take apart, to 'look' with their hands as well as their eyes. Looking closely means resisting the urge to turn too quickly to inference and interpretation.

Asking Questions (Wondering At, About and With)

Curious students ask questions which reveal an authentic engagement with the topic under consideration: "What makes a poem timeless?", "Why do we interpret the same work of art differently?", "How do we know the Big Bang Theory is right?" These questions about the learning are very different to questions about the work (Ritchhart, 2015), which are often clarifying or procedural in nature and may not indicate curiosity at all: "How long does this have to be?", "Am I doing this right?", "Will this be on the test?".

Authentic Inquiry (Exploring and Inquiring in an Effort to Learn More)

Authentic inquiry involves students actively engaging in meaningful exploration and investigation as they explore their wonderings individually or collectively. Inquiry is underpinned by a sense of perceived worth: students feel that their efforts are worthwhile, purposeful and intrinsically valuable (Ritchhart, 2015). They are not "doing it because the teacher told me to." During authentic inquiry, students may generate their own questions, engage with multiple resources, collaborate meaningfully with peers and share their findings with a broader audience.

FIVE KEY PRACTICES FOR CULTIVATING CURIOSITY

In schools across Australia, teachers from diverse subjects and age groups are placing curiosity at the heart of their classrooms. Now that I have established why this approach is desirable and illustrated what it might look like in practice, an important question remains:

What might we do as educators to cultivate curiosity?

After many years observing numerous outstanding practitioners, at least five key practices for cultivating curiosity are emerging.

Become a Curator of Curiosity Primers

Some years ago, I had the pleasure of working with an Australian Biology teacher who was about to embark on a unit exploring photosynthesis. Inspired by Cultures of Thinking ideas, he decided to begin the lesson with the Think Puzzle Explore thinking routine (Ritchhart, Church and Morrison, 2011). Students filed in from recess to find two pieces of butcher's paper on the wall, one headed up "What do you think you know about photosynthesis?", the other, "What questions or puzzles do you have about this topic?" With great enthusiasm the teacher shared these questions with his students, and waited. And waited. A small fragment of tumbleweed blew through the room. The students had nothing. Nothing came to mind for them that they wanted to share.

Luckily, this teacher had a built-in second chance with a parallel class that he taught the next day. This time, he decided to begin by showing a short, five-minute documentary about photosynthesis he had found on YouTube. Following this, he shared the same two questions as before. And this time, students were tremendously forthcoming with their thinking, both in terms of ideas and questions. Interestingly, they didn't just parrot back concepts they had taken from the video either. It seemed that the video had somehow served to awaken their curiosity. As Loewenstein (1994) posits, curiosity is often sparked when a small amount of information is shared, since this has the effort of raising learners' awareness of what they don't know, which motivates them to want more.

This is a phenomenon I call warm wondering. Curiosity needs to be primed. Asking students to wonder when cognitively cold is like trying to start a car with a dead battery.

Something I've noticed over the years is that teachers who value curiosity become curators of curiosity primers. By curiosity primers, I mean visual stimuli or provocations which will likely ignite students' curiosity.

As an English teacher, I've lost track of how many times I've taught George Orwell's *Nineteen Eighty-Four*. Many years ago, a colleague showed me a map of the novel they had found online (BigThink, 2024). It's a thought-provoking map. It distorts the shape of the continents, highlights experimental stations in South America and Western Australia, and re-badges the UK as 'Airstrip One'. Not only this, but the map has two contrasting keys: different allies and enemies are revealed depending on whether you view it via a landscape or portrait orientation. It is a fantastic curiosity primer. Spend a little time looking closely and it prompts numerous theories and wonderings.

Ancient History teacher Josh Levy also understands the power of curiosity primers. In a lesson on the Amarna Revolution at St Aloysius' College Sydney, Josh showed his students a series of typical images of New Kingdom Pharaohs, typically depicted with broad shoulders, a strong, muscular torso and an idealised, athletic build. After allowing his students time to describe what they noticed, he then shared some images of Akhenaten, Egyptian Pharaoh from 1353 to 1336 BCE. Josh's students were flabbergasted. The imagery is noticeably different: wide hips, a protruding belly, slender limbs, and an elongated neck and skull giving him an unusual, almost alien-like appearance. Why did he look like this? Was he an actual alien? If not, why this form of representation? Josh's students were alive with wonderings and a desire to unearth answers.

Reflecting on the examples above, and inspired by Daniel Berlyne's work on incongruity (1966), I would like to propose several characteristics of powerful curiosity primers:

- Ambiguity: Meaning is not immediately clear or is open to multiple possible interpretations
- Incongruity: Elements do not seem to belong or fit with expectations
- Complexity: There are layers of detail and different parts that relate to each other in a variety of ways
- Novelty: There are unfamiliar or unexpected elements which lead to new or different thinking
- Mystery: There is a sense of something not fully revealed (e.g. partially obscured objects or incomplete diagrams)
- Contradiction: Elements are in tension with one another or juxtaposed provocatively.

Teachers who seek to cultivate their students' curiosity are always on the hunt for curiosity primers like these, deploying them in class to provoke wonder and intrigue their learners.

Encourage Close Looking and Wondering

At Waitara Public School on Sydney's North Shore, Kath Boon's Year 5 Mathematicians are looking closely at an image she is projecting onto the screen.

At first glance, the image appears simple. There are five rows, with twelve units of one in the top row, six of two in the second, four of three in the third, three of four in the fourth and two of six in the bottom.

"I want you to have a really close look at this image" says Kath. "Tell me, what do you notice, and what do you wonder?"

Students are quick to share their observations.

"Red, white and blue go together."

"Yellow and green go together."
"I see twelfths, sixths, quarters, thirds and halves."
"I see fractions."
"Factors of twelve."
"I see only two prime numbers."
"Four out of five have a half."

As the students share their noticings, Kath documents their ideas on flipchart paper. Occasionally, she stops to press for elaboration.

"Four out of five have a half. Can you tell me what you mean by that?"

"Well, there are five different fractions, and you can see the line down the middle doesn't run through the thirds like it does for the other four, which can all be split exactly in half."

More noticings are shared.

"Anything you want to add, or build on, or wonder about?" asks Kath.

"Why aren't there any more fractions – why five?"

"I have a question - why isn't there a whole?"

"I have a wonder – how high could this go? – how small could it get? – and what are all of the steps on the way up?"

Kath Boon is a strong advocate for Noticing and Wondering, a thinking routine which encourages students to look closely, notice detail and ask questions. Part of its power lies in its utility as a low floor and high ceiling task, providing an entry point for all students as well as opportunities for more advanced exploration (Boaler, 2016).

Sitting at the back of her classroom, I find myself marvelling at just how much they see and how much thinking they share. There is a palpable sense of joy and playfulness in the room. Ideas jump like sparks from student to student. Community and collaboration fuels their wonder. Wonder sets the stage for an extended episode of inquiry, driven by students' desire to discover more. In one lesson, Kath's Year 5s go on to explore the difference between abundant, deficit and perfect numbers, making connections with the Aliquot sequence, challenging claims, exploring patterns and proposing theories.

On a practical note, readers interested in experimenting with Noticing and Wondering in Mathematics will find numerous powerful curiosity primers online at 'Multiplicity Lab', a website founded by Northwestern University School of Education and Social Policy (Multiplicity Lab, 2024).

Close Looking is not limited, of course, to the teaching of Mathematics. Project Zero's 'Artful Thinking' provides a number of thinking routines designed to facilitate observing and describing, which can be used to look closely at works of art or visual stimuli across the school curriculum (Artful Thinking, 2024). One of these routines, Looking Ten Times Two (Tishman, 2018), is a particularly powerful strategy for noticing more than first meets the eye, asking students to list ten words or phrases about anything they notice, and then another ten. I have sometimes engaged my learners in looking ten times three for particularly detailed images!

When creating opportunities for close looking, don't be frightened to have students leave their seats and come close. Sometimes, they may crowd around the screen where you are projecting an image, or sit together on the floor directly in front of it. Something about the act of communal leaning-in intensifies curiosity.

Practice using the phrase, "What else?", over "Anything else?"

"Anything else?" suggests within its own phrasing that there might be nothing else, particularly when asked with an upward inflection. Sometimes, "Anything else?" has a darker purpose behind it. We ask it when what we really want to do is wrap up: "Anything else, no, OK then, moving on…"

"What else?" signals to our students that we believe in them. We know they have it in them to notice more. Practice the "What else?" game. How many times can you ask "What else?" or "Something else?" when you are pressing for more noticings and wonderings? How much curiosity might this unearth that otherwise would never have seen the light of day?

Build Learning Opportunities around Prediction and Reflection

For me, one of the best things about being a father of young children was reading bedtime stories. It was a lovely opportunity for us to feel connected and relax together at the end of a busy day. Every night, they would take turns to select a picture book and I'd settle down to read it to them, silly voices and all.

As others have discovered however, it is a dangerous thing having a teacher for a parent. Before too long, I'd invented a bedtime-story thinking routine called 'What happens next?' with which to torment them on a nightly basis. Here was the idea: read until the moment they were completely immersed in the story, shut the book with a flourish and proclaim it is time for bed.

Much grumbling and bellyaching would inevitably ensue.

"Here's the deal," I would say. "We *can* read on if you like, but only if first you answer me this: what do you think will happen next in the story and why?"

Perhaps I was a mean Father.

The game would play out like this. My children would think about what had already happened and offer predictions for what they thought would happen next or how they thought the story would end. In doing so, I encouraged them to talk about their justifications: they might for instance refer to textual signposts they had noticed or what they intuitively understood about narrative structure. When predictions had been milked for all they were worth, we would finally read on. Having done so, we would then reflect back on our predictions and how accurate they were. Why did we think *that* was what was going to happen? How might we have predicted what actually happened? Which ending would have been best and why?

As you can see, there are two phases to "What happens next?"

- What happens next? What makes you think that?
- What actually happened? Compare and reflect.

There was, of course, method to my madness. Research shows that prediction is a highly effective strategy to improve reading comprehension (Miller, 2002). The process of making and then revisiting predictions encourages deep processing of information and enhances overall understanding (Duke and Pearson, 2002).

At the time, I was Director of Learning and Teaching at Masada College in Sydney and shared this routine with my colleagues. What happened next was interesting. Colleagues across the school took it up in different ways. Primary colleagues used it when reading storybooks to their classes. A Senior School History teacher used it during a unit on the Second World War, asking students to reflect on "What do you think Churchill did next?" at a key strategic moment. Physical Education (PE) teachers used the routine to help students explore tactical choices in rugby by pausing a video at a key point in a game. Inspired by their colleagues' stories, Science teachers adopted David Sadler's POE (Predict Observe Explain) thinking routine (1992), engaging their young scientists in making predictions, observing outcomes and explaining the results.

These teachers learned for themselves what the research already shows. When we encourage prediction, we activate prior knowledge, stimulate curiosity and engage cognitive processes that support deep learning and the development of understanding (McDaniel and Einstein, 2007; O'Reilly and Munakata, 2000).

Limit Excessive Explanation

According to Lipman *et al.*, 'Things are wonderful when we can think of no way of explaining them. It may be a magician's card trick, or a caterpillar turning into a butterfly, or a Schubert trio. But whatever it is, if we find it inexplicable, we are inclined to call it marvellous, and wonder at it' (1980, p. 32). Drawing rhetorically on imagery from a range of disciplines, the authors share a provocative idea: things are wonderful when they are inexplicable. But every moment of every day, in schools around the world, teachers explain things to their students. Is there a risk that we are explaining away the wonder?

Loewenstein (1994) offers a balanced perspective on the place of explanation. Yes, curiosity is often strongest when there are gaps in our knowledge and understanding, and once these gaps are filled the intensity tends to diminish. However, if we are exposed to information which is incomplete or raises new questions, it can also have the effect of prolonging or even intensifying our curiosity by challenging our existing thinking.

In other words, everything depends on timing. If our students are sitting there thinking, "Why are you telling me this?", we have gone wrong somewhere. If we can find a way to deliver our explanation at their point of need, it may well serve to enrich and sustain their curiosity.

At Ryde Secondary College in Sydney, Mathematics teacher Meg Bennett set about teaching her students the concept of simultaneous equations in a novel and engaging way. For Meg, it was not enough for her students to understand how just to 'do' simultaneous equations. She also wanted her students to appreciate the reason for their very existence.

To do this, Meg decided to involve her students in a real-life problem she was facing. Meg wanted to join a local gym and boiled her options down to a choice of two. Option A offered a set price of $22 per workout. Option B offered a monthly membership fee of $100 and only $10 per workout. Meg asked her students to use mathematics to help her decide which gym to join.

The problem was rich and challenging. Students drew on a number of problem-solving strategies, including listing, graphs, algebra and trial and error. Research suggests that mathematical tasks which ask the problem before teaching the method and involve multiple methods, pathways and representations are more likely to lead to engagement and deep learning (Boaler, 2016).

Meg's students soldiered on, but soon realised their current methods were inefficient. It became clear that the solution hinged on how many times per week Meg planned to work out, yet something still seemed to be missing. Their curiosity was piqued. "Is there an easier way to solve this?" they wondered.

This, of course, played right into Meg's hand. "What if I was to teach you something called simultaneous equations?" she said. "I've got a feeling that might be the missing piece you need." Meg was right of course. For her students, learning about simultaneous equations brought with it a sense of relief, positioned as it was as the antidote to their collective ills. Meg had delivered the explanation at their point of need. They now understood why humanity needs simultaneous equations. Without them, we'll never know what gym to join. Meg's students were keen to dig deeper into the topic and explore more applications for this mathematical concept.

Loewenstein (1994) was clearly correct. An appropriate amount of explanation delivered at the point of need can serve to increase our interest by satisfying our curiosity whilst simultaneously opening up more lines of inquiry. The key is how much and when. Excessive explanation can stultify the desire to learn and smother the flames of curiosity. A good question for us to ask ourselves as teachers is "Why am I telling them this?" Is this something they could work out for themselves if I primed their curiosity?

Create Time and Space for Curiosity

At Bellevue Hill Public School in Sydney's Eastern Suburbs, one way in which Year 5/6 teacher Belinda Kinross puts curiosity at the heart of her classroom is through a weekly learning routine she has established with her students known as 'Grej of the Day' (GOTD) (Hermansson, 2020).

In a nutshell, GOTD (pronounced 'Grey of the Day', meaning 'thing of the day') is a micro-learning strategy developed in 2009 by Swedish teacher Micael Hermansson. Each day, teachers give a short, intriguing presentation on a fascinating topic (about 8–10 minutes) aiming to spark curiosity and expand students' general knowledge through manageable, bite-sized information (Hermansson, 2020). At the end of the day, teachers provide students with a clue to get them thinking about the next day's topic, which they discuss speculatively with family at home. Next day, the session begins with students sharing their guesses for today's topic. GOTD topics range widely in theme, including people (e.g. Rosa Parks), places (e.g. The pyramids of Giza) and events/things of importance (e.g. The Titanic, chess, Apollo 11). After the presentation and resultant discussion, students organise their notes in a GOTD notebook and commit to sharing with their families what they have learnt today. The teacher prints an image for every topic and attaches it to a GOTD map of the world, with a thread running from the image to a corresponding place on the map.

It is bright and early on Monday morning and I am joining Belinda's class to witness GOTD in action. Belinda has been working with GOTD for some years now and has been immersed in Cultures of Thinking ideas for many more, so I am interested to see the fusion of pedagogy and practice in her classroom. Belinda runs GOTD once-weekly rather than daily with her class, sharing the clue with her students on Fridays to think about over the weekend.

This time, the clue is a series of three symbols arranged in a row: a cheetah, an upward-facing arrow and a flexed bicep. "What do you think the Grej of the Day might be today?" asks Belinda.

"I don't have a full answer, but cheetahs are the fastest animal, so perhaps it has something to do with that."

"John and I were thinking of Usain Bolt - he is fast, represented by the cheetah, and he is also tall and strong, represented by the arrow and the muscle."

"Cheetahs usually hunt using the high ground, represented by the upward arrow, so this makes me connect to Star Wars, when Obi-Wan defeats Anakin by taking the higher ground."

"I'm thinking about the Olympics motto - Faster, Higher, Stronger - and the images seem to connect directly to that."

Belinda listens to her students' many theories, occasionally pausing to reflect back and probe their thinking. As time passes, curiosity rises. It is clear that students are intrigued by each other's ideas and keen to hear the answer.

"Let's solve the mystery," says Belinda, advancing to her next slide. "It's the Olympic motto: Faster Higher Stronger."

The 2024 Paris Olympics are taking place during the time of my visit, so Belinda has taken the opportunity to connect to something current. On this occasion, one of her students guessed correctly: the clue was indeed the Olympic motto. It is not always the case that someone 'gets it right'. Regardless, Belinda is very careful to honour all of their theories: students understand engaging in the process of predicting is more important than getting 'the right answer'.

Belinda launches into her mini-talk. She has prepared a slideshow which is predominantly images and has used as few written words as possible. There is a sense that she is telling a story. Hermansson suggests that this phase should feel like a 'fairytale of facts' (2020, p. 16) and Belinda's students are enthralled. When she reaches the end, she highlights several key points and asks students what takeaways they have.

"For the first time, 50% of the competitors in 2024 are women."

"The five rings represent the five continents."

"Back at the oldest Olympics in 776 B.C. they used to fight to the death, naked!"

A little more discussion and clarification takes place.

When Belinda announces, "That is the end!", her students erupt into a spontaneous round of applause. There is a palpable sense of joy in learning. The class debates which part of the GOTD map today's image should connect with. Some argue for Greece, some for Paris. Belinda invites them to try to persuade the person sitting next to them of their opinion. "How about we say Paris," says Belinda, "since it is the first Olympics where there is a 50% representation for women."

The session moves towards a close. "I want you to go back to your devices," says Belinda. "I wonder... What are you still wondering about the Olympics? What questions do you still have?"

Later, Belinda shares with me a copy of their questions. There must be over 50, including "How can I get a sport included in the Olympics?", "Are the gold medals really made of gold?", "Why are the games in honour of Zeus and not the other Gods?" and "Is there skiing in the Paralympics?" Students are asked to pick somebody else's question, research it and answer in as much detail as possible in an online shared document. Belinda joins in, answering a couple herself, and submitting some of her own questions, some of which are answered by her students.

Spending the morning with Belinda, it is easy to see that she values curiosity and authentic engagement in her classroom. These are her non-negotiables, her goals as an educator, her 'Big Rocks' (Covey, 2020). In Belinda's own words, 'I want my students to have a love of learning and for learning to be fun, and I think that GOTD is a wonderful avenue for both of those things to come together' (Kinross, 2024). The benefits for her students are clear. 'I've seen them grow as thinkers on their own volition,' says Belinda. 'I give them the stimulus, but I can't be curious for them. What I love is that even though I'm the driver, they're the ones choosing to get into the car.' Highly effective teachers recognise that the way they choose to deploy time in the classroom is a statement of their pedagogical values (Ritchhart, 2015). In other words, if we want our students to become curious, we must be intentional in making space and time for them to feel curious.

Not all teachers will want to institute GOTD in their classrooms, but there are many other ways to make time for curiosity. One strategy is to develop the habit of pausing for think-time (Stahl, 1994). When teachers habitually pause for thought for at least three seconds before calling on a student to answer a question, or after they have shared an idea, student engagement increases, as does the quality of questions that teachers ask (Rowe, 1972). Frequent pausing for think-time sends messages to students that this classroom is a thoughtful place where curiosity is valued.

Over the years, I have tried to train myself out of asking, "Any questions?" I noticed that when I phrased it this way, I typically got questions about the work, such as "How long does this need to be?" or "When is this due again?", if indeed they asked any questions at all. Instead, I am training myself to ask, "What are you curious about?", or "What are you wondering?" The difference is amazing. When we press for wonderings, we get wonder.

What do we do, however, when our students share potentially tangential wonderings, questions we fear might send us down a rabbit hole from which we will never return? Do we ignore the question altogether? What messages might that send to our learners about curiosity and learning? What might unfold if we ventured down a few of those rabbit holes, so long as it serves the purpose of deeper learning? What would it be like if we were to create a 'Wonder Chart' in our classrooms, a piece of flipchart paper on which we record our students' wonderings as they come up, even if they are tangential? What if we followed Belinda's suggestion of having students go away and research answers to each other's wonderings and come back next lesson to share their findings? What impact might that have on the culture of our classroom?

STOKING THE FIRES

So, is it really possible for teachers to cultivate students' curiosity?

Whilst young children are renowned for their boundless questioning, studies show that curiosity typically takes a hit as soon as children go to school (Engel, 2015). A study by Tizard and Hughes (1984) found that although preschoolers ask on average 26 questions per hour at home, this rate dropped to two per hour when the same children were in the classroom. As Engel concludes, it seems that 'though children are curious, students are not' (2015, p. 89).

There is, however, a silver lining. As this chapter clearly shows, the extent to which learners demonstrate curiosity is highly dependent on the teacher in the classroom. Studies indicate that there is significant variation between classrooms in terms of expressions of student curiosity (Engel, 2015). Step inside Jenny's Biology classroom, Josh's History class, Meg's Maths lesson, or Belinda's Year 5/6 room, and there is no doubt that you'd instantly sense an atmosphere charged with curiosity.

Think of curiosity as flames, and information as firewood. Too much information and the fire is smothered. Too little, and the fire burns out. Just the right amount, and the fire burns brightly, new information satisfying existing wonderings whilst piquing more. Thinking is oxygen for the flame of curiosity. Gaps between the logs are essential if the flames are to breathe. Plenty of flames, and the fire of learning burns hot and bright.

Fundamentally, it is up to teachers to choose whether or not they wish to stoke the fires of curiosity. We all feel the pressures of coverage and time: there is just so much for us to get through every day as educators, and sometimes it feels almost impossible to make space for anything else. Is curiosity non-negotiable in your classroom? It's up to you. As Henry Ford famously put it, 'Whether you think you can, or think you can't, you're right' (Ford, 2024).

REFERENCES

Artful Thinking. (2024) *Overview*. [Accessed 25 September 2024]. Available from: http://pzartfulthinking.org/

Berlyne, D.E. (1966) 'Curiosity and exploration', *Science*, 153, pp. 25–33.

BigThink. (2024) *Orwellian cartography: how to tell two truths with one map*. [Accessed 24 September 2024]. Available from: https://bigthink.com/strange-maps/651-nil-orwellian-cartography-101-how-to-tell-two-truths-with-one-map/

Boaler, J. (2016) *Mathematical mindsets*. San Francisco: Jossey-Bass.

Covey, S.R. (2020) *The 7 habits of highly effective people: 30th anniversary edition*. New York: Simon & Schuster.

Duke, N.K. and Pearson, P.D. (2002) 'Effective practices for developing reading comprehension', in Farstrup, A.E. and Samuels, S.J. (eds.) *What research has to say about reading instruction*. Newark: International Reading Association, pp. 205–242.

Engel, S. (2006) *Open Pandora's box: curiosity and imagination in the classroom.* Child Development Institute. Occasional Paper Series. [Accessed 25 September 2024]. Available from: https://www.sarahlawrence.edu/media/cdi/pdf/Occasional%20Papers/CDI_Occasional_Paper_2006_Engel.pdf

Engel, S. (2015) *The hungry mind: the origins of curiosity in childhood.* Cambridge: Harvard University Press.

Ford, H. (2024) *Whether you think you can or you think you can't – you're right.* [Accessed 25 September 2024]. Available from: https://www.goodreads.com/quotes/978-whether-you-think-you-can-or-you-think-you-can-t–you-re

Gruber, M., Gelman, B. and Ranganath, C. (2014) 'States Of curiosity modulate hippocampus-dependent learning via the dopaminergic circuit', *Neuron*, 84(2), pp. 486–496.

Hermansson, A. (2020) *Grej of the day.* Sweden: Big Business Publishers.

Kang, M.J., Hsu, M., Krajbich, I.M., Loewenstein, G., McClure, S.M., Wang, J.T. and Camerer, C.F. (2009) ' The wick in the candle of learning: epistemic curiosity activates reward circuitry and enhances memory', *Psychological Science*, 20(8), pp. 963–973. [Accessed 24 September 2024]. Available from: https://doi.org/10.1111/j.1467-9280.2009.02402.x

Kashdan, T.B. and Silvia, P.J. (2009) ' Curiosity and exploration: facilitating positive subjective experiences and personal growth opportunities', *Journal of Personality Assessment*, 91(5), pp. 388–397.

Kinross, B. (2024) *Conversation with Simon Brooks*, 12 June.

Lipman, M., Sharp, A.M. and Oscanyan, F.S. (1980) *Philosophy in the classroom.* Philadelphia: Temple University Press.

Loewenstein, G. (1994) 'The psychology of curiosity: a review and reinterpretation', *Psychological Bulletin*, 116(1), pp. 75–98.

McDaniel, M.A. and Einstein, G.O. (2007) 'The power of predictions: the role of anticipation in learning', *Current Directions in Psychological Science*, 16(1), pp. 26–30.

Miller, D. (2002) *Reading with meaning: teaching comprehension in the primary grades.* Portland, ME: Stenhouse Publishers.

Multiplicity Lab. (2024) *Mathematical tasks worth doing.* [Accessed 24 September 2024]. Available from: https://multiplicitylab.northwestern.edu/

O'Reilly, R.C. and Munakata, Y. (2000) 'The role of prediction in learning and memory', *Psychological Science*, 11(6), pp. 430–434.

Ritchhart, R. (2015) *Creating cultures of thinking: the eight forces we must master to truly transform our schools.* San Francisco: Jossey-Bass.

Ritchhart, R., Church, M. and Morrison, K. (2011) *Making thinking visible.* San Francisco: Jossey-Bass.

Rowe, M.B. (1972) 'Wait-time and rewards as instructional variables: their effects on language, logic, and fate control', *Sociology of Education*, 45(1), pp. 63–75.

Sadler, D.R. (1992) 'The POE (predict-observe-explain) strategy', *Teaching Science*, 38(2), pp. 24–28.

Stahl, R.J. (1994) Using "think-time" and "wait-time" skillfully in the classroom. ERIC Digest. [Accessed 24 September 2024]. Available from: https://files.eric.ed.gov/fulltext/ED370885.pdf

Stephens, J. (2016) *Conversation with Simon Brooks*, 12 August.
Tishman, S. (2018) *Slow looking: the art and practice of learning through observation*. New York and London: Routledge.
Tizard, B. and Hughes, M. (1984) *Children learning at home and in school*. London: Fontana.
Zainal, N.H. and Newman, M.G. (2023) 'Curiosity does help to protect against anxiety and depression symptoms but not conversely', *Journal of Affective Disorders*, 323, pp. 894–897.

Shifting Paradigms
Section II

"There are three stories of learning we should examine before we can look at how to transform culture. The first is the old story – that is, the story each of us was told as a student. The second is the current story dominant in schools and classrooms today. The third is the new story we want to be telling" (Ritchhart, 2015, p. 21). This section zooms out to adopt a broader perspective, exploring the challenges and possibilities facing Australian education. By stepping back, we gain a clearer view of the systemic issues at play while also identifying potential pathways for our new story.

Education systems are increasingly failing to prepare students for an unpredictable future. The emphasis on standardised testing and rigid accountability measures stifles creativity and neglects the diverse needs of students. Education must acknowledge the unique experiences and backgrounds of each student, ensuring that it is not a one-size-fits-all approach but a rich tapestry woven from many threads.

Pasi Sahlberg argues that, despite significant increases in education spending, learning outcomes in the Western world have stagnated. This stagnation is attributed to escalating competition, rigid standardisation, and punitive accountability measures that diminish student engagement. Many Australian schools remain trapped in a cycle of compliance and fear of failure, relying on outdated methods and quick fixes rather than addressing the need for stronger relationships, wellbeing, and play.

Pasi advocates for transformative strategies to reshape education, including:

- Building Healthier Relationships through Teacher Looping
- Making More Time to Play
- Providing Daily Healthy Lunches

Indigenous educators **Melitta Hogarth, Justin Wilkey, and John Doolah** advocate for the integration of Indigenous knowledge into

DOI: 10.4324/9781003541745-5

teaching practices. They encourage educators to reflect on their own ways of knowing and to critique standardised testing, which often perpetuates deficit narratives about Indigenous students. Effective education should cater to diverse learning needs while fostering authentic relationships and a deeper understanding of shared histories. The authors call for a shift that values Indigenous knowledge, challenging the monocultural perspectives that dominate Australian classrooms. Readers are invited to explore different viewpoints and encouraged to embrace curiosity and take risks rather than maintain the status quo, as an inquisitive mind thrives on diversity.

REFERENCES

Ritchhart, R. (2015) *Creating cultures of thinking: the 8 forces we must master to truly transform our classrooms.* San Francisco: Jossey-Bass.

Restructuring Schools for Relationships,
Play, and Time to Think
Pasi Sahlberg

Three

THE PROMISE OF THE DISRUPTION

Thirty moons ago, the world was grappling with what would become the greatest disruption of a generation. The global health pandemic, officially declared by the World Health Organisation in March 2020, shocked the world, leaving over seven million dead and countless others suffering from a wide range of symptoms.

The COVID-19 pandemic, as it came to be known, changed the way most people worked, communicated, and learned. Bedrooms turned into office spaces, new relationships were forged, and millions of students were left, so to speak, to their own devices to study at home. A common sentiment during this global disruption was that, once it was over, nothing would be the same. Everything, it seemed, needed to be reimagined – a grand reset of how we lived and worked. This included education that many international organisations and leading researchers (Fullan, 2021; OECD, 2018; World Bank, 2018) viewed that time as being a global crisis. The global disruption was a perfect storm for a reset of education and to reimagine what schools could be in the future.

Every cloud has a silver lining, as they say. The pandemic, along with the profound disruption it caused, offered a unique opportunity to rethink our perspectives and habits regarding education. Many of us, whose contributions you will read in this remarkable book, seized that moment to think more deeply, read more broadly, and write more freely about the future, at a time when nearly all other aspects of normal life were restricted.

The tone of these writings – mostly essays and reflections – was one of optimism and hope for a better tomorrow. School closures, social isolation, and time for reflection prompted educators around the world to reconsider the true purpose of education and what schools could be when life returned to 'normal.' There were global calls for a new social contract in education, envisioning reimagined relationships within schools and more collaborative cultures within education systems. The

DOI: 10.4324/9781003541745-6

promise of that disruption was the co-designed school of the future, where every student would flourish through active engagement, greater agency, and meaningful learning.

In one of my own writings during that period, I argued that the COVID-19 pandemic was the greatest (natural) social experiment ever witnessed in Modern History (Sahlberg, 2021). The purpose of an experiment is to test the efficacy or likelihood of something previously untried. Contemporary education systems have evolved to serve various purposes, most centred around building human capital through carefully designed programmes and curricula for the betterment of individuals and societies. Consequently, many education systems are calibrated to achieve predetermined outcomes or standards – educating students for a predictable, likely future.

One immediate lesson from the pandemic was the stark contrast in how schools and education systems around the world were prepared to handle the unprecedented external shock. Prolonged school closures and the sudden shift from classroom instruction to remote learning exposed these differences. International organisations, such as the Organisation for Economic Co-operation and Development (OECD), the United Nations Educational, Scientific and Cultural Organization (UNESCO), and the World Bank (WB), have since reported insights about the schools that adapted well and the education systems that demonstrated resilience during the crisis. Schools that had equipped their students to be more self-directed in learning, and education systems that embraced trust and flexibility, often managed better in the face of the uncertainties brought on by the disruption.

GLOBAL LEARNING CRISES

The state of global education before the pandemic was already weak. The international organisations mentioned earlier had released reviews and analyses of education systems' performance on student outcomes, equity of these outcomes, and student attendance, engagement, and sense of belonging in school. In a synthesis of educational progress in the first two decades of the 21st century, the OECD concluded that "over the past decade there has been virtually no improvement in the learning outcomes of students in the Western world, even though expenditure on schooling rose by almost 20 per cent during this period" (OECD, 2018, p. 13). The WB's verdict in its annual Human Development Report in 2018 was that "there is a global learning crisis that amplifies educational inequalities and severely hobbles the disadvantaged youth who most need the boost that a good education can offer" (World Bank, 2018, p. 6). UNESCO's Global Education Monitoring Report in 2020 revealed that 260 million children, adolescents, and youth are not in school, and only half of them achieve the basic level of proficiency required for good life (UNESCO, 2020). It is worthy of note that the COVID-19 pandemic was not the reason for the global education crises, it made an already stark situation even worse.

Many efforts have been made to understand the drivers of this poor state of global education. Some evidence suggests, among them Jean Twenge's research on youth well-being (Twenge and Hamilton, 2022) and data from Australian students in OECD's Programme for International Student Assessment (PISA) study (De Bortoli et al., 2024) that the growing distraction caused by mobile digital technologies, especially social media, has led to the rapid erosion of children's mental health and well-being affecting their learning outcomes in school. Others criticise education policies and schools for their inability to adapt to new forms of learning and different kinds of learners, persisting with an old, uniform "grammar of schooling" (Zhao, 2024), instead of customising teaching and learning according to students' needs and interests.

For the past two decades, my interest has been in understanding how education systems worldwide respond to economic and cultural globalisation. The term *Global Educational Reform Movement* (GERM) has emerged to describe the policy priorities and assumptions that define national education reforms (Sahlberg, 2023). This chapter is not the place for a detailed description of GERM and how it operates, but here is a summary of its key elements during this century:

1. **Increasing competition between schools.**
   Rationale: When schools compete for enrolments, they focus more on improving teaching and learning outcomes. Assumption: Quality of education improves.
2. **Standardisation of teaching and learning in schools.**
   Rationale: Externally set high expectations for schools, teachers, and students are a precondition for improved learning and higher performance. Assumption: Common standards allow for better comparison of schools.
3. **Prioritisation of basic literacy and numeracy.**
   Rationale: Literacy and numeracy are the foundations on which good education is built. Assumption: Learning to read, write, and

perform mathematics well is essential for further learning and the development of higher-order competencies.

4. **Punitive test-based accountability.**
Rationale: Schools need more autonomy and flexibility to compete effectively, but this can only happen within clear accountability structures. Assumption: Standardised tests are the most reliable and fair way to hold schools accountable.

Research and policy analyses from around the world indicate that GERM has been a defining paradigm of education reform in many countries. While it is difficult to directly attribute the poor state of global education to these reform directions, they have not delivered the improvements they were intended to achieve. So, what does this mean for schools and education leaders in practice?

I offer two key conclusions for advancing education policy and school improvement. First, it makes no sense to keep doing the same things while expecting different results. This doesn't mean abandoning all healthy competition or teaching all children necessary basic skills or that schools should have no accountability for student learning. Instead, we need to rethink the purpose of schooling itself. As some education leaders are already doing, we should take a much closer look at today's students and how that influences what teachers do in schools. Transforming education requires adopting new rationales, assumptions, and values that drive alternative paradigms for future schooling.

Second, we must stay true to the promise of the past disruption. I would argue that most young people realised that the COVID-19 pandemic fundamentally changed their lives – the way they learn, communicate, collaborate, and live. Many students have told me how their lives were turned upside down during pandemic lockdowns, but despite promises to reimagine education after the disruption their schools have remained the same. Some feel that school education has even regressed. They tell me they find themselves doing less of what they are curious about and what truly matters to them, and more of what feels increasingly irrelevant. In short, most young people expected the pandemic to change their schools as many education experts and thinkers promised. Their disappointment that it didn't is reflected in statistics on student attendance, sense of belonging, and misbehaviour in schools.

Australia is no exception, unfortunately. Despite countless education reviews, declarations, and political reform rhetoric, educational performance has not improved, and in international comparisons, it has declined (ACARA, 2024; Sahlberg, 2024). Although Australian schools offer world-class learning to many, Australian education remains unfair and unequal, with significant learning gaps and disparities in educational opportunities between rich and poor students (Australian Government, 2023). Since the pandemic, the number of students unable or unwilling to attend school for various reasons has increased, student well-being has declined, and fewer students than before feel that school is a stimulating place to learn.

The issue is not a lack of professionalism or passion within schools to reverse these troubling trends. As in many other countries, the challenge lies in the fact that innovation and the drive for system transformation do not come from the top. They rarely have, and likely never will. The hope for change lies in schools and the individuals within them who have the courage and strength to lead the transformation from the ground up. The good news is that there are scores of schools and thousands of teachers and leaders, across all sectors and jurisdictions, who are already doing this (e.g., Cook, 2023). Some of them have written chapters for this book. The bad news is that most Australian education systems still operate within a culture of compliance, conformity, and fear of failure, which compels many schools to continue doing what they have always done.

In the following section, I will present three practical ideas that are already being implemented in some Australian schools, though they are far from mainstream practice. These ideas, when adapted to fit different school contexts, have the potential to transform the culture of schools – through relationships, play, and free school lunch – to enable students and teachers to think deeper about themselves and one another in school.

HOW TO CREATE TIME TO THINK IN SCHOOL?

Many years ago, I wrote in my doctoral dissertation that time is the greatest enemy of teachers. The cultures of teaching everywhere are defined by busy schedules, constant management of unexpected events, and dealing with hundreds of interpersonal relationships, often simultaneously, every day. I also concluded that time, when seen as a valuable resource used mindfully, can be the best solution to many challenges the teaching profession faces today.

The most common complaints I hear from teachers and principals are about overloaded school days, crowded curricula, and, consequently, a shortage of time to do what could truly improve schools. Teachers across the world express this concern, even though teaching schedules vary significantly from country to country. If we look at the number of school days in annual calendars, the differences aren't substantial. In most countries, children attend school for about 190 days a year. In Australia, it's 200 days (in government schools), and in the United States (US), it's typically 180 days, depending on the state. Another way to understand the amount of compulsory instruction students receive in different countries is to calculate the total number of hours during primary and lower secondary education. Figure 3.1 illustrates this comparison across several OECD countries.

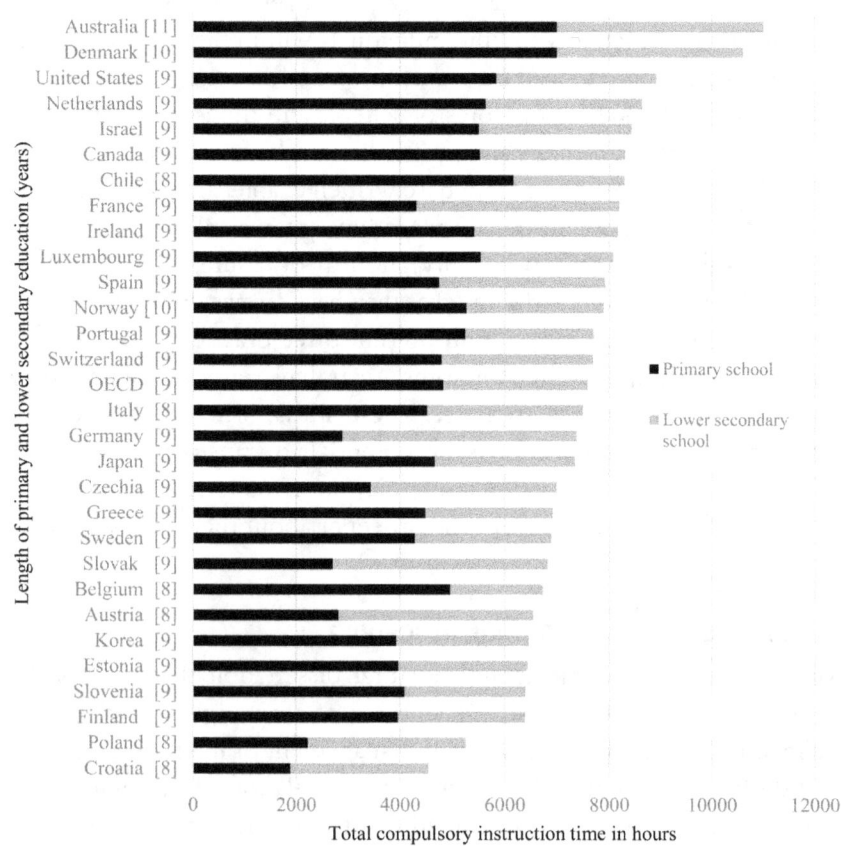

Figure 3.1 Total Compulsory Instruction Time During Primary and Lower Secondary Education in Some OECD Countries in Hours in 2022.
Source: OECD (2023).

It may be surprising that Australian children are required to have more formal instruction during primary and lower secondary schooling than their peers in any other OECD country, as shown in Figure 3.1. On average, students in OECD countries receive 7,580 hours of instruction in total, compared to 11,000 hours in Australia. Interestingly, the length of primary school (in hours) in Australia exceeds the entire first nine years of schooling in countries like Austria, Poland, Korea, Estonia, and Finland (OECD, 2023; Sahlberg, 2024). Such a heavy instructional load in Australian schools makes it difficult for students to do anything besides being taught during school hours. Time for students' independent activities is limited, and there's little opportunity for reflective thinking in schools that have such busy daily schedules.

So, what can be done? Extending school days by starting earlier or staying longer is often not an option. However, some schools and countries have successfully created time to cultivate cultures of collaboration, community, and belonging. One effective approach has been to restructure teaching in schools to foster deeper and sustained relationships between teachers and students. Another strategy, common in the Nordic countries, is to provide children with time for independent activities, particularly unstructured play. The key principle in building social capital in schools is the same as for building any other kind of capital: returns won't come without investments.

Time is the most effective resource to invest in social capital. Next, I describe what these approaches could look like in practice.

Building Healthier Student-Teacher Relationships Through Teacher Looping

A distinctive feature of Australian primary and secondary schools is the way teaching is organised from year to year. In most schools, teachers work with a new group of students each year, who were previously taught by another teacher. At the start of every school year, teachers get to know their new students, explain rules and expectations, set goals for the year, and address other important matters. The first week of Term 1 in many schools is focused on getting started and building new relationships between students and teachers.

Why so many schools operate this way is unclear. When asked, teachers often say, "This is the way it has always been." There is no strong evidence suggesting that this is the best way to organise teaching from a student learning and well-being perspective. Alternative models can be found in Australian Montessori or Waldorf schools, where children typically stay with the same teacher for several years. In some countries, mainstream education is organised such that teachers follow the same group of students for more than one year.

Teacher looping, or simply "looping," is an educational practice that dates back to the early 20th century. In looping, a teacher stays with the same group of students for consecutive years. Instead of receiving a new group of students each year, the teacher continues teaching the same students as they progress through school. Over multiple years, the teacher develops a deeper understanding of the students and builds stronger relationships with them.

Here are two examples of what teacher looping looks like in primary school:

- A teacher begins with a group of children in Year 1.
- Instead of transitioning to a new group of students the following year, the teacher continues teaching the same students as they move up to Year 2 and then Year 3.
- Depending on the school's practice, this arrangement can extend for several years, allowing the same teacher and group of students to progress together.

There is no single model for how looping can be arranged in schools. In Finland, for example, where all schools are designed on the principle of teacher looping to foster closer relationships between students and teachers, one teacher typically teaches the same group in Year 1 and Year 2, and then another teacher takes over and teaches the class from Year 3 through Year 6 (Sahlberg, 2021). Montessori and Waldorf schools often use different looping structures to serve the same purpose of building strong relationships. Figure 3.2 illustrates some common models of looping, with arrows indicating teacher mobility.

The main goal of looping is to build healthier relationships between teachers and students in schools. Looping also fosters closer relationships among teachers, parents, and carers. When teachers spend more than a school year with the same students, they can develop a better understanding of their students' individual needs and interests, which is essential for successful education. This enables more personalised learning and timely support for students. Stronger teacher-student relationships provide the support students need to thrive, learn, and grow (Ritchhart, 2023). Additionally, students benefit from a more stable and

Two 3-year loops:

Three 2-year loops:

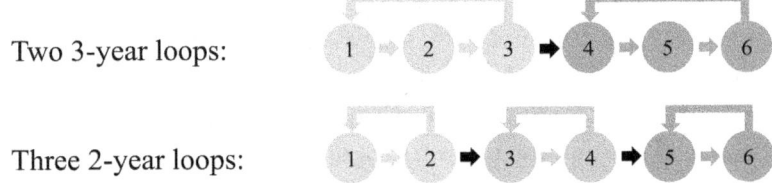

The Finnish Model

Y1–Y2 loop:

Y3–Y6 loop:

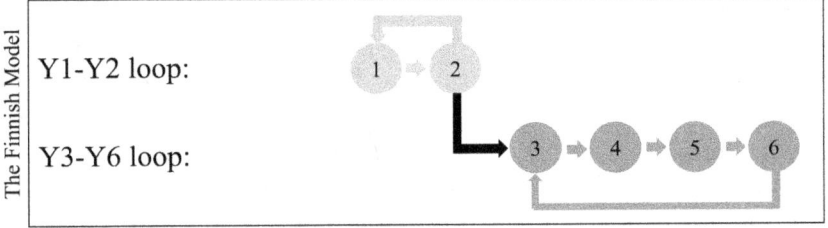

Figure 3.2 Different Models of Teacher Looping in Primary School.

consistent classroom culture, which can enhance both academic and socio-emotional outcomes.

Looping is a universal teaching arrangement in Finland, Japan, and Germany, and it is becoming common in primary schools in the United States. A growing body of research is providing evidence of positive impacts on classroom cultures, student achievement, and teacher job satisfaction (Wedenoja, Papay and Kraft, 2022). In practice, looping is a cost-effective method to cultivate healthier relationships and social capital in schools, benefiting students, teachers, and parents. Of course, looping is not a silver bullet to solve all challenges in schools, but it is a low-cost opportunity to improve schools by simply enhancing relationships within schools and between schools and homes. Looping requires principals with fluent organisational skills, flexibility from teachers, and direct communication with parents about the purpose and nature of sustained school-home relationships. It is important that no group of students would be saddled with an underperforming teacher for long periods of time while other students would excel. That's why good leadership and staff relations are paramount in making the most of teacher looping.

Making More Time to Play

One contributing factor to the excessive formal instruction in Australian primary schools is the uniformity of the school day schedule. Daily schedules may vary from school to school, but a common principle is that regardless of students' ages, school days follow the same sequence. Mornings typically start in primary schools at 9 a.m., for example, when students attend a two-hour block usually dedicated to two subjects (often literacy). After the morning tea break, another two-hour block of instruction follows. Lunch (box) break often includes time for outdoor play, followed by one more block of classroom instruction before the day ends at around 3:30 p.m.

For example, in Victoria, government schools are typically required to offer 300 minutes of instruction daily. In many other countries, the length of children's school days varies depending on their age. For instance, in Finland, primary school students have only about 200 minutes of instruction scheduled in four or five 45-minute lessons each day. The rest of the day is allocated for children to enjoy a longer lunch break, a 15-minute recess after every class, and play after the school day. Recently, some primary schools in Victoria and around the country have begun experimenting with more child-friendly daily schedules to improve student well-being, active engagement, and learning in school. Figure 3.3 shows how the current school day schedule could be adjusted to support recess and unstructured play in Australian primary schools.

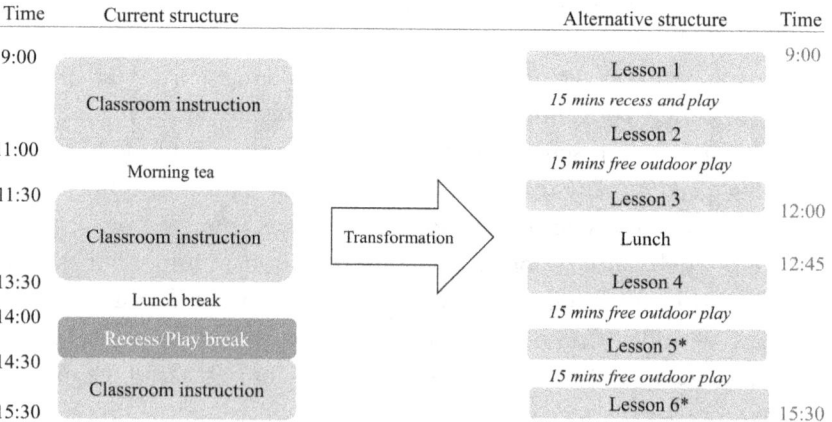

*Primary school days in Finland usually have only 4 or 5 lessons daily

Figure 3.3 Transforming Daily Structure in Primary Schools Towards the Finnish Model.

Based on education research and recommendations from paediatricians, here is the proposed alternative daily schedule:

- Limit each lesson to no more than 50 minutes. Children's attention span for productive learning in primary school ranges from 10 minutes to 25 minutes.
- Allocate 15-minute recess breaks after each lesson for free outdoor play promoting refreshment, socialisation, and building relationships.
- Schedule lunch around midday providing children and teachers time to eat, relax, and engage with one another.

This daily schedule aligns with practices in many other countries. Child health experts advocate for at least an hour of daily outdoor play for primary school children (Sahlberg and Doyle, 2019). A recent study by Peter Gray and colleagues in Boston argues that a primary cause of the decline in children's mental health is fewer opportunities today for them to play independent of direct oversight by adults (Gray, Lancy and Bjorklund, 2023). Better balance between instruction and free play can positively affect student well-being, a sense of belonging, and learning in school.

Giving Food for Thought Through Free School Meals

The Global School Meals Coalition, coordinated by the United Nations, is working to ensure that every child receives a nutritious school meal by 2030. Most parents understand that healthy children are happier and more effective learners. Yet, Australia has not joined this global movement, and the debate over the merits of universal school meals continues.

Globally, a growing trend is emerging: providing all children with a daily healthy lunch at school. Countries like Sweden, Finland, Estonia, and India already offer free hot meals to all students, and research consistently supports the wisdom of this practice (Cohen et al., 2021). So, why are healthy school meals so rarely offered in Australian primary schools? It's hard to believe that the barrier is financial.

There are at least two compelling reasons why we need to rethink universal school lunches in Australia. First, with one in six Australian children living below the poverty line, offering free, nutritious meals in schools would make our education system more equitable. This is not just a practical issue – it's a moral one. Do we want to build a better and fairer education system in the future or act on that commitment now? Providing universal school meals would also relieve the pressure on parents who struggle to fill lunch boxes every day, while eliminating the disparities that lunch boxes often highlight between students.

Second, lunch breaks can become a powerful tool for fostering connection, conversation, and community in schools, much like they do in many adult workplaces. Shared meals provide students – and their teachers – with a chance to pause, engage with one another, and build stronger relationships during school days. In Finland, for example, school meals are integrated into the national curriculum and play a key role in promoting the well-being of the entire school community. Daily school lunches offer opportunities to teach students about healthy, sustainable food choices, expose them to diverse cuisines and cultures, and build essential food literacy skills.

Some schools in Australia are already 'thinking outside the lunchbox' with new school meal programmes, and the results are promising. Tasmania is piloting a programme in 30 schools that provides students with a warm lunch from a set menu. The Northern Territory has improved access to nutritious meals in remote schools, and South Australia is working with Africola Canteen and Flinders University in Adelaide to serve tasty lunches at Annesley Junior School. Across the country, more schools are beginning to introduce daily lunches, and the benefits are clear: improved student attendance, stronger social relationships, and an enhanced sense of belonging.

FINAL THOUGHTS

In 1860, the first American female medical doctor Elizabeth Blackwell wrote in the *English Woman's Journal* that "our school education ignores, in a thousand ways, the rules of healthy development" (Blackwell and Blackwell, 1860). She was right in her time, and she would be right today if she observed many of our schools. But now is the time to change.

Schools are changing, though not always in ways young people might hope. One recent shift is the global trend of governments banning smartphones in schools. Many adults, me included, see this as necessary to create better learning environments. But removing smartphones alone will not make schools inspiring or engaging places for young people. Many teenagers view these bans as punitive, as something done to them rather than for them. As former Public Broadcasting Service (PBS) education reporter John Merrow (2024) asked, "What are adults offering in exchange?"

The challenge with blanket smartphone bans is that they oversimplify a complex challenge of our time. Instead of reacting with prohibitions, we need to respond with education that makes schools more curious, engaging, and safe places where young people *want* to be, not just *have* to be. When bans feel imposed, students often find ways around them, as young people have always done. What if, instead, schools offered activities that truly captured their curiosity and interest? Games, physical activity, music, and play could fill the gap left by smartphones, making school a place of joy and connection.

There's an even greater reason to cultivate new cultures in schools: the world that has emerged from the global disruption of the COVID-19 pandemic. The optimism and hope for a better and fairer world, which many educators and thinkers believed could be born from this crisis, has faded. In its place, we face brutal conflicts in Europe, the Middle East, and Africa, a planet in peril from climate change, and young people grappling with mental health challenges. Yet, instead of focusing on rebuilding relationships, improving well-being, or giving students time to play and reconnect, education systems are responding with top-down reforms, stricter discipline, and quick fixes that address symptoms, not causes.

In this chapter, I have proposed three ideas that can transform school cultures into places where young people could think and thrive. Our efforts for better educational futures should centre on creating schools where students' voices are heard, and they feel empowered to take agency and ownership of their learning (Ritchhart, 2023). These ideas – nurturing relationships, promoting play, and creating shared experiences – cultivate thinking, belonging, and engagement in schools. Healthier relationships foster independent thought and collaboration. Unstructured outdoor play encourages creativity, which can lead to meaningful, purpose-driven learning. And, perhaps most powerfully, the simple act of sharing a school lunch can build a sense of community and care. These are the foundations for deeper thinking, greater agency, and flourishing schools.

REFERENCES

ACARA. (2024) *NAPLAN 2024: National Results Commentaries.* Curriculum, Assessment and Reporting Authority. [Accessed November 2024]. Available from: https://dataandreporting.blob.core.windows.net/anrdataportal/ANR-Documents/NAP2024/2024%20NAPLAN%20National%20Results%20Commentary.pdf

Australian Government. (2023) *Improving outcomes for all: Final report of the review to inform a better and fairer education system.* Canberra: Australian Government. [Accessed November 2024]. Available from: https://www.education.gov.au/review-inform-better-and-fairer-education-system/resources/expert-panels-report

Blackwell, E. and Blackwell, E. (1860) The English Woman's journal (Vol. V). The English Woman's Journal Company.

Cohen, J.F.W., Hecht, A.A., McLoughlin, G.M., Turner, L. and Schwartz, M.B. (2021) 'Universal school meals and associations with student participation, attendance, academic performance, diet quality, food security, and body mass index: a systematic review', Nutrients, 13(3), p. 911. [Accessed November 2024]. Available from: https://doi.org/10.3390/nu13030911

Cook, S. (2023) *From the ground up. How a community with a vision and a principal with a purpose created a thriving state school.* Melbourne: Black Inc.

De Bortoli, L., Underwood, C., Friedman, T. and Gebhardt, E. (2024) *PISA 2022. Reporting Australia's results. Volume II: student and school characteristics.* Australian Council for Educational Research. [Accessed November 2024]. Available from: https://doi.org/10.37517/978-1-74286-726-7

Fullan, M. (2021) *The right drivers for whole system success (CSE leading education series no. 1).* Melbourne: Centre for Strategic Education Seminar Series.

Gray, P., Lancy, D. and Bjorklund, D. (2023) 'Decline in independent activity as a cause of decline in Children's mental wellbeing: summary of the evidence', The Journal of Pediatrics, 260, p. 113352. [Accessed November 2024]. Available from: https://www.jpeds.com/article/S0022-3476(23)00111-7/abstract

Merrow, J. (2024) Necessary but not sufficient. 24 September. The Merrow Report. [Accessed November 2024]. Available from: https://themerrowreport.com/2024/09/24/necessary-but-not-sufficient/

OECD. (2018) *World class: how to build a 21st century school system.* Paris: OECD.

OECD. (2023) *Education at a glance. Education indicators.* Paris: OECD.

Ritchhart, R. (2023) *Cultures of thinking in action: 10 mindsets to transform our teaching and Students' learning.* San Francisco: Jossey-Bass.

Sahlberg, P. (2021) *Finnish lessons 3.0. What can the world learn from educational change in Finland?* 3rd edn. New York: Teachers College Press.

Sahlberg, P. (2023) 'Trends in global education reform movement since the 1990s: looking for the right way', International Journal of Educational Development, 98, pp. 3–13. [Accessed November 2024]. Available from: https://doi.org/10.1016/j.ijedudev.2023.102748

Sahlberg, P. (2024) 'Australian Schools. Good different', Australian Educational Leader, 46(1), pp. 8–14.

Sahlberg, P. and Doyle, W. (2019) *Let the children play. How more play will save our schools and help children thrive.* New York: Oxford University Press.

Twenge, J.M. and Hamilton, J.L. (2022) 'Linear correlation is insufficient as the sole measure of associations: the case of technology use and mental health', Acta Psychologica, 229, p. e103696. [Accessed November 2024]. Available from: https://doi.org/10.1016/j.actpsy.2022.103696

UNESCO. (2020) *Global education monitoring report.* Paris: UNESCO.

Wedenoja, L., Papay, J. and Kraft, M.A. (2022) Second time's the charm? How sustained relationships from repeat student-teacher matches build academic and behavioral skills. *EdWorkingPapers*. pp. 22–590. [Accessed November 2024]. Available from: https://doi.org/10.26300/sddw-ag22

World Bank. (2018) *Human development report 2018. Learning to realize education's promise*. Washington: World Bank.

Zhao, Y. (2024) 'Artificial intelligence and education: end of the grammar of schooling', *ECNU Review of Education*, 0(0), pp. 1–18. [Accessed November 2024]. https://doi.org/10.1177/20965311241265124

Indigenous Knowledges – Valuing Different Thinking Paradigms

Melitta Hogarth, Justin Wilkey and John Doolah

Four

INTRODUCTION

The superdiversity of the Australian classroom today goes beyond the notion of multiculturalism illustrating the interconnectivity of the traditionally siloed conceptions of diversity – gender, religion, sexuality, ethnicity, disability, classism and so forth. Drawing on the works of Vertovec (2007) and Guofang Li (Li et al., 2021), Narungga, Kaurna and Ngarrindjeri scholar, Professor Lester Rigney states, "superdiverse classrooms are the new normal and resemble a mini-United Nations" (Rigney, 2023, p. 3). The increasing globalisation and rapid transience of the world's populations is creating new spaces providing opportunities to gain global perspectives, develop general capabilities and properties of an informed citizen such as empathy and understanding of self through others. The call for culturally responsive classrooms in Australia however remains silent on the privileging of a monoculturally sustaining pedagogical approach existing in our teaching and learning (Hogarth, 2022). In other words, educators are failing to recognise the funds of knowledge and multiliteracies that superdiverse students bring to the classroom and as a result, a radical change is needed. As Professor Geneva Gay in their seminal book, *Culturally responsive teaching: Theory, research and practice* (2000), shares, a predominant White monocultural teaching workforce teaches to the middle-class White student demonstrating gaps in the current Australian teaching and learning approaches.

The authors of this chapter are a collective Indigenous education team currently working together on a nation-building project, Ngarrngga, focused on supporting educators to showcase Indigenous Knowledge in their teaching and learning (Hogarth, 2024a). The first author is a Kamilaroi woman with almost two decades of experience working in all three systems in rural Queensland. The second author is a Ngarrindjeri man as well as Doctoral Candidate within the Faculty of Education. The third author is a Torres Strait Islander of Erubam le (Erub person) and Meriam le (Meriam person) heritage. He belongs

DOI: 10.4324/9781003541745-7

to the sager people (wind identity) of Mer and lectured in Aboriginal and Torres Strait Islander Studies courses, prior to joining the Faculty of Education. As a collective, we are dedicated to ensuring that schooling and other educational spaces provide meaningful educational opportunities for all students to learn about the contributions and achievements of Aboriginal and Torres Strait Islander Peoples to this country. While our primary focus is on Indigenous education, the universal aspirations of a culturally responsive approach are inclusive of all who sit on the margins, such as refugees, culturally and linguistically diverse peoples and so forth as well as the benefits of the dominant culture.

Therefore, our chapter speaks to the reflective professional practice and dispositions needed by teachers before seeking to explore students' thinking dispositions in areas such as truthtelling in an Australian context. What do we bring to the classroom? How do our ways of knowing, being and doing impact on what we teach? On how we engage with certain topics and themes? To support educators grappling with these questions and others, we will provide our definition of what is a 'good' education. In doing so, we are providing perhaps some different thinking paradigms for educators to consider. We will question the reliance on standardised testing and how it maintains a deficit logic and narrative about the educational attainment and futures of Indigenous youth. Reflection on the paradigmatic shift, not just in education but in education policy providing opportunity for the recognition of the complexity and value of Indigenous Knowledge in Australian classrooms and the possibility of embracing difference by valuing different thinking paradigms will occur. Finally, we consider the importance of the inquisitive mind for future Australian citizens through the delivery of a balanced curriculum that includes Indigenous Knowledge to promote [re]conciliation and to better understand the world in which we live.

'WHAT'S ANOTHER WORD FOR GOOD?': A WORD SALAD ABOUT QUALITY

In the Australian education context, the Federal overarching education policy, the *Alice Springs (Mparntwe) Education Declaration* (Education Council, 2019), henceforth referred to as the Declaration, sets the 10-year agenda for education in Australia. It's vision "is for a world class education system that encourages and supports every student to be the very best they can be, no matter where they live or what kind of learning challenges they may face" (Education Council, 2019, p. 2). Our interest lies in the definitions of *a world-class education system* and the assertion for an education system that *encourages and supports every student to be the very best they can be* with a particular emphasis on *every*.

Contrast these aspirations against the consistent messaging and deficit narrative of the dire educational attainment of Aboriginal and Torres Strait Islander students in the national testing programmes and the questioning of *every student* becomes more poignant. More notably, the value of education and its impact on Australian youth's potential futures become clearer when considering that "school education often functions as a sorting mechanism more appropriate to workforces of the past, and so leaves many students without the knowledge and competencies their futures will require" (Masters, 2022, p. 3). How then are schools ensuring that every student achieves their full potential? How then are schools promoting excellence and equity? How are we supporting all young Australians to be lifelong learners? If the vision and purpose of education is to ensure that all young Australians are able to transition to employment or further education and yet, the research literature, policy and reviews continue to speak of a failure to improve the educational attainment of Indigenous students and/or provide an educational experience where Indigenous students see themselves and their cultures and histories valued and respected, could a culturally responsive and relationally strong approach provide some solution?

Education Quality in Policy Discourse

What is a *world-class education system*? What makes education – *good*? In this section, we want to explore the aspirations within the Declaration's vision statement (Education Council, 2019). We will explore the broader concept from a Western lens, prior to sharing from an Indigenous lens. In doing so, we are not intentionally centring Western knowledge, but moreover, setting the scene of what *is* currently maintained so as to be able to speak back to current practice. As a consequence, we are able to contrast and compare the different thinking paradigms to identify similarities and differences and identify what we believe is currently missing from an Indigenous standpoint, to answer the question: what is a 'good' education for Aboriginal and Torres Strait Islander children and youth?

In their report, *Building a world-class learning system*, Masters (2022) outlines the findings of a joint study conducted by the National Center on Education and the Economy (NCEE) and the Australian Council for Educational Research (ACER) that investigated five jurisdictions – British Columbia, Estonia, Finland, Hong Kong and South Korea – that perform well on measures used in international surveys, such as the Programme for International Student Assessment (PISA), to better understand what they have learnt and what interventions they have enacted to provide a world-class education system. One of the key findings was that "as a general principle, these jurisdictions have pursued equity not by ensuring that all students are treated equally, but by better identifying and responding to individual learning needs" (Masters, 2022, p. 12). He continues by sharing how these jurisdictions provide targeted resources to support students to thrive as they recognise that the conventional structure of schooling creates an environment where not every student will be successful or achieve high standards.

It is also important for us to note that Indigenous education policy today goes further illustrating the criticality of ensuring that Indigenous Knowledge is evident within Australian classrooms and broader Australian society. This is a relatively new phenomenon with most policies only including Indigenous Knowledge since the early 2000s. The Declaration, released in 2019, emphasises the contributions of Indigenous cultures and knowledge to Australia's social and economic future (Education Council, 2019, p. 16). Regarding curriculum, the inclusion of the Aboriginal and Torres Strait Islander Histories and Cultures cross-curriculum priority within the Australian Curriculum in 2014 provides opportunities for all students to "deepen their knowledge of Australia by learning about the world's oldest continuous living cultures" (para 3). The introduction of the Australian Professional Standards for Teachers (AITSL, 2022a) in 2014 also has been stated to "reflect the characteristics of quality teaching" (AITSL, 2018, p. 2), and provides distinct advice around the considerations of Indigenous Knowledge but also, the Indigenous students and their needs. While not explicitly stating the term of reference, *a 'good' education*, each of these policies speaks to the contributions and benefits of the inclusion of Indigenous Knowledge as well as ways of knowing, being and doing. However, none of these policies state how this should be achieved or implemented or provide advice or guidance to educators and systems on the 'how' (Hogarth, 2022). It is this gap that interests these authors.

Such a gap in the translation of policy to practice was identified in the *National Aboriginal and Torres Strait Islander Curricula Project* led by Professor Marcia Langton (2017–2019) and has since been further pursued and addressed by Ngarrngga (2021–ongoing). Educators have reported that they are afraid of making mistakes (Booth, 2014; Hogarth, 2022; 2024a), of being tokenistic in their approaches (Bishop and Durksen, 2020; Morrison et al., 2019) and/or offending as a result (Ma Rhea, Anderson and Atkinson, 2012; Morrison et al., 2019; Riley, Monk and Van Issum, 2019). Such apprehensions illustrate the cultural gap (Hogarth, 2020; 2022), the ever-widening chasm in the lack of cultural understanding of educators where the predominant Australian teaching workforce is non-Indigenous, and therefore, it is not surprising when considering the purposeful exclusion of Indigenous Knowledge, cultures and histories in the Australian classroom that there has been an impact on educators' conviction to confidently showcase Indigenous Knowledge in classrooms today. Nonetheless, this does not excuse inaction or the deafening silence. We believe that every teacher, every educator and every person engaged in education have a role to play in enacting change and transformation in the provision of education in Australia as called for in current education policies (Hogarth, 2024a).

Furthermore, the call for the inclusion of Indigenous Knowledge in teaching and learning is not new. Indigenous leaders have been formally calling for the inclusion of Indigenous Knowledge into the Australian education system since the 1930s (Hogarth, 2024b). Exasperated questioning by esteemed Indigenous Elders such as Uncle Jack Patten of untrained teachers being given the responsibility of educating Indigenous children and youth on the missions and stations and the racist policies of the past excluding Indigenous students from the classroom up until the 1970s are evident throughout the literature (Hogarth, 2024b). What is often overlooked here though, as it counters the deficit logics maintained within the status quo of disengagement and disempowerment, is the fact that these calls are evidence of the engagement of Indigenous Peoples in schooling and education spaces (Hameed, Shay and Miller, 2022). Our children's futures matter and we see education as key to achieving their dreams, their aspirations and their future goals.

Steps Towards A 'Good' Education

So, with this in mind – what is 'good' education? We believe this is a particularly important question to answer – from an Indigenous perspective – especially when considering our work focuses on how to best support educators to showcase Indigenous Knowledges through a practical and sustained approach. In this section, we will provide our definition of what a 'good' education could look like. In a Gaps Analysis report (Langton, 2019) completed by colleagues in the *Aboriginal and Torres Strait*

Islander Curricula Project, the first iteration of Ngarrngga, it was affirmed that most Aboriginal and Torres Strait Islander parents, grandparents and great grandparents have a burning desire for their young people to learn in school about their cultures and achievements, and feel proud of them. They also expressed the need for all Australian children to know that "contemporary Aboriginal and Torres Strait Islander communities are strong, resilient, rich and diverse" (ACARA, 2024).

Therefore, we argue that a 'good' education and the hope for the future of Aboriginal and Torres Strait Islander education may well depend on a number of important factors. First and foremost, there is the need for the showcasing of Indigenous Knowledge in Australian educational spaces (ACARA, 2024; Hogarth, 2024). This will be dependent on significant investment in Indigenous representation in the education ecosystem. This is beyond the Diversity and Inclusion targets, often aligned to population parity, but moreover, ensuring that Indigenous Peoples are sitting at each and every table where decision-making is made (in schools, in early childhood centres, in departments, government and so forth), and their voices heard (Australian Government, 2020; Taylor and Habibis, 2020).

Second, Indigenous educators, inclusive of academics and teachers, play a quintessential role in supporting the showcasing of Indigenous excellence in education – as the saying goes 'you can't be what you can't see' (Office for Learning and Teaching, 2014). The training of all educators, inclusive of pre-service teachers, to effectively showcase Aboriginal and Torres Strait Islander histories and cultures in their classrooms in a meaningful and culturally responsive way is necessary (AITSL, 2022b). Educators need to be given opportunities to demonstrate cultural sensitivities and maturity to recognise that there will be times where it is appropriate and necessary to include Indigenous Peoples (Sambono, 2021). That is, for example, when they are looking to include cultural examples and local insights within their classroom, culturally responsive teachers recognise where their role ends, and Indigenous voices and representation are needed. The inclusion of Indigenous Peoples and the valuing of their knowledges evidenced in the classroom can only work to further engage Indigenous students and demonstrate the valuing of different worldviews and thinking paradigms to others.

Finally, as Rigney (2015) stated in a presentation at the *Learning to Live Together in Culturally Diverse Societies Conference* in South Australia, 'curriculum didn't arrive on a boat, pedagogy didn't arrive on a boat, it was always here'.

Indigenous Peoples have successfully educated peoples for generations ensuring that subsequent groups had the necessary knowledges, beliefs and practices to enable them to navigate diverse and dynamic ecosystems (Price, 2012; Rigney, 2002). The intergenerational transmission of Indigenous Knowledge centres a holistic approach (Kirkness and Barnhardt, 2001). The showcasing of Indigenous Knowledge in Australian education requires educators to have a solid understanding about our shared histories so that they can build authentic relationships with Indigenous students, from a place of understanding about the impact of our shared histories. They should also have a strong foundational understanding about the history of education, both pre- and post-contact, for Indigenous Australians. The inclusion of Indigenous Knowledge in Australian classrooms promotes reconciliation (ACARA, 2024). If these initial factors, at a meta-cognitive level, are addressed, we argue that schools will be moving towards a more inclusive and welcoming space – making steps towards a place of 'good' education.

BEYOND THE DEFICIT: A PARADIGMATIC SHIFT

Further to the shifting mindsets and the acknowledgement of the contributions of Indigenous Knowledge in the teaching and learning, educators and schooling need to go beyond the deficit narrative maintained by NAPLAN testing in the Australian context about Indigenous youth. NAPLAN testing occurs every year and involves students in Years 3, 5, 7 and 9 (National Assessment Program [NAP], 2024). It is nationwide and seeks to measure the skills of Australian students in literacy and numeracy. It is argued that NAPLAN testing provides schools with the necessary information and evidence about the supports necessary in the teaching and learning of literacy and numeracy.

Despite government initiatives such as the National Agreement on Closing the Gap (Australian Government, 2020) signalling its intention to improve Indigenous lives by addressing the social determinants inclusive of education, the 2024 NAPLAN data show, 'Aboriginal and Torres Strait Islander children are failing at four times the rate of non-Indigenous children and up to 90 per cent of students in remote communities are failing to reach minimum standards of literacy and numeracy…' (SNAICC, 2024). The persistent messaging of 'failure', highlighting the gap between Aboriginal and Torres Strait Islander and non-Indigenous students in literacy and numeracy standards, provides evidence of the discrepancies and inequity in the Australian education landscape. Whilst the latest NAPLAN results about Aboriginal and Torres Strait Islander children and youth's engagement and outcomes are concerning, they are hardly new; given that in 2008, NAPLAN data indicated that the system was 'failing' many Indigenous students (Vass and Chalmers, 2015). The lack of progression opens space for questions about what information and data are valued and through which lens are the data interpreted? The issue facing Aboriginal and Torres Strait Islander engagement in education, when considered from the standpoint of an Indigenous worldview, becomes more than the process of schooling but the process of learning – valuing different thinking paradigms – different ways of internalising ways of knowing, being and doing to thrive and survive.

Although speaking in terms of higher education, we see the need for education provision to shift, as explicated by Kirkness and Barnhardt, where there is "the need for a higher educational system [read as educational system] that *respects* them [read as Indigenous students] for who they are, that is relevant to their view of the world, that offers *reciprocity* in their relationships with others, and that helps them exercise *responsibility* over their own lives" (Kirkness and Barnhardt, 2001, p. 2 [original emphasis]). As a result, this paper seeks to ponder on the 'how' of learning beyond examinations and recollection of facts. Indigenous approaches to education and learning are more holistic (Kirkness and Barnhardt, 2001). Historically, mastery of Indigenous Knowledge ensured survival. The translation of knowledge to new circumstances to demonstrate understanding, proficiency and in some cases, mastery, required demonstration and application of skills and knowledge in situ (Price, 2012).

Creating spaces in classrooms for deep learning beyond rote practices provides space for curiosity and active learning and the translation of knowledge to produce something new. Critique of NAPLAN testing inclusive of the validity of the tests has occurred since its inception (see, for example: Polesel, Dulfer and Turnbull, 2012). Aboriginal and Torres Strait Islander representative bodies have reported that the privileging of Standard Australian English in the Literacy tests fails to recognise the multiliteracies of Indigenous youth and the benefits of being multilingual. Through this lens, rather than presenting data about Indigenous failures, an alternative narrative of such data is to understand how and why some Indigenous students do exceptionally well in these standardised tests? Because, despite the endless headlines of failure, "In 2022 51.9, 45.8, 30.5 and 26.0 per cent of Aboriginal students in

Years 3, 5, 7 and 9 achieved in the top three bands for reading respectively" (Victorian Government, 2023).

Furthermore, McGaw and colleagues identified that "the lack of validity of the NAPLAN tests lies in the exclusion of Aboriginal and Torres Strait Islander knowledge [...] that NAPLAN falls short of reporting some really important attributes in how Aboriginal students see the world" (McGaw, Louden and Wyatt-Smith, 2020, p.78). In other words, the assessment of a monocultural worldview fails to acknowledge, recognise and value multicultural Australia and the beauty of the differing worldviews. What results is the failure of education systems to value different thinking paradigms and instead, enables the consistent critique of 'teaching to the test' (Polesel, Dulfer and Turnbull, 2012). In other words, we need to go beyond surface learning (Ritchhart, Church and Morrison, 2011). Flipping the deficit logics, we argue that education systems will be making steps towards a place of a paradigmatic shift not just in education but in the provision of educative spaces if they were to provide opportunity for the recognition of the complexity and value of showcasing Indigenous Knowledge in Australian classrooms as beneficial for all Australian students.

THE INQUISITIVE MIND: EMBRACING DIFFERENCE

In this chapter, we have made explicit some of our thinking – questioning and considering differing viewpoints in contrast to evidence from an Indigenous theoretical position drawing on the likes of global and national Indigenous scholars such as Kirkness and Barnhardt (2001) and Rigney (2002; 2015; 2023), respectively, to justify our conclusions. Our own curiosity about the positioning of Indigenous student educational attainment to maintain a deficit narrative and how that narrative is maintained was flipped to a strengths-based approach to celebrate the successes of Aboriginal and Torres Strait Islander students utilising evidence and explicating our reasonings makes visible our thinking. We have dug 'deeper into ideas' explicating our analyses of the current context in Indigenous education and making connections to our own work and that of others. We have also questioned and wondered about the potential futures of Indigenous students and what could be done to address issues of equity. In doing so, we are inviting educators and yourself to consider a differing viewpoint – "to look beyond [your] own perspective and to consider others' experiences" (Project Zero, 2022). We have begun to untangle some of the complex structures set within the

Australian education system that consistently appear to ignore the voices of Indigenous educators.

Curiosity about the world in which we live, understanding the way things *are* and questioning the reasons *why* are all attributes that lend themselves to active and engaged learning. Our work in Ngarrngga is focused on showcasing Indigenous Knowledge in teaching and learning in all educative spaces; "providing opportunity for all Australian students to learn about the achievements and contributions of Aboriginal and Torres Strait Islander peoples to Australian society" (Hogarth, 2024a). As articulated previously, the inclusion of Aboriginal and Torres Strait Islander histories and cultures within teaching and learning is mandatory in education policy and it is with this knowledge that we centre our work in supporting educators to confidently showcase Indigenous Knowledge in their teaching and learning. We invite educators to be curious and to 'be brave and have a go' rather than maintaining the status quo and silence; for an inquisitive mind embraces difference.

REFERENCES

Australian Curriculum, Assessment and Reporting Authority [ACARA]. (2024) *Australian curriculum v9.0: understand this cross-curriculum priority – Aboriginal and Torres Strait Islander Histories and Cultures.* [Accessed 3 September 2024]. Available from: https://v9.australiancurriculum.edu.au/teacher-resources/understand-this-cross-curriculum-priority/aboriginal-and-torres-strait-islander-histories-and-cultures

Australian Government. (2020) *National agreement on closing the gap.* [Accessed 1 September 2024]. Available from: https://www.closingthegap.gov.au/sites/default/files/2022-09/ctg-national-agreement_apr-21-comm-infra-targets-updated-24-august-2022_0.pdf

Australian Institute for Teaching and School Leadership. (2022b) *Building a culturally responsive Australian teaching workforce: final report for Indigenous cultural competency project.* Available from: https://www.aitsl.edu.au/docs/default-source/comms/cultural-competency/aitsl_indigenous-cultural-competency_final-report_.pdf

Australian Institute for Teaching and School Leadership [AITSL]. (2018) *Assessment criteria for graduate teacher standards 1.4 and 2.4P supporting the accreditation of initial teacher education programs in Australia: standards and procedures.* Melbourne: AITSL. [Accessed 1 September 2024]. Available from: https://www.aitsl.edu.au/tools-resources/resource/assessment-criteria-for-graduate-teacher-standards-1.4-2.4

Australian Institute for Teaching and School Leadership [AITSL]. (2022a) *Australian professional standards for teachers.* [Accessed 30 August 2024]. Available from: https://www.aitsl.edu.au/standards

Bishop, M. and Durksen, T.L. (2020) 'What are the personal attributes a teacher needs to engage indigenous students effectively in the learning process? Re-viewing the literature', *Educational Research*, 62(2), pp. 181–198.

Booth, S. (2014) Teaching Aboriginal curriculum content in Australian high schools [Master thesis, Edith Cowan University]. [Accessed 15 September 2024]. Available from: https://ro.ecu.edu.au/theses/1522/

Education Council. (2019) *The Alice springs (Mparntwe) education declaration*. [Accessed 30 August 2024]. Available from: https://www.education.gov.au/alice-springs-mparntwe-education-declaration/resources/alice-springs-mparntwe-education-declaration

Gay, G. (2000) *Culturally responsive teaching: theory, research and practice*. New York: Teachers College Press.

Hameed, S., Shay, M. and Miller, J. (2022) "Deadly leadership' in the pursuit of indigenous education excellence', in Netolicky, D.M. (eds.) *Future alternatives for educational leadership: diversity, inclusion, equity and democracy*. London: Routledge, pp. 93–110.

Hogarth, M. (2020) 'Research-informed teacher learning as professional practice', in Beckett, L. (eds.) *Research-informed teacher learning: critical perspectives on theory, research, and practice*. London: Routledge, pp. 1–11.

Hogarth, M. (2022) 'An analysis of education academics' attitudes and preconceptions about indigenous knowledges in initial teacher education', *The Australian Journal of Indigenous Education*, 51(2), pp. 1–18.

Hogarth, M. (2024a) *Australian teachers shouldn't be afraid to teach indigenous knowledge*. Pursuit. [Accessed 12 September 2024]. Available from: https://pursuit.unimelb.edu.au/articles/australian-teachers-shouldn-t-be-afraid-to-teach-indigenous-knowledge

Hogarth, M. (2024b) *The history of advocating for indigenous knowledge within Australian education*. Ngarrngga blog. [Accessed 12 September 2024]. Available from: https://www.ngarrngga.org/stories-news/the-history-advocating-for-indigenous-knowledge-within-education

Kirkness, V.J. and Barnhardt, R. (2001) 'First nations and higher education: the four R's – respect, relevance, reciprocity, responsibility', in Hayoe, R., and Pan, J. (eds.) *Knowledge across cultures: a contribution to dialogue among civilizations*. Hong Kong: University Press.

Langton, M. (2019) *Gaps analysis report*. Unpublished manuscript.

Li, G., Anderson, J., Hare, J. and McTavish, M. (2021) 'Introduction: superdiversity, emergent priorities, and teacher learning', in Li, G., Marom, L., Anderson, J., Hare, J., and McTavish, M. (eds.) *Superdiversity and teacher education: supporting teachers in working with culturally, linguistically, and racially diverse students, families, and communities*. New York: Routledge, pp. 1–16.

Ma Rhea, Z., Anderson, P.J. and Atkinson, B. (2012) *Improving teaching in Aboriginal and Torres Strait Islander education: national professional standards for teachers standards focus area 1.4 and 2.4*. [Accessed 9 September 2024]. Available from: https://www.aitsl.edu.au/tools-resources/resource/improving-teaching-in-aboriginal-and-torres-strait-islander-education-australian-professional-standards-for-teachers

Masters, G.N. (2022) *Building a world-class learning system*. Centre for Strategic Education (CSE). [Accessed 9 September 2024]. Available from: https://research.acer.edu.au/tll_misc/40/

McGaw, B., Louden, W. and Wyatt-Smith, C. (2020) *NAPLAN review final report*. [Accessed 11 September 2024]. Available from: https://naplanreview.com.au/pdfs/2020_NAPLAN_review_final_report.pdf

Morrison, A., Rigney, L.I., Hattam, R. and Diplock, A. (2019) *Toward an Australian culturally responsive pedagogy: a narrative review of the literature*. University of South Australia. [Accessed 30 August 2024]. Available from: https://childrensa.sa.gov.au/wp-content/uploads/2023/03/Annex-3-Morrison-Rigney-Hattam-Diplock-2019.pdf

National Assessment Program (NAP). (2024) *NAP: National Assessment Program*. [Accessed 2 September 2024]. Available from: https://www.nap.edu.au/naplan

Office for Learning and Teaching. (2014) *'Can't be what you can't see': the transition of Aboriginal and Torres Strait Islander students into higher education – Final report 2014*. [Accessed 15 September 2024]. Available from: https://ltr.edu.au/resources/SI11_2138_Henderson_Yates_Final_Report.pdf

Polesel, J., Dulfer, N. and Turnbull, M. (2012) *The experience of education: the impacts of high stakes testing on school students and their families*. [Accessed 12 September 2024]. Available from: https://www.whitlam.org/publications/2017/10/17/the-experience-of-education-the-impacts-of-high-stakes-testing-on-school-students-and-their-families

Price, K. (2012) 'A brief history of aboriginal and Torres Strait islander education in Australia', in Price, K. (eds.) *Aboriginal and Torres Strait Islander education: an introduction for the teaching profession*. United Kingdom: Cambridge University Press, pp. 1–20.

Project Zero. (2022) *Project zero's thinking routine toolbox*. Harvard Graduate School of Education, United States. [Accessed 10 September 2024]. Available from: https://pz.harvard.edu/thinking-routines

Rigney, L. (2002) 'Indigenous education and treaty: building indigenous management capacity', *Balayi: Culture, Law, and Colonialism*, 4, pp. 73–82.

Rigney, L. (2015) *Learning to live with Aboriginal Australians*. Paper presented at the Learning to live together in culturally diverse societies conferences, University of South Australia.

Rigney, L. (2023) 'On the need for new culturally responsive pedagogies', in Rigney, L. I. (eds.) *Global perspectives and new challenges in culturally responsive pedagogies: super-diversity and teaching practice*. London: Routledge, pp. 3–9.

Riley, T., Monk, S. and Van Issum, H. (2019) 'Barriers and breakthroughs: engaging in socially just ways towards issues of indigeneity, identity and whiteness in teacher education', *Whiteness and Education*, 4(1), pp. 88–107.

Ritchhart, R., Church, M. and Morrison, K. (2011) *Making thinking visible: how to promote engagement, understanding, and independence for all learners*. United States: John Wiley & Sons Inc.

Sambono, J. (2021) 'The Aboriginal and Torres Strait Islander histories and cultures cross-curriculum priority: cultural responsiveness in science education', *SASTA Journal: Teaching Indigenous Science – A resource guide for science educators*, 1, South Australian Science Teachers Association, pp. 4–13. [Accessed 9 September 2024]. Available from: https://indd.adobe.com/view/78697e1f-b411-4d6a-9b2e-8666dbd16500

Secretariat of National Aboriginal and Islander Child Care (SNAICC). (2024, September) *NAPLAN results highlight need for early years and transition to school support for Aboriginal and Torres Strait Islander children*. [Accessed 12 September 2024]. Available from: https://www.snaicc.org.au/2024-naplan-results-reveal-need-for-early-years-and-transition-to-school-support-snaicc-in-the-news/

Taylor, P.S. and Habibis, D. (2020) 'Widening the gap: white ignorance, race relations and the consequences for aboriginal people in Australia', *Australian Journal of Social Issues*, 55(3), pp. 354–371.

Vass, G. and Chalmers, G. (2015) 'NAPLAN, achievement gaps, and embedding indigenous perspectives in schooling', in Lingard, B., Thompson, G., and Sellar, S. (eds.) *National testing in schools: an Australian assessment*. London: Routledge, pp. 139–151.

Vertovec, S. (2007) 'Superdiversity and its implications', *Ethnic and Racial Studies*, 30(6), pp. 1024–1054.

Victorian Government. (2023) *Victorian government: aboriginal affairs report 2023*. [Accessed 12 September 2024]. Available from: https://www.firstpeoplesrelations.vic.gov.au/sites/default/files/2024-07/VIC-GOV_Aboriginal-Affairs-Report_2023.pdf

Transforming Classrooms
Section III

This section provides a reflective exploration of transformative teaching practices that foster collaborative learning environments and empower students as active participants in their education. The chapters emphasise nurturing key dispositions that drive intellectual growth and establish thriving cultures of thinking. Each contributor shares practical approaches to creating more inclusive, engaging, and thoughtful classrooms, highlighting the importance of student agency, meaningful collaboration, and reflective thinking as cornerstones of effective learning.

Simon Brooks examines the distinction between surface-level motivation and deep motivation in education, advocating for the cultivation of a learning culture rather than just a work culture. He underscores that such a culture leads to improved academic outcomes and enhances student wellbeing. He also examines how purposeful, expansive learning opportunities promote deep engagement and foster greater understanding.

Milica Savic is committed to fostering a collaborative learning environment grounded in the belief that we learn best when we learn together. She places a strong emphasis on building meaningful connections and active listening during discussions. At the end of each lesson, Milica incorporates reflective questions that encourage students to recognise and appreciate their peers' contributions, reinforcing the value of collaboration. Through her practice, Milica has observed the profound impact that collaboration has on her students' exploration of their identities and their process of constructing knowledge.

Lana Fleiszig has evolved her teaching approach from the traditional "I Do, We Do, You Do" model to a more student-centred philosophy that encourages greater engagement and ownership of learning. Central to her approach is the belief that students should first engage in independent thinking before any teacher-led instruction. This process allows students to construct their own meaning and understanding. Lana advocates for a culture of thinking that embraces struggle as an essential part of learning, using open-ended questions to promote conceptual understanding.

DOI: 10.4324/9781003541745-8

April Taylor explores her journey in fostering independent learners at OneSchool Global. She uses thinking routines like Compass Points and Connect-Extend-Challenge to promote curiosity, reflection, and metacognition. By building trust and creating safe spaces for risk-taking, she enables students to tackle complex topics with confidence. April's use of scaffolding tools like the Understanding Map empowers students to think critically, write analytically, and develop a sense of agency in their learning.

Five

"Will This Be on the Test?": How Teachers in Australian Schools Help Students Focus More on Learning and Less on Work

Simon Brooks

Every day in every classroom in every school around the world, teachers give their students something to do. Perhaps they are assigned pages from a textbook to read and comprehension questions to answer. Maybe they are given a problem to solve. Perhaps they are invited to bake a cake, design a product, play a game, conduct an experiment, analyse a poem, or have a discussion. Perhaps they are instructed simply to listen and take notes. In every scenario I can imagine, students are given something to get on with and do.

There is a risk in equating activity with productivity. Sure, we all want our students to be busy. I haven't met a teacher yet who comes to school in the morning with a plan for their students to do nothing that day. But in a Culture of Thinking, busy work is not enough. It is wholly possible for our students to be very busy indeed whilst learning very little (Ritchhart, 2015). Work is not synonymous with learning.

Many years ago, I was teaching a unit on postmodernism to a class of Year 12 English Literature students. One day in particular stands out in my memory. Sitting at my desk, I noticed one of the students getting to his feet and coming to the front. There was a hushed silence on his approach. Heads turned and eyes followed intently. He reached my desk.

"Mr. Brooks," he said, "on behalf of the whole class…" My blood froze. A phrase like that is never going to end well. The seeds of revolution had been planted there and then.

"Mr. Brooks, on behalf of the whole class, please would you not worry so much about making learning interesting. With great respect, we don't need creative tasks or whole class discussions. Please - just tell us what we need to know in order to get top marks in the exam."

The die had been cast. Here was a student who no longer seemed interested in learning, or at least not the kind of learning I describe in this chapter. Here was a student who simply wanted me to deliver as much information as I could, in the most expedient way possible, in service of his misguided belief about the best way to prepare for examination success.

DOI: 10.4324/9781003541745-9

When I share this story with fellow teachers, I am usually rewarded with nods of recognition. It seems that many of us have experienced something similar: students who are keen to cast us in the role of knowledge transmitters rather than facilitators of learning. Students often believe they learn best by listening to lectures and taking notes, since from an early age 'they have been enculturated that this is learning' (Ritchhart, 2023, pp. 102–103). However, although this perception is widespread, research shows that they actually learn much more when actively engaged in thinking through discussion, experimentation, and problem-solving (Deslauriers et al., 2019).

You might be pleased to know that I didn't give in to my student's request. Many years of teaching have shown me that students do not always know what is in their own best interests. Instead, I took the opportunity to initiate a playful discussion with the whole class about how we learn, sharing some of the research on the power of thinking and active approaches to learning. Going forward, I took every opportunity I could for us to reflect not just on what we had learned but how we had learned it, opening up ongoing dialogue and debate about the nature of powerful learning.

LEARNING OVER WORK

In *Creating Cultures of Thinking* (2015), Ron Ritchhart identifies several key expectations that we as teachers might have for our students, rather than of them. The prepositional distinction here is important. Expectations of our students tend to be behavioural in nature: we might expect our students to remain silent while we speak, or sit in a seating plan, or submit their homework on time. There is nothing wrong with these expectations of course, but expectations for our students are grander in scope and much more interesting. Perhaps we have an expectation for them to develop growth rather than fixed mindset, or to become independent rather than dependent, or to develop understanding over just knowledge.

One such expectation we might have for our learners is that they engage in learning over work. According to Ritchhart (2015), work is something we do for someone else because we have to. In contrast, learning is something we do for ourselves because it carries with it a sense of perceived worth and intrinsic value. When we are at work, it is difficult to see the purpose of what we are doing beyond task-completion. When we are learning, the work exists in context and in service of the learning; it is a means to an end rather than an end in itself.

THE BENEFITS

Why should we as educators care about creating a culture of learning over work?

Several decades ago, Professor John Biggs from the University of Newcastle in New South Wales made a clear distinction between surface motivation and deep motivation (1985). Surface motivation is underpinned by a utilitarian mindset and is typified by a desire to attain minimal outcomes or invoke rote memory for short-term gains such as passing a test. In contrast, deep motivation occurs when the student is intrinsically motivated to engage in learning, where the goal is to develop understanding through studying widely, reading, and making connections. My contention is that surface motivation closely aligns with a focus on work, while deep motivation aligns with a focus on learning.

Over the years, many studies have explored the relative effectiveness of teaching approaches that leverage deep as opposed to surface motivation. In terms of effect size, the evidence is clear. When teachers emphasise surface motivation, there is a negative effect size of −0.14 (Hattie, 2023). However, when the emphasis is on deep motivation, the effect size is 0.57, well above Hattie's hinge point of 0.40. In other words, an emphasis on learning is particularly impactful in terms of student academic progress, while an emphasis on work over learning may have a negative influence on student achievement.

The benefits of cultivating a culture of learning over work go well beyond higher academic achievement. Some years ago, I was teaching the poetry of Peter Skrzynecki to a group of Year 11 students. We were a few weeks in, and energy levels had dipped, both for my students and for me. Without even realising, I had fallen into the age-old routine of 'covering' a poem a lesson and dutifully working my way through the anthology. I could tell from their faces that they were over it. Lessons were starting to feel less like learning and more like work. As always, they were well behaved, but they were doing the work for me, not for an intrinsic love of learning.

I decided something needed to change and went to visit my colleague in the Art department for inspiration. She furnished me with some gorgeous, high-quality art paper and coloured pastels. Next lesson, my instructions were as follows. "Students, for some time now we've been exploring the poetry of Peter Skrzynecki and we've looked at a number of his poems. Today, I want us to pause and slow down. What's resonating with you from the poems we have studied? What big ideas have stayed with you? What insights into the human condition have they offered? Here's what I'd like you to do. I want you to pick one poem from the collection that you find particularly interesting and create a visual representation of that poem using this paper and these colours. Be playful. Breathe. Try to allow the process of representation to deepen and enrich your understanding of your chosen poem. Go!"

That was my focus for the lesson. I found some relaxing classics to play in the background. To their credit, my students embraced the opportunity, engaging quietly and thoughtfully in the process. Halfway through the lesson, I noticed one of my students was crying. She wasn't sobbing uncontrollably, but there were definitely tears in her eyes. I made a mental note to check in with her at the end. Once students had finished, we created a gallery walk so that they could all look at one another's efforts. They were intrigued by each other's thinking and artistic choices. Rich, respectful, authentic discussions ensued. Everybody was involved in the conversation. There was a sense of meaningful engagement and deepening understanding. More than in any other lesson over the past few weeks, I felt that they found real value in the poetry. This was learning, not work.

At the end of the lesson, I quietly checked in with the student who had been crying. I told her that I had noticed her tears and just wanted to ask whether everything was alright. Here is what she said: "Mr. Brooks, every day at school is just so busy. We move from class to class with very little time in between to rest. Every lesson feels urgent. All my teachers are on a mission to get through the content and all of them say they are running out of time. It's exhausting and it's all we know. So today, when you said that you wanted us to slow down, and breathe, and be creative, it was almost more than I could bear, and that's why I was crying."

I have never forgotten this moment. This student was caught in an institutional cycle of work over learning, which was slowly breaking her spirit. I believe that as educators we must focus on building a culture of learning over work, not just because of the obvious cognitive benefits, but also because of the impact on wellbeing. Are we content with perpetuating school cultures where a focus on work over learning is so exhausting that they no longer remember that schooling should be a joyous experience that inspires a lifelong love of learning?

Ultimately, when teachers and schools prioritise a culture of work over learning, student apathy is the inevitable outcome. According to a survey of 3000 teachers, 95% of 5-year-old children love school, a result that dips drastically to 37% by Grade 9 (Jenkins, 2016). These are devastating numbers. Are we happy that nearly two-thirds of 14-year-olds no longer love school? When our emphasis is on work completion, the will to learn decreases to such an extent that students no longer care about learning. In the words of Lyle Jenkins, 'It is nearly impossible to teach students who just do not care to learn' (2021).

SHIFTING THE EMPHASIS

How might we keep the emphasis on learning over work in our classrooms?

Here's an incredibly powerful question to ask our students every day:

"What are you learning by doing this?"

Imagine that your students are getting on with a task. Perhaps you are circulating around the room, supporting, and keeping them on track. What would it be like if you were to say, "OK everyone, let's stop what we are doing for a moment. I'd like us to pause and take stock. What are we learning by doing this?" I wonder what they would say. Challenge yourself to slow down and document their thinking on butcher's paper. "What else are you learning by doing this? And what else?" Invest time in the experience. Be curious about their responses. How have they surprised you with their thinking? Once ideas are documented, you can revisit their thinking in future lessons. "How has your thinking changed since that lesson last week when I asked you what you were learning and you said this."

"What are you learning by doing this?" works both for individual and whole-class conversations. If you have your own children, it is also a question you can ask while they get on with their homework in the evening (Ritchhart, 2013). If they are like my own children, be prepared for them to say, "I have no idea what I'm learning, but I do have to get this handed in tomorrow, so please let me get on with it!" Just sometimes, however, interesting conversations ensue.

When we ask this question, we shift the emphasis from work to learning. We encourage them to remember that activities are vehicles that take us to the learning. Another question you might ask is: "What different activity might we have done today to learn the same thing?" (Wright, 2009). A side benefit of asking this question is that they often come up with great ideas that we can use next time around. Engage them in discussion about the difference between learning and work and why this distinction is important.

Over the years, I've had the privilege of spending many hours in Australian schools where teachers are dedicated to building cultures of thinking. Three key characteristics stand out in classrooms where the focus is on learning over work: *purpose, play,* and *reflection*. Although impoverished versions of these characteristics might be observed in work-oriented classrooms, I believe they exist in a meaningful way only when the emphasis is on learning and not on work.

PURPOSE

At the Australian International School Malaysia, Steven Webster's Year 10 History students are welcoming guests to their 'Echoes of the Vietnam War' museum exhibition. There is a sense of excitement and anticipation in the air. For some weeks now, they have been building up to this special day.

To explore diverse perspectives on the Vietnam War, Steven has invited his students to create various artefacts that provide insight into the experiences of those who lived through it. Students have been given the option to compose an original song, create a visual artwork, write diary entries, design a military artefact, produce a short documentary, create a collection of photographs, or produce a radio broadcast that could have been aired during the war. Having done so, they have then worked collaboratively to curate a museum-style exhibition of their efforts, hosted in the school's Black Box Theatre.

As I wander through the exhibition, I am struck by the thoughtful and respectful way students are conducting themselves. The exhibits have been thoughtfully curated, each one accompanied by a written reflection explaining its historical context and intended purpose. The exhibition lasts all day and is attended by students from other classes and grades, teachers, parents, and other community members. Steven's students act as guides, accompanying visitors and answering their questions. A haunting student composition entitled 'Free From My Memories' plays in the background and provides a soundtrack for the exhibition. Visitors are invited to share their thinking using See Think Wonder (Ritchhart, Church and Morrison, 2011) as a scaffold for their own reflections.

'Echoes of the Vietnam War' is wonderful example of learning over work, not least because these students see purpose behind their actions. Creating a sense of purpose goes well beyond teachers simply sharing pre-determined learning intentions and success criteria (Ritchhart, 2015). From the outset, Steven's students understand that their study of the Vietnam War is leading to a culminating project that holds special importance for them. As one of Steven's students shared in his reflection, 'The experience was incredibly valuable to me. It allowed me to engage deeply with the subject matter [and was] personally meaningful' (Webster, 2024). True purpose is underpinned by a sense of perceived worth, a feeling that what we are doing matters and is intrinsically valuable (Ritchhart, 2015).

Another reason for the success of 'Echoes of the Vietnam War' is the expansive rather than narrow framing at the heart of this learning opportunity. When topics are introduced with a narrow framing, there is often a sense that the purpose of schooling is to prepare for an examination or fulfil the requirements of a curriculum (Chua et al., 2017). For example, a teacher might begin a lesson by saying, "Today we need to cover chemical bonding ready for the test next week."

In contrast, expansive framing encourages students to situate their learning within a larger context, making connections both within and across learning areas, and fostering a deeper understanding of themselves and the world around them. In Steven's own words, 'it's important that as history teachers (or any teachers), we do not teach with bias; we must present students with the facts and allow them to learn, grow, and develop critical thinking skills through their own interpretation of these facts' (Webster, 2024). This is expansive framing. Steven's students are not just learning *about* the Vietnam War in order to prepare for a test. They are learning *with* the Vietnam War in their journey to become thoughtful, truth-seeking, critical, empathetic young historians.

One way in which to frame learning expansively is through the use of driving questions (Larmer, Mergendoller and Boss, 2015), sometimes described as generative questions (Ritchhart, 2015) or essential questions (McTighe and Wiggins, 2013). According to McTighe and Wiggins, driving questions 'are not answerable with finality in a single lesson or a brief sentence… Their aim is to stimulate thought, to provoke inquiry, and to spark more questions… They are provocative and generative' (2013, p. 3). For example, in Mathematics we might ask, "How does algebra make life easier?" In Science, we could ask, "Is aging a disease?" (McTighe and Wiggins, 2013). In Business Studies, we could offer this provocation: "What's more important: people or profit?"

At Albion Park High School in New South Wales, English teacher Casie Horton engaged her Year 11 students with a driving question during their study of Shakespeare's *Othello*: "The Paradox of Tragedy: Why can't we look away?" Before students even approached the text, they explored this driving question and shared their thoughts on the compelling nature of tragedy:

- "We can't look away because we are naturally curious: tragedy piques our interest because of the excitement of the unknown"
- "Fear is primal. It has been with us since the beginning because of necessity, but in our evolved environment it is no longer so prevalent. Now we purposefully seek it out for the rush of happy chemicals like dopamine and serotonin that follow"
- "Tragedy often creates unity by connecting people that wouldn't usually find community with one another"
- "Without ever feeling sadness how would we ever know true happiness?"

(Horton, 2024)

Driving questions create a hook for learning. They encourage engagement with the big ideas of a unit from the outset and are revisited repeatedly in the weeks to come as student understanding evolves and deepens. For Casie, it was important that her students gained more from their studies than simply learning the plot of *Othello* and preparing to write essays for assessment. The driving question became a way for students to synthesise the content and concepts explored during the term. It gave structure and purpose to the unit, allowing students to make rich connections between the text, themselves, and the world around them.

Purposeful learning happens when students understand the why behind what they are learning and find value in the journey of getting there. When the emphasis is on work over learning, students may know what they're expected to learn but are unlikely to experience the process as meaningful and engaging. Finding meaning in what we do is an essential facet of feeling purposeful. As Simon Sinek says, 'Working hard for something we don't care about is called stress; working hard for something we love is called passion' (2012). Ultimately, being told the purpose and finding purpose is a key distinction between work and learning.

PLAY

At St. Aloysius' College in Sydney, French teacher Karen Downes is on a mission to improve her Year 10 students' conversational French. It is a couple of months after the 2018 G7 summit in Canada, often remembered for the viral photograph of Angela Merkel and other world leaders standing over a seated Donald Trump. Karen knows that the boys in her class have an interest in global politics and uses this to her advantage.

In recent months, Karen has established a new routine in her classroom. Every week, she finds an image of interest and shares it with her students using the Zoom In thinking routine (Ritchhart, Church and Morrison, 2011). Zoom In is a routine that encourages close observation and interpretation. The teacher gradually reveals portions of an image, one stage at a time, prompting students to make interpretations based on each new detail. After each reveal, the teacher asks, "What do you see or notice?", and "What do you think might be going on here based on what you are seeing?" Students are aware that their predictions are tentative and could change at any moment. As such, the routine is a powerful tool for generating engagement and curiosity.

Today, Karen shares the Trump G7 photo with her class, but there is a twist. The whole routine is conducted in French. "What do you see or notice?" Karen asks, in French. "What is going on here?... What makes you say that?" After each reveal, her students respond, also in French. Playful learning mode is engaged. Karen's students are enjoying themselves. It feels like a game. Sometimes, the boys have enough French to describe what they see and think; other times they do not. Karen seizes opportunities to correct their grammar and introduce new vocabulary as needed, writing each new word or phrase in French on the board as she goes. Examples include 'a surprised look', 'coffin', 'I think it's a factory', 'Everybody seems depressed', and 'receding hairline'. The atmosphere in the room is light-hearted but focused. The boys are learning at their point of need, playing with language in ways of their own choosing.

Once the whole image is revealed, Karen hands out laminated copies of the photograph and students work in groups to write French captions in speech marks, which they stick onto the photo. They are playful but appropriate in what they come up with. I enjoy listening to their questions, some of which they ask Karen and others of which lead them to consult dictionaries:

- "Miss, how do you say drama teacher?"
- "How do you say nuclear proliferation?"
- "How do you say moustache care kit?"

It is clear to see that Karen's weekly routine encourages these young students to play with French and speak at length in the target language. There is a lot of laughter and fun in the room. There is a sense that the boys might want to play this game, even if Karen was not there to lead it. A key indicator of playful learning is when what students want to do aligns with what their teachers want them to do (Mardell et al., 2023).

The following year, Karen emails me with her students' DELF speaking test results (Downes, 2019). In the previous year, prior to the Zoom In intervention, 72% of her students had scored in the basic range, and 28% in the independent range. For this post-intervention group, the numbers had flipped: now 38% were basic, and 62% were independent. In real terms, this means that most of her students had moved from being able to handle short social exchanges and making themselves understood in simple interactions, to engaging in spontaneous conversations with some degree of fluency and clarity, even on complex subjects. Of course, other variables might have been at play here, but Karen puts this improvement down to Zoom In and a whole year of her students being playful with language.

So what do I mean by play? I define playful learning as tinkering with ideas with open-mindedness and a lightness of touch, embracing mistakes as opportunities to learn. For Karen's students, playing with language in this way was motivating and enjoyable, leading to much improved proficiency in spoken French. For Steven's students, playing with ideas took the form of representing aspects of the Vietnam War in a multiplicity of different forms, including songs, artefacts, and photographs. In my lesson on the poetry of Peter Skrzynecki, students played with the key ideas of the poems by representing their developing understanding in a visual form. As Mardell et al. argue, 'When people play, they are engaged, relaxed, and challenged - states of mind highly conducive to learning. Through play, children and adults try out ideas, test theories, experiment with symbol systems, better understand social relations, take risks, and reimagine the world' (2023, p. 19).

It is difficult to imagine what playful learning might look like with an emphasis on work over learning. True play is characterised by a spirit of authentic experimentation coming from within, whereas work by its nature is extrinsically motivated. Perhaps it is impossible for playful learning to exist in a culture of work. For educators interested in cultivating a culture of learning over work, creating opportunities for playful learning is a must.

REFLECTION

When teachers place the emphasis on getting through the work rather than learning, reflection is often the first thing to go. After all, when there is already too much to get through, and not enough time to do it, how can we possibly make time to think more about what has already been covered? One of the beliefs at the heart of this book is that 'coverage is the enemy of understanding' (Gardner, 1993, cited in Brandt, 1993). It is all too easy for us as teachers to become consumed by a work-completion mindset, driven by a goal of 'getting through the stuff', but if we choose to allow this to happen, learning suffers.

When we make time for reflection, we shift the emphasis to learning over work. Mardell et al. (2023) define reflection in schools as 'thoughts or questions that result from thinking critically about a learning experience to strengthen current or inform future learning' (p. 71). When we reflect, we wander mentally through where we have been already to make sense of the journey and our discoveries along the way.

Try asking your students this question: "What was something interesting that you learned today?" I wonder what they would say. Will their takeaways be the same as your understanding goals for the lesson? When we give our students the opportunity to reflect, we personalise their learning experience. If our emphasis is on work, there is a sense that we are marching our learners like-it-or-not towards the pre-determined learning intentions we have deemed important. When we provide meaningful opportunities for reflection, we allow for the fact that what they have learnt may or may not be what we intended. In doing so, we create a culture of learning over work, in which we value our learners as individual human beings, in all their complexity, diversity, and uniqueness.

Figure 5.1 The 8 to 1 Thinking Routine: A Routine for Capturing the Essence of Learning

There are many thinking routines to facilitate rich opportunities for reflection, including 'I Used To Think… Now I Think', '3-2-1 Bridge', and 'Connect-Extend-Challenge' (Ritchhart, Church and Morrison, 2011). At Albion Park High School, Legal Studies teacher Brayden Neaves makes use of the 8 to 1 thinking routine (Brooks, 2017) to help his students capture the essence of what they are learning. In 8 to 1, students reflect on the key ideas and themes from what they have read, seen, or heard, then craft an eight-word sentence that captures the heart of what should be remembered. They then condense this sentence: first to four words, then to two, and finally to one. Ultimately, students share their eight, four, two, and one-word summaries with a partner or the group, explaining and justifying their choices. Scan the QR code above for a more detailed description of the 8 to 1 thinking routine along with tips for facilitation.

It is the final term of 2014 for Brayden and his Year 11 class. After two weeks exploring the criminal investigation process, his students have engaged with a range of complex concepts, including the role of the police, the scope of their powers, the use of warrants, the right to bail, and remand. Brayden now needs them to slow down, synthesise their learning, and take stock. The 8 to 1 thinking routine proves to be a game-changer in facilitating reflection and fostering a culture of learning over work.

Students in Brayden's classroom are familiar with the use of mini-whiteboards to make their thinking visible, so they use these to draft and document their 8 to 1s. Leo decides to create a list of eight rather than a full sentence, and chooses Police, LEPRA, Bail, Discretion, Dean, Skaf, Prevention, Purpose. After the process of distillation, he selects LEPRA as his single word, an acronym of his own invention for the Law Enforcement (Powers and Responsibilities) Act 2002. For Leo, this is the single most important piece of legislation in relation to the criminal investigation process, and therefore the most important part of the topic to remember. When asked what made it important than the other words, he explains and justifies his choice at length.

To enhance the depth and breadth of discussion, Brayden sets up an in-class gallery walk for students to view and reflect on each other's 8 to 1s. As they move from table to table, students explore each other's reasoning for the selection or cutting of particular words. In 8 to 1, much of the learning takes place in students' discussion of the choices they have made. Brayden facilitates this by asking well-chosen reflective questions. *What made you chose this word over that one? Which words were the hardest to sacrifice? How has your thinking changed? What seems most important now about the criminal investigation process having gone through the journey of 8 to 1?* Inspired by Brayden's questioning, students begin challenging each other in similar ways. The discussion feels authentic and meaningful. It is clear that Brayden's students value and appreciate the experience of collaborative reflection.

As with the other two characteristics of learning-focused classrooms, *purpose* and *play*, reflection in its truest form cannot exist in a culture of work. Of course, in a work-oriented classroom, we could give our students a thinking routine like 8 to 1, and most likely they would dutifully comply. However, if the emphasis in our classroom is on work over learning, they will only share what they think we want to hear, not what they have truly learned. When students are empowered to reflect meaningfully, filtering their experiences through the lens of their own identity, they embrace a culture of learning rather than a culture of work.

NEXT STEPS

"Will this be on the test?" – a question that sends a shiver down the collective spine of teachers around the world. And don't forget its close allies: "Am I doing this right?", "Should I underline the title?", "What do I need to write?", and "Do I have to show my work on this?"

When students ask questions like these, it is clear that they are focused on the work over the learning. They are questions that reveal a preoccupation with succeeding at the game of school rather than a true desire to learn.

In this chapter, I have shown that an emphasis on learning over work enhances academic achievement, improves student wellbeing, and lays the foundations for lifelong learning. I have presented several different approaches that might help us achieve this goal, by leveraging three central characteristics of learning over work: *purpose, play,* and *reflection.*

Keeping students busy is not enough and was never enough. School is more than just a passport to tomorrow. As educators, let's want more for our students than task completion and preparing for the test. Let's cultivate an environment where every student sees their work as a meaningful step in their journey of personal growth and discovery, because true learning is not something we do for others, but something we do for ourselves.

REFERENCES

Biggs, J.B. (1985) 'The role of metalearning in study processes', British Journal of Educational Psychology, 55(3), pp. 185–212.

Brandt, R. (1993) 'On teaching for understanding: a conversation with Howard Gardner', ASCD, 50(7). [Accessed 15 October 2024]. Available from: https://ascd.org/el/articles/on-teaching-for-understanding-a-conversation-with-howard-gardner

Brooks, S. (2017) 8 to 1: a routine for capturing the essence of learning. [Accessed 10 December 2024]. Available from: https://www.simonbrookseducation.com/_files/ugd/22452f_f02f7adfecbf46b6ac5b69e6541ab55b.pdf

Chua, F., Morrison, K., Perkins, D. and Tishman, S. (2017) Portable knowledge: a visible thinking bundle to foster transfer of content and 21st century skills. [Accessed 8 November 2024]. Available from: https://pz.harvard.edu/sites/default/files/Portable%20Knowledge%20for%20ISV%202017%2006%2023_CreativeCommonsLicense.pdf

Deslauriers, L., McCarty, L.S., Miller, K., Callaghan, K. and Kestin, G. (2019) 'Measuring actual learning versus feeling of learning in response to being actively engaged in the classroom', Proceedings of the National Academy of Sciences, 116(39), pp. 19251–19257. [Accessed 8 November 2024]. Available from: https://doi.org/10.1073/pnas.1821936116

Downes, K. (2019) Email to Simon Brooks, 11 June.

Hattie, J. (2023) Visible learning: the sequel. New York: Routledge.

Horton, C. (2024) How can I help my students value the study of literature and embrace the opportunity to gain new insights about themselves and the world? [Poster]. Inquiry Action Projects: A Celebration of Learning, 4 September, Albion Park High School.

Jenkins, L. (2016) Optimise your school: it's all about the strategy. Thousand Oaks: Corwin Press.

Jenkins, L. (2021) Education's greatest challenge: children start their education full of enthusiasm, but as they progress that enthusiasm fades badly. Education Today. [Accessed 8 November 2024]. Available from: https://www.educationtoday.com.au/news-detail/Education-5477

Larmer, J., Mergendoller, J. and Boss, S. (2015) Setting the standard for project based learning. Alexandria: ASCD. [Accessed 8 November 2024]. Available from: https://files.ascd.org/staticfiles/ascd/pdf/siteASCD/publications/books/Setting-the-Standard-for-PBL-sample-chapters.pdf

Mardell, B., Ryan, J., Krechevsky, M., Baker, M., Schulz, T.S. and Liu-Constant, Y. (2023) A pedagogy of play: supporting playful learning in classrooms and schools. Cambridge: Project Zero. [Accessed 8 November 2024]. Available from: https://pz.harvard.edu/sites/default/files/PoP%20Book.pdf

McTighe, J. and Wiggins, G. (2013) *Essential questions: opening doors to student understanding*. Alexandria: ASCD.

Ritchhart, R. (2013) *9 apps for parents*. [Accessed 8 November 2024]. Available from: https://pz.harvard.edu/sites/default/files/9%20Apps%20for%20Parents%20.pdf

Ritchhart, R. (2015) *Creating cultures of thinking: the eight forces we must master to truly transform our schools*. San Francisco: Jossey-Bass.

Ritchhart, R. (2023) *Cultures of thinking in action: 10 mindsets to transform our teaching and students' learning*. New Jersey: Jossey-Bass.

Ritchhart, R., Church, M. and Morrison, K. (2011) *Making thinking visible*. San Francisco: Jossey-Bass.

Sinek, S. (2012) *Working hard for something we don't care about is called stress; working hard for something we love is called passion*. [X]. 28 February. [Accessed 8 November 2024]. Available from: https://x.com/simonsinek/status/174469085726375936?lang=en-GB

Webster, S. (2024) *Email to Simon Brooks*, 21 September.

Wright, T. (2009) *How to be a brilliant teacher*. Abingdon: Routledge.

Exploring Collaborative Learning
Milica Savic

Six

LEARNING TO STEP BACK

As a Middle Years educator, I have always found the final two weeks of the school year to be magical. It is that sweet spot where we get to enjoy our time with students and colleagues without the regular pressures of the school year. It is around this time, following exams and report-writing, that the end of year 'thanks' and Christmas wishes start coming in. Over the years, the walls of my office have become adorned with these beautiful messages. There are the students who make an effort to say thank you at the end of each lesson, those who share cards with an existing message and add a simple 'to' and 'from', and those students that you've created a strong rapport with who will clearly articulate their experiences in the classroom and their gratitude for particular approaches or moments. As educators, we pour our hearts and souls into what we do, and there is something incredibly special about a child taking the time to acknowledge this. However, there is one category that I am always blindsided by – the *unexpected* 'thank you'.

Sam* had been my student in Year 7 and again in Year 9. She had matured a lot in this time and various peer group pressures meant that she was no longer the bubbly and confident risk-taker that I first taught. Regardless of this, Sam had a strong sense of justice that I could carefully and regularly tap into in the language classroom. As the year's end rolled around, Sam appeared at my office door with a handwritten letter.

> "You've taught me so much in the few years I've known you and I could go on and on about the memories and moments, however, one of my most significant lessons was in Term 3 when we were playing 'Beat the Teacher' and I was the only one to say the word, I knew I was right but the class was trying to explain why they were correct. Instead of jumping in, you watched

DOI: 10.4324/9781003541745-10

and allowed me to stand up for myself (I was, in fact, right). Although you possibly did this unintentionally it taught me that you believed in me and to stick up for what is right (especially in 'Beat the Teacher')".

Sam's letter was the first time I was compelled to consider how I view my role in the classroom. Here was this student telling me that the best experience she had in my class, was one that required me stepping back. I wished in that moment that the interaction she was referring to was intentional. That I had planned to provide this wonderful provocation for discussion. Even though it wasn't, and I didn't, it became my mission to make more of those moments for all of my students. The longer I sat with this reflection, I realised that the interaction Sam referred to would only be possible if my classroom culture was one of collaboration and valuing the thinking of each individual in my classroom. Valuing it by providing opportunities for students to share, justify and build on each other's thinking.

Equal parts thanks to my upbringing and my schooling experience, my engagement with the Cultures of Thinking (Ritchhart, 2023) mindsets has always seen me circling back to the sixth mindset – that *learning and thinking are as much a collective enterprise as they are an individual endeavour.* Diving further into this, I began to experiment by making small tweaks in my own practice. The closer I looked, the more opportunities I found to amplify the conversations that my students were having in the classroom. The more value I placed on us being a *community of learners,* the less pressure I felt to *perform.* For the first time in my teaching career, students would hear the bell and exclaim: *"that went really quickly!".*

THE MANY FORMS OF COLLABORATION IN THE CLASSROOM

Given that this chapter focuses on my own exploration of collaboration in the classroom, it's important that we unpack what is meant here by the term *collaboration*. Lev Vygotsky's early work on social constructivism suggests that knowledge, or our understanding of how the world works, is socially constructed (Hausfather, 1996). That is, that we develop through social interaction and communication. Jerome Bruner (1996, p. 126) shares a philosophy similarly rooted in our relationship with others, referring to collaboration as the 'sharing of human resources of all those involved in the mix of teaching and learning' (note the absence of the words 'student' and 'teacher' here). These initial interpretations of collaboration are powerful as they are not linked to a task or particular outcome, rather a way of being and learning together. Bringing the focus back to what this might look like in the classroom, Zorich, Waibel and Erway's (2008) Collaboration Continuum, despite being outside of a school context, articulates a progression from contact to convergence:

- **Contact** is when groups first meet up to open dialogue. No joint efforts or projects at this stage.
- **Cooperation** is when groups work informally on an activity that offers small but tangible effort. This might be sharing info or helping each other out with an activity.
- **Coordination** is when the work requires a framework to organise the group into everyone knowing what they have to do, when and where.
- **Collaboration** moves to become a process of shared creation. Something is new that wasn't there before, including transformation among the collaborators.
- **Convergence** is a state of collaboration that has become so extensive, engrained and assumed, it is no longer really recognised as a collaborative undertaking. It has matured to become infrastructure – a critical system we rely on without considering the collaborative effort that makes it possible. We might consider this to be the enculturation of collaboration into our classroom.

Main's (2016, p. 106) work shares a similar delineation between cooperative and collaborative learning, stating that 'in collaborative learning, students work together to construct a common or collective understanding through the total combined efforts of the group'. However, they add that a key difference between cooperation and collaboration 'depends on the amount of student ownership of the learning process'. This shift in ownership would spark intrigue (outrage?) in many who see it as the teacher's role to own the learning. What might it look like if students were supported to take the reins and alter the direction? I am confident that they would exceed our expectations more often than not, challenging some of the narratives we may carry around the roles of student and teacher.

WHAT'S IN IT FOR US?

Understanding how collaboration can be defined is essential but none of these definitions matter unless they are applied effectively in a classroom context. The Australian Curriculum, Assessment and Reporting Authority (2024) states that 'intercultural understanding is an essential part of living with others in the diverse world of the twenty-first century... learning to value and view critically their own cultural perspectives and practices and those of others through their interactions with people, texts and contexts across the curriculum'. Main et al.'s (2017) research into Middle Years Schooling shares further insight into the positive impact that collaboration can have on engagement by sharing that their meta-analyses have consistently shown that the use of collaborative learning strategies resulted in positive effects for students in the areas of achievement, socialisation, motivation, peer relationships as well as their personal development. We can no longer refer to collaboration as a *soft skill* as we have in the past. As Ron Ritchhart (2023) calls them, these are *success skills*, and collaboration is one of many core competencies that we have a responsibility to future generations to nurture in our young people. So, how do we start this process of building an expectation of learning together? What might a scaffolded approach to collaboration look like in the classroom?

PICTURES OF PRACTICE: THINGS WE KNOW TO BE TRUE

This activity, which I have grown used to calling 'things we know to be true' has become one tool in supporting respectful and informed discussions in our classroom. In order to justify their thinking, students are asked to stay in the thinking space a little longer. What tells them they might be right? What is some proof that could support this thinking? How do they know what they think they know? In Year 9, students are exploring the perfect tense in French. Following various examples of the tense in context, they create a list of indicators to help them articulate their understanding:

1. *It can be conjugated with avoir or être*
2. *The endings of infinitives change (er à é, ir à i, re à u)*
3. *You have to first conjugate avoir or être correctly in present tense*
4. *They go in the order of subject pronoun + auxiliary (etre/avoir) + past participle*
5. *When you use 'être', the ending might need an extra 'e' (feminine) or 's' (plural)*

While this may look complicated to a non-French speaker, this important discussion and resulting list means that students are able to break down a challenging concept into its various parts and refer to these when justifying their responses.

PICTURES OF PRACTICE: CREATING AN EXEMPLAR

Developing their reading comprehension skills, students complete a reading task independently. Following this, in groups of 3–4, they are tasked with submitting one completed question sheet. Some students gather, standing, around the laboratory benches, while others pull their chairs around to sit in small groups. The one constraint applied to the task is that no response can be written on the final question sheet until there is unanimous agreement. Going through one question at a time, students share responses and challenge each other using the modelled language on the wall:

How do you know?
Can you tell me more about that?
Can you show me using another example?
Where does this link to the 'things we know to be true'?

Rich, and at times passionate, discussion occurs in small groups, before students submit their final work as a group.

STUDENT 2: *"It's got something to do with the ending."*
STUDENT 1: *"Are you sure? Are your 3 and 4 right?"*
STUDENT 2: *"I don't know"*
STUDENT 1: *"There's no point writing it if it's not right. *Turns to another student* Are your 3 and 4 right?"*
STUDENT 3: **Gestures uncertainty**
STUDENT 4: *"Oh, she made some money – it's there in the text."*

The next stage of conversations is then facilitated by two student volunteers who seek responses to each question from the group, while holding the accurate response sheet for the task.

PICTURES OF PRACTICE: CREATIVE QUESTION STARTS

As Year 9 students begin their inquiry into the prevalence of loneliness in society, they use the Creative Question Starts protocol to unpack lines of inquiry and build connection to the topic at hand. They know that part of their inquiry will be the creation of a game to support their learning. The lesson starts with a provocation – a statistic relating to the percentage of young people reporting feelings of loneliness following the COVID-19 pandemic. Students then see the Creative Question Starts and sit silently for a couple of minutes. One student begins:

STUDENT 1: *"Why do people feel lonely?"*

The ice has been broken, and students have an idea of the types of questions they might ask.

STUDENT 2: *"What if there were ways to minimise those feelings?"*
STUDENT 3: *"What is the purpose of the data collected?"*
STUDENT 4: *"How would it be different if we looked at pre-pandemic data?"*
STUDENT 1: *"What if we knew how to help people?"*
STUDENT 5: *"What would change if people spent more time together?"*

With a range of questions to provoke thinking, students are then asked whether they see a particular question that they want to unpack further. These students raise their hands. Those who haven't, are invited to find another link into the topic.

TEACHER: "That percentage equates to about 20 students in this class. 20 of us that are reporting increased feelings of loneliness following lockdowns. What do we need to know more about?"
STUDENT 6: *"How people spend their time, maybe?"*
TEACHER: *"I wonder whether that has changed in the past few years."*
STUDENT 7: *"How do board games help?"*
TEACHER: *"Are all boardgames made equal?"*
STUDENT 7: *"Maybe look at which ones help the most?"*
TEACHER: *"Reflecting on your own experience, which games come to mind?"*

This protocol provides a range of ways for students to engage with the same topic, through a line of inquiry that is most interesting to them. It models how ideas can be linked to each other and promotes curiosity through giving students greater agency.

PICTURES OF PRACTICE: SHARING STORYBOOKS

In Year 9, after lengthy exploration of the perfect tense in French, students are asked to connect their learning to a form of community service, viewing community in the context of our school and its various parts. Students put forward two ideas. The first is to run a 25-minute lesson for the class focusing on one area of the grammar. The second idea is to create a storybook for a younger year level.

Those who are creating a storybook are asked to specify a group of younger students to work with. Choosing learners in the Early Childhood Learning Centre, one pair then takes a piece of paper and a pen to research the students' interests, returning with a list of characters and within minutes, have the bones of a short story about Bluey's lost mermaid. Sharing one of my children's favourite books with them, I urge them to consider the impact of repetition in children's narratives. With this, and two additional planning lessons, they are ready to read both French and English versions to their new young friends.

While students see the focus of their learning here being the creation of a new 'artefact', reflection helps them to learn that the communication and presenting skills developed provide a more transferrable and holistic opportunity to further their learning. One student uses a prop telephone in the room to "call Bluey" while another student looks at me in horror as he realises the little ones don't quiet down at his expected rate. Students who normally avoid each other are smiling and chatting, sharing their impressions of the younger students. In their semester reflection, one of the students in the above examples shares that providing "more activities to share our learning through teaching, like with the books" would be a good focus for my teaching moving forward.

FINDING THE RIGHT FIT

While I have found this exploration of collaboration to be overwhelmingly rewarding, it has not always been smooth sailing. As with any inquiry into practice, a healthy level of risk-taking is needed and an even greater dose of humility and patience. A key challenge I have found in my practice is identifying where and when collaboration will amplify student learning. In the language classroom, collaborative tasks have been most impactful in exploring ways of transferring grammar and vocabulary to unfamiliar contexts. In Design, however, powerful collaboration can happen at the very beginning of a topic, tapping into the cohesive knowledge of the group to drive inquiry.

Lotan (2003) defines 'group worthy' tasks as having the following five design features:

- They are open-ended and require complex problem-solving
- They provide students with multiple entry points to the task and multiple opportunities to show intellectual competence
- They deal with discipline-based, intellectually important content
- They require positive interdependence as well as individual accountability
- They include clear criteria for the evaluation of the group's product

Main et al. (2017) affirm this view of group-worthy tasks, reminding us of the role that whole-class teaching plays in a Middle Years classroom, including the teaching of new and complex concepts and skills or using whole-class discussion to generate ideas. It may also be best suited when conducting demonstrations or working to create an atmosphere in the classroom through music or narratives. We understand that not all tasks are collaborative tasks, but even so, a culture of collective learning can be supported through intentional questioning, approaches to feedback and classroom agreements for behaviour.

Another key consideration is the way in which the environment communicates the need for collaboration. I am fortunate to have had my own children experience the Reggio Emilia approach to early learning, introducing me to the idea of the environment as the *third teacher*. When I am hosting school tours, I urge families to read the stories of the school's walls. How do the classroom walls demonstrate the value of collaboration? Whose thinking is on display? A commitment to promoting learning as a collective enterprise comes with an acceptance that no two classrooms will look the same and letting go of the 'picture perfect' spaces. Learning together is beautifully messy. I have embraced the competing fonts of different students' handwriting and have worked to ensure that their thinking is as visible as any 'final product' itself. This isn't just a challenge for teachers but for our students as well. The first time I asked one student to put our mind maps on the wall, he responded with *"Are you sure you want to put this up? It doesn't look that good"*. Another opportunity to remind him that learning and thinking can look like a lot of different things and highlight the focus on process over product.

My interest in how the classroom environment can support students' thinking has included trying to understand whether any one particular seating configuration better supports student learning. Unsurprisingly, this research resulted in the same outcome that most binary suggestions in education do: there is no one size that fits all. For this reason, it's important that we look closely at what we are trying to achieve with different tasks and then ask how the environment might support us in facilitating the kinds of interactions we desire.

Thornburg (2013) shares several provocations to support teachers in the transition from teacher to student-centred environments:

The Campfire: the traditional 'lecture style' set up which places the teacher as expert
Watering Holes: space for small group or pair interactions
Caves: opportunities for quiet reflection and individual work
Life: opportunities to apply what students have learned

The most common response I hear from teachers is that it takes too long for students to move tables into different configurations. I challenge this thinking, having done this myself with Middle School students and seeing it work in a Year 4 classroom. I have seen teachers play the song 'Beat It' by Michael Jackson to see if their students can beat the song. I have timed students each week with the goal of bringing their time taken to rearrange the tables down. I have asked students to ensure our classroom is ready by the time I make it from one space in the school to the next. Regardless of the time taken to move tables and chairs, we should resist seeing this as 'lost' time and instead as yet another opportunity for teamwork and communication.

BUILDING THE TEAM FIRST

As I wrote about earlier in this chapter, I have learnt that relationships can make or break any well-planned learning engagement in the classroom. The cultural force of *interactions* is incredibly important here in building trust and psychological safety in which the *modelling* and *routines* of collaboration can be embedded. One of the best pieces of life advice I have received and regularly share with my own children is that trust is earned by the inch and lost by the mile. It is earned in every interaction of just a few seconds, just as it is in the deeper conversations we have with students about their lives and challenges. Failed attempts at introducing collaboration as a *tool* have taught me to be patient with building a culture that can sustain such tools when ready. Understanding when and where to employ different thinking routines has been crucial, and a steep learning curve when trying to use one without first establishing positive and respectful relationships. From insisting on eye contact when saying hello, to including their names in sample sentences and tapping into their interests, I have found that a student who feels *seen* is a student who will more openly accept an invitation to collaborate.

GETTING FROM HERE TO THERE: CHALLENGES AND NEXT STEPS

Having established a clear why and how, the question then turns to how will we measure it? While I am sceptical of the need to measure everything that we do in education, I do find myself asking whether we are putting enough emphasis on finding ways to measure what we value and using these data to further support our learners (Biesta, 2009). This said, what does a skill progression for collaboration look like at different developmental stages? And once we've got it, what do we do with it?

The Australian Council for Educational Research has produced a skill development framework for collaboration, with the purpose of establishing a common terminology for describing collaboration (Scoular et al., 2020). The framework begins by breaking collaboration down into three strands. Each of these strands is then further divided into three or four various associated aspects. The three strands are:

- *building shared understanding*
- *collectively contributing, and;*
- *regulating.*

The University of Melbourne's New Metrics Program has made great strides in this space, working towards measuring a more holistic and transferable set of skills. It defines collaboration as a *complex competency* — a set of 'skills, attitudes and values that learners are expected to develop to thrive at school and in the future' (University of Melbourne, 2024, p. 6). The New Metrics Program is in the process of developing learning progressions for each complex competency, which will take into account a broad range of stages of development and will 'represent the qualitative leaps in development of competence; reflecting the growth in sophistication of application of competence that arises as learners develop in age and throughout typical stages of schooling' (p. 14). The strides taken here to make the seemingly immeasurable now measurable are promising in the shift towards reporting on student learning.

You do not have to look far for a reminder of the importance of collaboration. 'The whole is greater than the sum of its parts' (Aristotle, 1906). 'It takes a village' (African Proverb). Helen Keller's 'Alone we can do so little; Together, we can do so much' (American Foundation for the Blind, 2015). 'We're all in this together' (High School Musical Cast & Disney, W., 2006). Interdependence has always been and remains crucial to sustaining and growing communities. Developing the belief that learning and thinking are as much a collective enterprise as they are an individual endeavour emphasises the value that others can have on our growth, as well as the crucial role we play in the learning of others (Ritchhart, 2023). Watching students graduate from our classrooms with an enhanced appreciation of the other and the richness of engaging with diverse perspectives affirms to me that we're on the path to providing an education that really matters, and it goes a hell of a long way beyond a score out of 100.

REFERENCES

American Foundation for the Blind. (2015) *Script for Helen Keller and Anne Sullivan Macy's Vaudeville performances.* [Accessed 12 November 2024]. Available from: https://www.afb.org/HelenKellerArchive?a=d&d=A-HK01-04-B095-F09-030.1.5&srpos=3&e=-------en-20--1--txt--Alone+we+can+do+so+little------3-7-6-5-3-------------0-1

Aristotle. (1906) *Metaphysics. Book VIII, Part 6.* Translated by W.D.Ross. [Accessed 12 November 2024]. Available at: https://classics.mit.edu/Aristotle/metaphysics.8.viii.html

Australian Curriculum Assessment and Reporting Authority (ACARA). (2024) *Intercultural understanding (version 8.4).* [Accessed 12 November 2024]. Available from: https://www.australiancurriculum.edu.au/f-10-curriculum/general-capabilities/intercultural-understanding/

Biesta, G. (2009) 'Good education in an age of measurement: on the need to reconnect with the question of purpose in education', *Educational Assessment, Evaluation and Accountability,* 21(1), pp. 33–46.

Bruner, J. (1996) *The culture of education.* Cambridge: Harvard University Press.

Hausfather, S.J. (1996) 'Vygotsky and schooling: creating a social context for learning', *Action in Teacher Education,* 18(2), pp. 1–10.

High School Musical Cast & Disney, W. (2006) *We're all in this together.* Disney Music.

Lotan, R. (2003) *Group-worthy tasks.* Association for Supervision and Curriculum Development. [Accessed 12 November 2024]. Available from: http://tafstem.pbworks.com/w/file/fetch/67621837/Group-worthy-tasks-Lotan.pdf

Main, K. (2016) 'Cooperative learning', in Main, K., Pendergast, D., Lee, D. and Bahr, N. eds. 2017. *Teaching middle years: rethinking curriculum, pedagogy and assessment.* Abingdon: Unwin, p.106.

Main, K., Pendergast, D., Lee, D. and Bahr, N. (eds.) (2017) *Teaching middle years: rethinking curriculum, pedagogy and assessment*. Abingdon: Unwin.

Ritchhart, R. (2023) *Cultures of thinking in action: 10 mindsets to transform our teaching and Student's learning*. New Jersey: Jossey-Bass.

Scoular, C., Duckworth, D., Heard, J. and Ramalingam, D. (2020) *Collaboration: skill development framework*. The Australian Council for Educational Research, pp.1–16.

Thornburg, D. (2013) *From the campfire to the holodeck: creating engaging and powerful 21st century learning environments*. San Francisco: Jossey-Bass.

University of Melbourne. (2024) *Assessing agency in learning*. [Accessed 22 July 2024]. Available from: https://education.unimelb.edu.au/__data/assets/pdf_file/0009/4841910/Sample_AGENCY-IN-LEARNING_2024_edition.pdf

Zorich, D., Waibel, G. and Erway, R. (2008) *Beyond the Silos of the LAMs: collaboration among libraries, archives and museums*. Dublin: OCLC Research.

Encouraging Learners to Do the Heavy Lifting
Lana Fleiszig

Seven

Sometimes, you've just got to go with your gut! I'm rewinding my memory to a turning point in my Year 4 classroom some thirty years ago. At the time, being a graduate, I enthusiastically and gratefully attended our weekly planning meetings firmly grasping onto every recommendation that my knowledgeable and experienced colleagues generously shared. We were all required to teach the same thing, at the same time, in the same order, to all of our students – as the focus was on getting through the curriculum outcomes at a pace that would allow us to finish teaching the required content by the end of the school year. The focus was mostly on curriculum outcomes and teaching. There was far less of a focus on individual students and learning.

For the first half of the year, I duplicated what was shared by my colleagues and loved spending hours making the worksheets look more appealing, decorating the classroom with my handmade posters, and finding unique ways to reward my students for 'good' behaviour or when they did well on the test. However, it was what unintentionally happened in one spelling lesson that planted my career-long essential question 'what might happen if I did less and my students did more?' At the time, I had not thought about 'thinking' – yet alone developing a Culture of Thinking in my classroom – however, starting with that one spelling lesson I experienced a shift in my students, their learning, and my belief about my role as a teacher!

Our lesson started like any other spelling lesson, with me following my curriculum document. I proceeded to neatly write words with the long A sound on the blackboard. However, unlike previous weeks, the sheet of words from which I was copying had not classified the words into columns based on a pattern, so I randomly listed them as they appeared on the paper – disgrace, claim, migrate, portray, weigh, aphid, etc. As I was writing with my back to the class, I heard whispers; 'What's the rule?', 'There is no rule', 'I can see the magic e', 'these words are hard', 'I think they all have a long sound'. I smiled to myself as I couldn't believe my students were focused on the words I was writing rather than talking quietly amongst themselves. I vividly remember thinking this was like a puzzle – my learners were trying to guess what was going on as they were familiar with our spelling lesson format and this list of words looked different from previous weeks. They were noticing, questioning, making connections, and enjoying the challenge. They were curious… about spelling! Before long Robbie bellowed, "Miss Raizon don't tell us the rule - we want to guess!"

Diverting from one's lesson plan is often hard to do – especially as a graduate teacher. I felt comfortable with Fisher and Frey's (2008) I Do, We Do, You Do approach (IWY) where firstly I would model exactly how to do something new, then the whole class would practise what I had shown them whilst I guided them and finally I would give my students some other examples to practise on their own. Through this gradual release of responsibility, they seemed to learn what I was teaching and they tended to do well on the weekly spelling tests where only words following a particular rule were assessed. Yet that lesson, my gut told me to listen to Robbie and I'm so glad that I did!

I stopped what I was doing, I ditched my lesson plan, and I asked my learners one simple question, "Looking at these words, what do you notice?" I remember the feeling of freedom as I made my way around the room, not having to do the talking, visiting groups, and eavesdropping on their rich conversations. They were noticing much more than words with the long A sound! Jemma shared her observation that some of the words had 'ei' in them, rather than 'ie' as we'd explored the week prior. I used Jemma's observation as a springboard for the students to explore what the ei words had in common with the other words on the board and then asked, "how else might we group some or all of these words?" The students returned to their table groups and continued to problem-solve, hypothesise, and collaborate with others. I remember feeling happily redundant – even though I recognise now that I was a crucial player in the success of their learning. I was crystal clear about the learning destination – what I wanted my students to know (i.e. multiple ways to represent the long A sound). I didn't yet understand the importance of conceptual understanding so my destination was still narrow – but over time that would change. Whilst I knew the learning destination, I did not know the route that the lesson would take and that was where the magic happened!

I had planned to introduce the multiple ways of making the long A sound through a story I wrote which used many of the words included on the blackboard. I had spent a lot of time writing the story – thinking that if I contextualised the words in the list then my students were more likely to be engaged. Next, I had planned to colour code the words on the board so the students could see the patterns and together we would group them and classify them. Finally, my plan was to ask them to copy the classified words into their books, adding some of their own to each group. Thanks to Robbie, I ditched my carefully planned IWY lesson and handed the thinking over to the students without knowing exactly what was going to be revealed. There was not only one correct answer, in fact it was not even about the answer and at first that scared me. I Do, We Do, You Do had been flipped and there was no going back!

WHY

That day in 1993, there was something my gut was telling me to repeat, yet I wasn't able to name it until many years later. Simon Sinek refers to it as The Golden Circle which places why people or companies do what they do at the core – impacting every decision that is made with regard to what they do and how they do it. He claims that 'people don't buy what you do, they buy why you do it' (2009, p. 41). I had briefly witnessed buy-in from my learners that was intrinsic and I needed to investigate why. So I'm going to start with a vision for education which sits front and centre of why you might consider using the flipped You Do, We Do, I Do approach in your school setting – where Learners Think First (LTF).

Schools need to be places where all students flourish and attain a lifelong love of learning. In addition, 'the goal of quality education is to develop students as powerful thinkers and learners who possess robust understanding ready to take their place in the world as active agents' (Ritchhart, 2023, p. 151). This is a school's overarching purpose – it's why. This vision of education is the filter allowing principles, decisions, and actions, to be audited to ensure that everything, both inside and outside the classroom, is done with intention and with this end goal in mind. By everything I'm referring to pedagogy, timetabling, excursions, the way we speak to students, assessment, resources, reporting, professional learning, homework, meetings, camps, student groupings, and all other school-related 'activities'. If this goal is what we are striving to achieve for every student, then we need to explore how we might action our why.

HOW

Over the years, researchers have shared many principles, mindsets, tools, and actions as a means of realising a school's why like the one we have just brought to mind. Ron Ritchhart has gifted us a few frameworks, which we can use to help enact this vision – of which I'm going to draw on two. The first are 8 Cultural Forces that we must master to truly transform our schools (2015) and the second are 10 Mindsets to transform our teaching and student's learning (2023). These frameworks work together in synergy and I will be referring to some of their parts as we explore how we might bring our why to life.

To transform schools and classrooms into communities where learners are powerful thinkers with dispositions that enable them to take action, we need to change the role of the teacher, the role of the students, and the opportunities provided (City et al., 2009). LTF is one way to do this! I'd like to unpack the three elements in this approach – highlighting how to use this flipped view of teaching and learning whilst drawing on some of Ritchhart's tools and mindsets for transformation. Most of my experience over the last two decades has been in the Maths classroom so in light of this I will unpack each of the elements with practical tried and tested strategies showcasing what we might do in our classrooms to give life to our why.

You Do

In the traditional IWY approach, You Do describes the final phase where students eventually have the opportunity to independently practise what the teacher has taught through direct and then guided instruction. The reasoning for this approach is that students learn best through gradual release of responsibility, placing the teacher at the centre of the learning process. However, if one of our goals of quality education is 'to develop students as powerful thinkers and learners' (Ritchhart, 2023, p. 151) then we need to switch I Do with You Do, ensuring that students have the *opportunity* to think and construct meaning rather than passively wait for the learning to be 'done to' them instead of 'by' them.

David Perkins states that 'learning is a consequence of thinking' (1992, p. 8) and Ritchhart names this as one of the 10 core mindsets that educators need to adopt to inform action. Thinking includes noticing, making connections, wondering, explaining, forming theories, reasoning with evidence, and uncovering complexities, amongst others. Placing You Do first involves teachers holding high *expectations* for students and the learning process. Educators focus on students: learning rather than working, developing conceptual understanding rather than gaining knowledge, taking ownership of their learning rather than depending on the teacher, and developing a growth mindset rather than a fixed mindset. It upholds the belief that thinking is highly valued and necessary – not an extra or an add on.

Positioning You Do first is intentional and I will share most of my suggestions for action around this part of the approach. So let's get practical – how might we send these inspiring messages about learning to our students? What teacher moves might we use to ensure that our students take centre stage in a purposeful educational journey?

HOW? #1 BUILD A CULTURE OF THINKING.

Cultures of thinking are 'places where a group's collective, as well as individual, thinking is valued, visible and actively promoted as part of the regular, day-to-day experience of all group members' (Ritchhart, Church and Morrison, 2011, p. 219). In his book Creating Cultures of Thinking: The 8 Forces We Must Master to Truly Transform Our Schools (2015), Ritchhart identifies the forces that shape culture and delves deeply into how each of the forces contributes towards developing Cultures of Thinking. LTF is a powerful way to shift the role of the teacher to ensure that student thinking is at the core of learning.

WHAT might educators do to action this?

- **Frame the lesson's learning intention as a guiding question.**

  What I have learnt first-hand is that students learn more effectively when they are clear about the purpose. Framing the learning intention as a question and sharing it in writing with students at the beginning of a lesson is a powerful way to spark inquiry and it conveys the *expectation* that students are required to think. 'What might be the connection between subtraction and division?' is an example of a guiding question. The *language* is intentional. The word 'might' sends a message to students that the aim is to explore possibilities, form conjectures, and actively construct meaning through reasoning.

  We often learn more about student thinking from the questions they ask rather than their answers to our questions. As a result, a student's question can become the guiding question for a whole-class investigation or a small group targeted teaching workshop. I usually credit these questions with the student's name, signalling that question posing is highly valued.

- **Make struggle an *expectation*.**

    Placing You Do first pushes students straight into what James Nottingham (2017) describes as the Learning Pit. As educators we need to let students know that this is our aim – as there is no learning without struggle. When visiting classes I share this, followed by my 'rules' (inspired by Tierney Kennedy from Back-to-Front-Maths) which include: there is no such thing as a wrong answer, erasers are banned, you must have a guess, and you are allowed to change your mind. Based on Jo Boaler's research (2016), I often highlight my 'favourite mistakes' (conceptual not numerical errors) sending the message that mistakes are encouraged, valued, and celebrated!

- **Ask a standard Maths question BEFORE students who have been shown how to solve it.**

    For example, You Do is the time to ask students to solve $16.2 + 18.8$ if they have not yet been shown how to add decimal numbers. In this way, they will need to think first, using prior knowledge and schema, to possibly find a method based on their conceptual understanding of adding whole numbers.

- **Use a thinking routine** to structure students' thinking and to make their thinking visible. In their book *Making Thinking Visible* (2011), Ritchhart *et al.* explore many *thinking routines* in depth, identifying the thinking moves required in each. A frequently used routine in my Maths classroom is Claim-Support-Question (pp. 191–198). By attaching this routine to any question, the focus becomes one of forming conjectures, reasoning with evidence, identifying generalisations, and asking deep questions – rather than merely finding the correct answer. Using $16.2 + 18.8$, students would firstly make a claim regarding the sum of these two numbers or the method they might use. They would then justify their thinking to convince a sceptic and perhaps ask a question to take the thinking further. In my class, Brad's question, "how would it work if each number had a different amount of digits after the decimal point?" was used as a provocation for the whole class to investigate in the following lesson.

- **Launch with a challenging open-ended problem** without any explanation or teacher direction as 'learning is enhanced when students work on mathematics problems that they don't yet know how to solve' (Sullivan, 2018, p. vi). Ritchhart names this mindset 'learning occurs at the point of challenge' and recommends looking 'for occasions where you can step back so that students can step forward' (2023, p. 70). There are many websites that teachers can use to find rich, open Maths tasks, my favourites being NRICH and YouCubed. However, teachers can easily become designers and modify existing closed problems to promote thinking and understanding. For example, instead of asking students to find the perimeter of a 10 by 2 rectangle, challenge them to draw shapes with a perimeter of 24.

- **Use extending prompts** to add complexity. 'What if...' questions work well. For example, in the perimeter prompt above we could ask 'what if the shape resembled a letter in your name?'
- **Talk less and listen more.**

    According to Barnes (2013), a teacher should speak for no more than 5 minutes in a row in order to provide students more time to think and learn independently. I often display a large 5-minute sand timer and ask students to remind me to stop talking as soon as time is up. By then taking the role of active listener, I have the opportunity to collect data to inform next steps in a responsive and intentional manner.

- **Curate an *environment* that invites student interaction.**

    Ritchhart describes the physical environment as a 'culture shaper' (2015, p. 227). When I enter a classroom, the first thing I do is arrange the desks into groups so that students see that *interaction* with others to learn is an *expectation*. I try to ensure that there is space in between the table clusters so that students can walk around easily – when needing to seek inspiration from others' thinking. Liljedahl's research (2021) advocates for students using vertical non-permanent surfaces to make their thinking visible to everyone and I have found this to be a powerful way to promote interaction and collaboration.

HOW? #2 FOCUS ON LEARNING WITH CONCEPTUAL UNDERSTANDING

Concepts are big ideas and students with conceptual understanding know more than isolated facts and procedures. They understand why an idea is important and how it can be transferred to other contexts.

Boaler's research shows that 'students learned at significantly higher levels when taught mathematics through a conceptual approach focussed on connections and communications' (2016, p. 68). If understanding is the goal of thinking, then it only makes sense to teach conceptually. Placing You Do first is an effective way to do this.

WHAT *might educators do to action this?*

- **Use guiding questions that are conceptual.**
    Rather than rewording a curriculum outcome as a question, think about the big idea and create a question around that. For example, in the Australian Curriculum a Year 5 Content Description requires students to *identify and describe the properties of prime, composite, and square numbers*. Instead of using the guiding question 'What are squared numbers?' which is very narrow, consider asking the question 'How might numbers be classified?' which opens up a pathway to conceptually understand that numbers have unique properties and can be grouped accordingly.
- **Encourage students to seek patterns and make connections**
    Conceptual understanding is demonstrated when students find connections, apply to a new context, and form generalisations. One of my best concept attainment games is called 'In the Club, Out the Club'. The aim of the game is for students to uncover a secret rule created by a leader. Cards with words, pictures, or numerals are revealed one at a time and placed by a student into one of the two groups – 'in' or 'out'. As cards are moved, their correct placement is confirmed by the leader and students independently form and refine theories, without sharing until all cards have been sorted. At this stage, students predict the rule for cards 'in the club', with reasoning.
- **Start the lesson with a student's misconception**
    Using a student's misconception as a prompt for others to explore, honours process over product and creates a purpose for learning. Using the *thinking routine* Claim-Support-Question (Ritchhart, Church and Morrison, 2011, pp. 191–198), students make a claim about whether they agree or disagree with the prompt, give supporting evidence for their claim, and ask further questions. I then introduce my claim with supporting evidence for them to explore and question.

HOW? #3 ENCULTURATE DISPOSITIONS

In order for students to flourish in school and beyond, we need to place emphasis on how they learn alongside what they are learning. Murdoch refers to skills as 'what the learner is doing' and dispositions as 'what the learner is being' (2015, p. 97). By starting with You Do, we prioritise student dispositional development and create a culture where learners cultivate the skills and dispositions required for a lifetime, including persistence, curiosity, metacognition, and resilience. 'We can't directly teach dispositions; we must enculturate them' Ritchhart (2023).

WHAT *might educators do to action this?*

- **Use 'split screen' guiding questions**

    Prior to introducing a You Do provocation, consider sharing a second guiding question with students. In addition to a content understanding goal, introduce a skill or dispositional goal focusing on learning to learn. Claxton et al. (2011) refer to this as 'split screen' teaching. 'What does it mean to be open minded?' is an example of a guiding question, which brings a disposition to the fore so that it can be explored and discussed alongside the development of students' content understanding.

- **Spotlight a disposition**

    During You Do, observe students closely and identify a disposition as a focus for a week or two. In addition to using it as the 'split screen' question in your lessons, share this with parents and other teachers in the school community so that learners have the opportunity to build this disposition in multiple settings.

We Do

In the IWY approach, We Do usually describes the second phase where teachers lead students through guided practice of a skill. With the flipped approach, We Do is redefined to mean students collaborating with each other and it is not a phase, rather an *expectation*. There is much research to support the benefits of student collaboration rather than working in co-operative groups, where the workload is merely divided amongst members or where students take on specific roles assigned by the teacher. Ritchhart refers to some of this research in Cultures of Thinking in Action (2023) where he identifies and explores the mindset 'learning and thinking are as much a collective enterprise as they are an individual endeavour' (p. 123).

If another goal of quality education is for learners to flourish, then we need to recognise that 'flourishing' is 'an interplay between our best individual selves and our best environment' (Street, 2018, p. 7), which includes interacting effectively with those around us. We Do is time for students to develop social skills such as communicating respectfully and listening actively – in context. It sits hand in hand with You Do and must not be seen as a separate phase in the model.

I Do

In the IWY approach, I Do describes the first phase where teachers use direct instruction and students learn by listening and repeating what the teacher has modelled. In the flipped approach, I Do is the last element where teachers spend the least amount of their time directly teaching a method or providing information to students. It is the time where teachers *model* thinking and help students with a misconception, to change their minds. It only takes place after students have had time to; experiment and work out their own strategies, form conjectures, and discuss them as groups and as a class.

Over the years, I have noticed that once students have had the opportunity to struggle they are often more curious, excited, and open to being shown a strategy or concept. Kath Murdoch advocates growing inquiry learners by 'challenging students to discover something new on their own and some intentionally placed direct instruction - it's 'and' - not 'or'' (2015, p. 14).

When reflecting back to that auspicious spelling lesson some thirty years ago, I have come to appreciate that the success of that lesson was not just about students learning how to spell words with the long A sound or them successfully guessing the common link between the 20 words I'd written on the board. It was about me rapidly rather than gently releasing responsibility so the students could think, develop understanding, productively struggle, and collaborate thus developing skills and dispositions, in addition to gaining knowledge. The focus was on developing the whole child, not just the speller! Students were thinking rather than passively absorbing information I had spent hours sourcing and preparing. What unintentionally happened in that spelling lesson has ironically led me to the importance of intentionality and starting with why. If we want schools to be places where all students flourish and attain a lifelong love of learning and if 'the goal of quality education is to develop students as powerful thinkers and learners who possess robust understanding ready to take their place in the world as active agents' (Ritchhart, 2023, p. 151), then swap I with You and trust your gut!

REFERENCES

Barnes, M. (2013) *The 5 minute teacher: how do I maximize time for learning in my classroom?* Alexandria: ASCD.

Boaler, J. (2016) *Mathematical mindsets: unleashing students; Potential through creative math, inspiring messages and innovative teaching.* San Francisco: Jossey-Bass.

City, E.A., Elmore, R.F., Fiarman, S.E. and Teitel, L. (2009) *Instructional rounds in education. A network approach to improving teaching and learning.* Cambridge: Harvard Educational Publishing Group.

Claxton, G., Chambers, M., Powell, G. and Lucas, B. (2011) *The learning powered school: pioneering 21st century education.* Bristol: TLO Ltd.

Fisher, D. and Frey, N. (2008) *Better learning through structured teaching: a framework for the gradual release of responsibility.* Alexandria, VA: ASCD.

Liljedahl, P. (2021) *Building thinking classrooms in mathematics, grades K-12: 14 teaching practices for enhancing learning.* California: Corwin Press.

Murdoch, K. (2015) *The power of inquiry.* Victoria: Seastar Education.

Nottingham, J. (2017) *The learning challenge: how to guide your students through the learning pit to achieve deeper understanding.* Thousand Oaks: Corwin Press.

Perkins, D. (1992) *Smart schools: from training memories to educating minds.* New York: The Free Press.

Ritchhart, R. (2015) *Creating cultures of thinking: the 8 forces we must master to truly transform our schools.* San Francisco: Jossey-Bass.

Ritchhart, R. (2023) *Cultures of thinking in action: 10 mindsets to transform our teaching and students' learning.* New Jersey: John Wiley & Sons.

Ritchhart, R., Church, M. and Morrison, K. (2011) *Making thinking visible: how to promote engagement, understanding and independence for all learners.* San Francisco: Jossey-Bass.

Sinek, S. (2009) *Start with why: how great leaders inspire everyone to take action.* New York: Penguin.

Street, H. (2018) *Contextual wellbeing: creating positive schools from the inside out.* Subiaco: Wise solutions.

Sullivan, P. (2018) *Challenging mathematical tasks: unlocking the potential of all students.* Victoria: Oxford.

Creating a Culture of Self-Directed Learning: Risk-Taking, Feedback, Goals, *Repeat*

April Taylor

Eight

Sitting in the front row of Mrs. Clare Savedge's Year 9 Honours World History class in Chesapeake, Virginia, I was eager to write down every big question she asked and everything she wrote on the overhead projector or chalkboard. Mrs. Savedge's reputation was that of a strict, yet warm teacher who had high expectations for her students. She was my 'magic weaver' (Jones, 2009). She asked challenging questions without always giving us the answers, she expected us to write well-researched and well-written essays, and she made us love History. Time stood still in those 90-minute periods as we learned about the Nile River Valley, dressed up to *Be Somebody* from the past, or ate cakes shaped like ziggurats to learn about Mesopotamian architecture. I became a teacher because I wanted to foster a love of History in others as Mrs. Savedge had done for me. Nearly 26 years after being her student and 20 years after being her student-teacher, I know I don't just want students to love History – I want them to be confident individuals who love *learning*. Helping students develop the disposition of independence became a theme throughout my teaching.

Learning is different today. Students can simply Google the answers to any question they have about the past – or really most topics. They can generate responses using Artificial Intelligence (AI), thus completely bypassing the need for any thinking if they choose. They are inundated with information constantly, and it is often misinformation. It's not enough to say that I want students to be critical thinkers, or independent learners, or even self-directed learners. Their world is quite different to the one in which I was brought up. I must provide them with opportunities and time to engage in the relevant thinking. I must model different processes for making thinking visible by being 'involved in the process of learning' (Hattie, 2012, p. 29). And I must be patient and trust in the process. Listening to Sir John Jones in a conference room in Sydney in 2016 talk about 'Magic Weavers' made me realise if I wanted to 'connect physically, cognitively, and emotionally' to my students I needed to shift

DOI: 10.4324/9781003541745-12

my practice (Jones, 2009, p. 16). When first introduced to Harvard's Project Zero and the work of Ron Ritchart through Simon Brooks in the same year, I felt this was THE answer to the puzzle of how to teach in the 21st century.

BUILDING A CULTURE OF TRUST AND HEALTHY RISK-TAKING

OneSchool Global is an independent school with 120 campuses spread out across the globe, of which 31 are in Australia, where I have worked since 2012 in various roles including teacher, principal, and New South Wales (NSW) compliance coordinator for senior subjects. Walking into a classroom in OneSchool is a unique experience, as our classrooms are often hybrid – meaning our students may be physically in front of us or on large screens joining via Zoom from one of 11 campuses across NSW. When I first started teaching this way in 2015, I felt a real disconnect with my remote students. OneSchool Australia enlisted the help of Simon Brooks to create a culture of thinking a year on, and I signed up to be a trained facilitator. Countless hours later, I was excited and empowered to turn any classroom, whether it was face to face or with students across the state, into one where the 8 Cultural Forces were 'marshalled' (Ritchhart, 2015). In those early days, it was somewhat easier, as all of the teachers in OneSchool were trained and practising, with Wednesday afternoon Professional Learning Groups to share our experiences and the thinking of our students in facilitated protocols.

OneNote became the physical space in our hybrid environment and shared annotations on Zoom became the space for modelling. I decided to embed thinking routines into the first five minutes and found improved interactions. This was where I built connections and provided opportunities for metacognition using thinking routines such as Take Note – what has challenged you about what we have learned? What are you still wondering? (Ritchhart and Church, 2020, p. 140). This was what made the students want to come to class quickly in fear of missing something important to their understanding of the topic or skills. They enthusiastically shared their 'voice'. Broadening the range of warm-up activities became the space to build self-regulation and responsibility in my students.

I started with thinking routines such as Compass Points to build the structures for metacognition, and over time have learned that ending with the EXCITES positions the students to be more positive about their learning and eager to continue (Ritchhart, Church and Morrison, 2011, p. 93). Not all students are comfortable with this process, so taking it slow and meeting each student where they are in their journey has been important. When teaching topics that are confronting, this thinking routine has created the tone of a safe space, such as when introducing the depth study of The Holocaust. The following is the reflection of a Year 10 student in Stage 5 History:

What worries you? The horror of how people were treated.
What do you need to find out? The perspectives of the Jewish people and how they were treated.
What is your stance or suggestion? I believe the Holocaust was terrible as a minority was almost completely wiped out in Europe.
What excites you about the topic? It is Modern History and we will learn about Jewish lives.

It was not enough to simply provide students with the questions to guide their thinking; the role of the teacher is to facilitate the thinking process. Ritchhart and Church identified questioning, listening, documentation, and thinking routines as "integrative practices that enhance and complement one another" (2020, p. 24). This is where many teachers became stuck – they were seeing a culture of thinking as something we do, and thus they were not seeing the shifts. Once students had been given time to reflect, the 'floor' opened for them to share. In Zoom-teaching, this became through the chat, using a WhiteBoard, or one at a time verbally sharing. It was slow early in the process of creating this culture of students sharing, so I began using responses like "someone has an idea that hasn't been mentioned" to show that not all answers had been given. Doing this over time, I noticed the more opportunity for this type of thinking meant more students were eager to share to the whole class. I frequently asked for a show of hands (Reactions in Zoom) for students to share the worries.

- What could you do to learn more about what you need?
- Where could you start?
- Can you report back to us by X date?

There was always the risk students would share their ideas and they would be confronting to hear. Being armed with responses such as "What makes you say that?" and "How do you know that idea is your own?" fostered an atmosphere of accountability and the need for justification.

Likewise, it was effective to model active listening with phrases like "thank you for sharing" or by repeating their contributions. As misinformation becomes more widespread, I know this habit encouraged many to be more sceptical, thus equipping them with the tools needed to avoid conspiracy theories and stop divisive speech.

My students knew they could freely express their ideas and feelings in my class. Creating similar opportunities for reflection and accountability for learning pushed the students to move past knowing what they needed to making a plan on their own. The following is the reflection from another student from Year 9 History. I noticed how the student had identified a rational way of pushing through his challenge without my directing him. Expecting students to build their own glossary became a simple way of nurturing the skills for self-directed learning.

What is something you have found interesting in this topic? The German citizens were victims of the Holocaust as well.
What is something that is challenging for you relating to this topic? Some of the words in the lessons are hard to pronounce.
What strategies and activities do you think will help you to overcome your challenge? Add them to my glossary and use Google to learn to pronounce them confidently.

Once a culture of trust was established, students expected opportunities to reflect and share their thinking with classmates. This has looked like the aforementioned thinking routines and questions, or even placing their thesis statements in a shared collaborative table for all to see. It was critical the trust was built, but likewise norms were established for respectful interactions. Providing each student with time and space to share their thinking, acknowledge and address challenges, and choose their pathway for overcoming difficulties is what began the process of self-directed learning. I knew I had found the right recipe when I asked students to reflect on one habit they had learned in History lessons that they will continue with, and one Year 12 student replied, "asking questions I am not sure of, without caring whether I look silly!"

ENCULTURATING THE DISPOSITION OF CURIOSITY

Over time, fewer teachers in my school were trained facilitators of creating a culture of thinking in the classroom and school. I led professional development workshops for teachers across OneSchool Global Australia to create a culture of thinking in their classrooms. The Wednesday Professional Learning Groups took on new focus areas as new teachers and leaders joined. The mindset of our school being a culture of thinking for teachers remained as inquiry-based practices continued, as reinforced by Ritchhart (2023). In NSW, our syllabuses tend to be quite content-heavy and prescriptive. This became a point of frustration and fear for those trying to meet curriculum requirements while also creating a culture of thinking. Teachers felt they had to make a choice – trust the process and the students or go back to more traditional ways of teaching that were proven to get strong results.

In *Cultures of Thinking in Action*, Ritchhart (2023) discusses the importance of curiosity in driving inquiry and learning. He collates the research of numerous studies to show that this disposition affects "happiness, creativity… increased personal growth after traumatic experiences, and enhanced perception that one's life has meaning" (Ritchhart, 2023, p. 33). Likewise, my own experience in trying to help my students develop the skills to be self-directed learners has proven the need to make learning matter. I knew I had to make it relevant. In the context of OneSchool, this equated to me helping my students see how the skills I was teaching them would matter after school. I also found that with certain thinking routines, I could hold the students in the state of curiosity by leveraging the cultural force of time and not giving them the answers to their questions (Ritchhart, 2015). Erickson, Lanning and French argue for 'teaching inductively to the concepts…using topics, facts, and skills as supporting tools rather than final destinations' (2017, p. 44). When showing videos, I quickly found the Connect, Extend Challenge routine (Ritchhart, Church and Morrison, 2011) would either leave the students wanting more information about a topic or eager to begin a class discussion at the end of the video. I have one memory of Year 9 students watching a video about crime and punishment in the Industrial Revolution in London, and a few actually bouncing in their seats eager for the video to finish so they could ask their questions. They became even more frustrated when I asked them to go away and find the answers themselves to the questions. The next lesson multiple students were eager to report back. My withholding of answers proved beneficial as the students were hooked. The video and the thinking routine were merely a tool to help my students ask questions and find their own answers.

It became expected that I would not quickly answer the students' inquiries, but that did not stop the students from asking questions. I soon found ways to give the students opportunities to share their thinking and wonderings, such as in their notes. Those students who made this habitual were the ones who excelled. For example, in a set of notes on the impact of convicts and settlers on Indigenous peoples, one Year 10 girl wrote boldly and quite largely (in comparison to the rest of her notes) "WHY DIDN'T THEY BOTHER TO LEARN ABOUT THEM?" I knew then that giving my students both time and opportunity to ask questions would increase their curiosity and drive to learn more – and in some cases, increased empathy and understanding of others.

A CULTURE OF SELF-DIRECTED LEARNING IN ACTION

A few OneSchool teachers and leaders maintained a network with Project Zero, and I volunteered to be a workshop presenter at the PZ Sydney Cultures of Thinking: Puzzles of Practice conference in Sydney in 2017. I shared my experiences of using thinking routines to help students make connections in their learning. It was encouraging to see how broad the network in Australia had become.

In NSW, the Higher School Certificate (HSC) measures students' performance using six bands, with Band 6 being the top. To achieve top bands, students must show complex thinking and synthesis of ideas. I quickly found that Parts, Purposes, and Complexities (PPC) from the PZ Toolkit could be adapted to the humanities subjects to accomplish this (Harvard Graduate School of Education, 2022). In 2020, the HSC question for Conflict in the Pacific asked students to "Evaluate how effective Allied strategies were in combatting Japanese aggression in the period 1942 to 1945." The next year, I changed how I taught this using PPC, where one student, who normally struggled to write complex thesis statements, argued on a collaborative table:

> *The relationships of the strategies is that they all work together very effectively and complement each other. Take the US bombing, they couldn't have known where to bomb without intelligence. Then take how the US was easily able to island hop, this is due to their naval power and submarines in taking out any barricades and major defences.*

Over time, my role shifted from classroom teacher, to teaching Principal. While I maintained a History class, I also found the routines for engaging students and pushing them to be challenged translated to any subject area. At OneSchool Global, students are provided time in each course to work at their own pace on set tasks in our Learning Centre. Teachers have timetabled periods in the Learning Centre where we are teachers of all students and all subjects – the guide on the side. I once was watching a couple of Year 8 girls on the floor who had moved the tables aside to draw a maze with masking tape. I asked them "why are you doing this?" One girl quickly answered, "it's a formative task." I knew I needed to be mindful of my questioning strategies so I asked, "is problem-solving involved?" The girls smiled at me like that was obvious. I asked what method they were using and why they were persevering. The second girl said "experimenting. It's fun because it's a challenge." Over a number of days, I observed the girls trying new ways of coding to successfully make their Spheroes navigate their maze. They did not want teachers to give them the answers, but they often used teachers to explain their thinking, pose their questions, and share their ideas.

I learned how to give the students space to explore with the types of questions I asked.

- What is challenging you about the task?
- How can you pull yourself out of the learning pit? (Nottingham, 2022)
- What tools are available to you? What will you try next?

This supported the idea that "students…actually like and value a degree of cognitive complexity as well as the feeling of being pushed and challenged" (Ritchhart, 2023, p. 155). In my experience, teaching students to slow down their thinking by zooming in on details goes a long way. One morning, while walking around the Learning Centre looking for students who needed help, I observed one Year 11 girl completing a source analysis for her Modern History unit, The Construction of Modern Histories. She was looking at a photo from the Warsaw Ghetto in 1941 of a Jewish man tipping his hat towards the cameraman. The student had to identify the perspective of the photographer, what was happening in the photo, and why the photo was taken. Her initial responses were quite simple, so I asked her to zoom-in on each area of the photo. She was easily able to identify clues such as the tipped hat, fearful faces, and lack of shoes on the people. When we zoomed-out, she noticed the body language and the streaks making her think the people were rushing past the photographer. I introduced her to Claim Support Question (Ritchhart, Church and Morrison, 2011). I could see her confidence grow as she sat up straighter, started becoming animated with her hand gestures, and her written responses became more justified with evidence: "The perspective of the photographer is a Nazi because the Jew is tipping his hat in the photographer's direction. He looks scared and reluctant to do so because he is leaning away." We moved onto the next question of what was happening in the photo:

STUDENT   The Jews are walking on a street in a ghetto. They are badly dressed, and one is barefoot.
ME   *What makes you say the Jew is badly dressed?*
STUDENT   Well, they aren't really badly dressed. One person has a coat, one is wearing a shirt dress, and another is barefoot.
ME   *Why comment on the layers of clothes?*
STUDENT   It's cold and maybe close to winter. There are actually a few in coats. This signifies that they are not getting the supplies they need and their living standard is inadequate.
ME   *So why was the photo taken?*
STUDENT   To feel satisfied?
ME   *What makes you say that?*
STUDENT   To see the progress they are making with removing the Jews from society.

FEEDBACK, GOALS, *REPEAT*

Early in my career, I felt confident I was a good teacher. I met the syllabus requirements, my students enjoyed my class, and there was a healthy buzz when they were learning. I integrated different professional development courses into my practice. The world changed halfway through my career as social media took hold and life outside of the school was often tumultuous: politically, socially, or economically. I knew teaching students to think critically was crucial to developing students who could interrogate information with a healthy scepticism. So how did this fit into my teaching practice?

Teachers have always given students feedback, both oral and written. I have participated in many professional development courses and activities on the role of feedback and how to give effective feedback. I was introduced to the Ladder of Feedback (Ritchhart and Church, 2020) in one of the initial workshops with Simon Brooks with a video of a teacher using the tool. I had already discovered that I could get more out of my students when they make their thinking visible to their peers. I decided to embed this tool into my own practice. I started with helping students to write clear and concise thesis statements. Providing them with a collaborative table in OneNote, each student was given time to put their statement in. I then provided time for students to ask clarifying questions, express what they liked about the statement using language such as "I appreciate", state their concerns using language such as "I wonder", and make suggestions for improvement. Initially, the students were hesitant, but soon they found this to be a valuable tool and would ask for it regularly.

Creating a culture of giving and accepting feedback, my next step was to teach the students what to do with the feedback. When I was a child, I often played the Warm/Cool game. One of my siblings would hide something and the other would have to find it. The only clues we were given were "warm" if you were getting close, "cool" if you were not, "hot" if you were right next to it, and "cold" if you were not even close. I turned this into a tool for my students in their digital notebooks. Each time they received feedback from either a peer or me, they had to take it and put it into the table. I regularly monitored the tables to ensure students were on the right track. I would also leave notes or suggestions. Hattie identified feedback as a tool 'acknowledging errors allows for opportunities,' and that is what I was aiming to accomplish (Hattie, 2012, p. 130). An example is a student who identified cool feedback from his peers in a Ladder of Feedback session regarding the need to write more concisely as his thesis statement was repetitive.

Following on from the Warm/Cool table, I provided students with a separate table for goal-setting. Initially, I had them identify one of the 16 Habits of Mind, where they usually used striving for accuracy, questioning and posing problems, and applying past knowledge to new situations (Costa, Kallick and Zmuda, 2022). They had to set a goal, identify a habit to sustain it, provide steps they would take, and resources they would need to achieve it. Finally, I asked them to return to the table regularly to write down evidence of when they achieved the goals. The student above who was working on writing more concisely identified "In further developing [his] thesis [he] was able to write more concisely in an 80-word summary in a more restricted time limit." Over time, this became a routine in my classroom. It was repeated multiple times throughout each topic we studied. I gave my students time at the end of lessons to check on their Warm/Cool tables and their goal-setting tables. One Year 12 Modern History student frequently used her table, and by the end of the course was sending me daily emails requesting I look at drafts that were linked to her table as evidence she had achieved her goal! The students were thinking about their thinking, setting goals they wanted to achieve, and using feedback. They were becoming self-directed in their learning.

PREPARING OUR STUDENTS FOR THE FUTURE

If we want students to be prepared for the future, we must develop the dispositions of risk-taking and curiosity, and self-directed learning skills. We may be fortunate to have some students who have naturally acquired these; however, the majority of our students need support. It is our responsibility as educators to give them time, opportunity, and modelling to show how this is done. In a world with rapid-fire information, students need reminders to zoom in then zoom out. Additionally, expecting students to justify their ideas with evidence by asking "What makes you say that?" encourages them to interrogate the world around them. Whether it is through giving them opportunities to be challenged and work through problems, holding them in curiosity instead of quickly answering all of their questions, or providing scaffolding for reflecting and setting goals, our role as teachers is as important as ever. The world around them is filled with misinformation, which they must be prepared to interrogate and navigate. While it may be easier to fall back into traditional teaching methods to help students get the top results, it isn't why I became a teacher. And it isn't going to produce a better future for the next generation.

REFERENCES

Costa, A., Kallick, B. and Zmuda, A. (2022) *Teachers habits of mind explanation.* [Accessed 28 December 2024]. Available from: https://www.habitsofmindinstitute.org/wp-content/uploads/2022/02/Teacher-HOM-Explanation-1.pdf

Erickson, H.L., Lanning, L.A. and French, R. (2017) *Concept-based curriculum and instruction for the thinking classroom.* California: Corwin.

Harvard Graduate School of Education. (2022) *PZ's thinking routines toolbox.* [Accessed 28 December 2024]. Available from: https://pz.harvard.edu/thinking-routines

Hattie, J. (2012) *Visible learning for teachers: maximizing impact on learning.* New York: Routledge.

Jones, J. (2009) *The magic-weaving business: finding the heart in learning and teaching.* London: Leannta Publishing.

Nottingham, J. (2022) *A short guide to the learning pit.* [Accessed 28 December 2024]. Available from: https://www.learningpit.org/wp-content/uploads/2022/04/Learning-Pit-Overview-Guide-22-07-Online-version.pdf

Ritchhart, R. (2015) *Creating cultures of thinking: the eight forces we must master to truly transform our schools.* San Francisco: Jossey-Bass.

Ritchhart, R. (2023) *Cultures of thinking in action: 10 mindsets to transform our teaching and students' learning.* New Jersey: Jossey-Bass.

Ritchhart, R. and Church, M. (2020) *The power of making thinking visible: practices to engage and empower all learners.* New Jersey: John Wiley & Sons.

Ritchhart, R., Church, M. and Morrison, K. (2011) *Making thinking visible.* San Francisco: Jossey-Bass.

Leading Professional Growth
Section IV

This section underscores the fundamental importance of cultivating school cultures that prioritise thinking and inquiry for educators as well as students. As Ritchhart argues, "the work of developing a culture of thinking is not about training teachers in one-off workshops, but engaging them in ongoing, embedded learning over time" (2023, p. 3).

In an informational learning paradigm, new practices are introduced to enhance teaching without questioning existing belief structures or the system of schooling. In contrast, a transformational learning paradigm is one in which we reflect on our practice and question our assumptions, often leading to significant changes in how we perceive our goals and purposes as educators (Ritchhart, 2023).

Leading for professional growth involves fostering personalised teacher inquiry, emphasising continuous learning, and creating opportunities for meaningful collaboration.

Nicole Mockler explores the first of Ron Ritchhart's mindsets for transforming teaching and learning: for classrooms to be cultures of thinking for students, schools must be cultures of thinking for teachers. She highlights how this mindset positions teachers as agentic and transformative. Nicole challenges the assumption that education should be the same for everyone, arguing that this confuses equality with equity. She contends that the messiness of human experience makes standardised, scripted approaches inadequate for fostering confident, successful lifelong learners. In conclusion, she offers three principles for building a transformative professional learning culture: encouraging professional curiosity, cultivating trust and risk-taking, and embracing creativity.

Ryan Gill and Carla Gagliano reflect on the long-term journey of creating a Culture of Thinking at Masada College. They emphasise that nurturing this culture is an ongoing process rather than something to be 'done', framing their efforts in terms of inquiry rather than implementation. At Masada, teachers are empowered to investigate personalised

DOI: 10.4324/9781003541745-13

areas of inquiry, identifying and exploring puzzles of practice as part of a community of learners. Ryan and Carla also offer a compelling example of Cultures of Thinking in action through the 'Living Historians' project, highlighting a powerful learning opportunity for students at Masada College.

Samantha Gooch examines the intersection of adult learning principles and Cultures of Thinking ideas, arguing that opportunities for teachers to reflect on lived experiences are the hallmark of powerful professional learning. She demonstrates how activations are used to initiate reflection and outlines several strategies for making teachers' thinking visible. For Sam, effective professional learning involves risk-taking, is relevant to everyday practice, and is framed as a collective endeavour.

Similarly, **Kara Baxter** presents a model for empowering educators through professional learning communities, inquiry-action, and peer observation. She emphasises the role of collective efficacy and teacher collaboration in fostering Cultures of Thinking. Kara believes that it is the responsibility of schools to show a commitment to creating an effective learning culture, in which teachers reflect on their practice and develop their pedagogy with peer support. She shares examples from her school, where professional learning communities help teachers explore ways to promote student thinking.

School meetings can often feel frustrating and fall short of expectations. **Doug Broadbent** explores why collaboration can be so challenging and outlines several ways that school leaders and teachers might begin to collaborate more effectively. A key point in this chapter is that collaboration is not the same as cooperation; meaningful collaboration goes far beyond simply dividing and assigning tasks. Doug argues that a clear purpose is essential for powerful collaboration and introduces several protocols that can be used to clarify not only why we collaborate, but how to do so effectively. At the heart of this chapter is the belief that genuine collaboration requires meaningful cultural change, not just quick fixes.

REFERENCES

Ritchhart, R. (2023) *Cultures of thinking in action: 10 mindsets to transform our teaching and students' learning.* New Jersey: Jossey-Bass.

Pathways to Cultures of Thinking in Troubled Times
Nicole Mockler

Nine

In the first chapter of his 2023 book, Cultures of Thinking in Action, Ritchhart makes the argument that in order for classrooms to be cultures of thinking for students, schools need to be cultures of thinking for teachers. He contends that cultures of thinking in classrooms require teachers who are knowledgeable, curious and creative, "willing to take risks and question the status quo" (2023, p. 4), and oriented to what Marilyn Cochran-Smith and Susan Lytle have termed 'inquiry as stance' (2009): an openness to a robust questioning and ongoing transformation of practice. Later in the book, he suggests a series of 'role shifts' for teachers that will serve to support cultures of thinking in classrooms, captured in Table 9.1.

This shift, encompassing orientations to teaching and pointing to different ways of 'doing' classroom teaching, suggests a particular vision of teacher professionalism, one that positions teachers as agentic and transformative, and that privileges teacher autonomy and professional judgement. Furthermore, these ideas are resonant with notions of transformative teaching and learning advanced by others over the decades, including, to name a few, Ted Sizer (1984), and Grant Wiggins and Jay McTighe (1998). They also stand in tension with prevailing views,

Table 9.1 Changing the Roles of Teachers

Old Teacher Roles	New Teacher Roles
Information deliverers	Orchestrators
Managers of students' time and work	Mentors and promoters of agency
Disciplinarians	Builders of community
Evaluators	Feedback providers
Authoritative fonts of wisdom	Fallible, ongoing learners
Speakers	Listeners
Rescuers	Providers of challenge with support
Deliverers of the curriculum	Co-constructors of curriculum

Source: Adapted from Ritchhart (2023, p. 56).

DOI: 10.4324/9781003541745-14

embedded in education policy and discussions of education in the public space, in Australia and elsewhere, about what it is to be a teacher and, concomitantly, what education is actually for. Given that so much about the creation and sustainability of cultures of thinking in Australian schools rests on the capacity, willingness and support of teachers and school leaders, it seems appropriate to ask what the enabling and constraining factors might be to this form of teacher professionalism in Australia today.

This chapter engages with this question, working from contemporary framings of teachers' work in the public space (and particularly as expressed in education policy and media reporting) to ask how far they are consistent with Ritchhart's vision, and to suggest constraining and enabling factors for achieving this vision.

FRAMING TEACHER PROFESSIONALISM: GOING BACK TO PURPOSE

In the opening chapter of *Creating Cultures of Thinking*, by way of framing the argument for cultures of thinking, Ritchhart challenges us to ponder the greater purpose of education, citing Diane Ravitch's (2009, p. 5) observation that:

> The single biggest problem in education is that no one agrees on why we educate. Faced with this lack of consensus, policy makers define good education as higher test scores.

In the same article, Ravitch goes on to argue:

> Why do we educate? We educate because we want citizens who are capable of taking responsibility for their lives and for our democracy.

These questions about the purpose of education are not confined in their consequences to debates around educational philosophy. The way we, as educators, school communities and societies form answers to these questions, fundamentally shapes our education systems and ultimately, the educational experiences of our children and young people. Furthermore, our answers at a broad social level to the 'why' question shape the preferred image of the 'good' teacher (Connell, 2009) and the teaching profession at any given time. For teachers at an individual and collective level, the 'why' is often articulated around a sense of moral purpose, a desire to make a contribution through work with young people.

Over 30 years ago, Michael Fullan argued that "teaching at its core is a moral profession. Scratch a good teacher and you will find a moral purpose" (Fullan, 1993, p. 12), and subsequent research has found that this moral centre for teachers persists, despite pressures and tensions that sometimes undermine it (e.g. Pring, 2005; Santoro and Hazel, 2022). But we don't talk enough about the 'why' of education and what it means for educators' practice. In the public space, discussions of education are often infused with the assumption that standardisation of curriculum, pedagogy and other practices of schooling is the ultimate means by which a good education system is achieved. Take, for example, current and ongoing discussions of the 'lesson lottery' (Hunter, Haywood and Parkinson, 2022) Australian students are said to be subject to:

> For too long, governments have taken curriculum planning in schools for granted. This has saddled teachers with unrealistic expectations and exacerbated their workloads. Even more worrying, it has created a lesson lottery that impedes student achievement.
> (Hunter, Haywood and Parkinson, 2022, p. 6)

The argument here goes that because governments leave decisions about curriculum enactment and pedagogy up to schools and teachers, not exactly the same thing happens in, for example, every Year 8 History class at the same time, thereby creating a "lesson lottery" that should be stamped out. Furthermore, teachers' curriculum and pedagogical work is positioned as unnecessary 'admin' and banks of downloadable 'lessons' are proffered as the solution to both teacher workload and the 'lesson lottery' (Mockler and Stacey, 2024, in press). Meanwhile, politicians declare teachers to be "rudderless" (The Australian, 2022, p. 10) and stories in the media about teachers being left to "fend for themselves" (Carroll, 2024a; Carroll and Heffernan, 2022; Heffernan, 2022; Jenkins, 2022) proliferate.

This is one example, among many, of how our public discussions of education start from the 'commonsense' assumption that education can and should be the same for everyone, everywhere. In more extreme examples, this assumption underpins scripted lessons and curriculum and also claims about "explicit teaching", often placed in a false dichotomy with "inquiry-based learning" as the 'no brainer' preferred pedagogical pathway: in the words of the New South Wales (NSW) Education Minister, "Explicit teaching works in the classroom. Period."

(Carroll, 2024b). It sometimes takes the form of arguments for "high fidelity" pedagogy and "low variance" curriculum (Del Rio et al., 2023) adopted by some school systems in other parts of Australia, including the Australian Capital Territory (ACT).

There are a number of problems with this assumption, but to my mind the main and immediate one is that it confuses equality with equity. Ideas about curriculum differentiation and the need for teachers to work with students' 'virtual schoolbags' (Thomson, 2002, p. 1) are an educational expression of the foundational principle of equity: the recognition that we do not all start from the same place and that we thus need different pathways. Ideas about standardisation and scripting are built on the notion of equality: the idea that fairness and justice in schooling will be delivered via the same experiences being provided to all students. Within this framework, any 'variances' in learning (based on the principles of equity) are, therefore, to be treated with suspicion and avoided.

The confounding issue here is, of course, what I have previously referred to as the "messy humanity" (Mockler, 2023, p. 17) of teaching, perhaps best expressed by Raewyn Connell in her now foundational piece on the consequences of the marketisation of education:

> To say that education involves nurture is important. Education involves encounter between persons, and that encounter involves care. Learning from a computer is not education; the machine does not care. Learning from a person behaving like a machine is not education; that person's capacity for care is being suppressed. It is care that is the basis of the creativity in teaching, at all levels from Kindergarten to PhD supervision, as the teacher's practice evolves in response to the learner's development and needs. Encounter between persons implies people capable of encounter; that is, people with significant autonomy. The more that power relations impinge on a situation, the less scope there is for encounter and therefore for education.
>
> (Connell, 2013, p. 104)

Good education is about encounter, between students and teachers, and students and students. It requires space for teachers to use their expert judgement and knowledge of their students and their discipline to engage in curriculum enactment rather than mere 'delivery' or 'implementation' (Poulton and Mockler, 2024, in press; Ritchhart, 2015). Impoverished versions of encounter are the outcomes of subtracting teachers' capacity to engage in curriculum work that provides a robust intellectual and affective frame for their pedagogical encounters with students; scripting lessons and other interactions; and removing the capacity for and expectation that teachers will employ their professional judgement to shape learning opportunities for their students. Ultimately, these strategies undermine the intention to support the development of "citizens who are capable of taking responsibility for their lives and for our democracy" (Ravitch, 2009, p. 5), or, in the words of the Mparntwe Declaration, for "all young Australians [to] become confident and creative individuals, successful lifelong learners, and active and informed members of the community" (Education Council, 2019, p. 6). The cultivation of cultures of thinking (Ritchhart, 2015; 2023) in schools is entirely consistent with these expressions of the purpose of education which are critical in the contemporary context of climate emergencies, fractured international politics and post-truth distrust, all of which mean that now, possibly more than ever, we need future leaders with high-level creative and advanced problem-solving capabilities.

TEACHER PROFESSIONALISM FIT FOR PURPOSE

So what does this mean for our teaching profession? If our goal is to support young people to take up these challenges, and along the way to foster cultures of thinking within schools, cultures that are consistent with these broader democratic aims of education (which stand against standardisation of practice), then how might we support the development of teachers equipped to rise to the challenge?

Over 20 years ago now, Judyth Sachs (2001; 2003) wrote expansively about what she saw at the time to be two competing forms of teacher professionalism at work in Australia and elsewhere. She argued that these two discourses of teacher professionalism were both informing and reflective of different forms of education policy and practice which existed in tension with each other. She named these two forms of teacher professionalism *managerial professionalism* and *democratic professionalism*, and the following table, reproduced from the work of Day and Sachs (2004, p. 7), highlights their differences and points of tension.

Sachs argued that managerial teacher professionalism was embedded in the 'new public management' approaches to education popular in the early 2000s, which consequently came to inform the 'corporate models of change' that form one of the pillars within Sahlberg's

Table 9.2

Managerial Teacher Professionalism	Democratic Teacher Professionalism
System driven/ends	Profession driven/ends
External regulation	Professional regulation
Drives reform agenda	Complements & moves beyond reform agenda
Political ends	
Competitive and market driven Control/compliance	Professional development
	Collegial and profession driven
	Activism

Source: Adapted from Day and Sachs (2004, p. 7).

conceptualisation of the Global Education Reform Movement (GERM) (Sahlberg, 2016). She also argued that this version of teacher professionalism was strongly fused into regimes of standards and performative accountability (Lingard, Sellar and Lewis, 2017) that were beginning to proliferate throughout the world.

In tension with this account she placed democratic teacher professionalism, associated with the development and careful use of teacher professional judgement, itself associated with professional autonomy and based on high levels of social trust. Importantly, Sachs' conceptualisation of democratic teacher professionalism encompassed an active and engaged profession, self-regulated and driven towards democratic ends fuelled by the moral purpose and commitment of its members. Her aspiration of an 'activist' teaching profession encompassed professional engagement; what Ritchhart subsequently referred to as "tough collegiality" (2023, p. 4); a bent towards transformation of individuals and communities as well as schooling itself; and a valuing of professional knowledge and practice.

Reflecting over a decade later on this tension, Sachs (2016, p. 424) drew attention to the expansion of performance cultures, performative accountability and narrowly rendered teaching standards, arguing that together, in the intervening years, these "have created the conditions for a more conservative and risk-averse teaching profession" to develop, with managerial professionalism on the increase and conversely, democratic professionalism becoming less prominent. She recognised the critical role of teacher professional learning in supporting teachers to develop dynamic and democratic forms of professionalism, and specifically forms of professional learning and development that are "inquiry oriented, personal and sustained, individual and collaborative" (2016, p. 423), supported by cultures of inquiry within schools and school systems.

In her picture of democratic and activist professionalism, and the role of learning in teachers' professional development, Sachs' views echo Ritchhart's:

> Transformational learning calls on us to question the assumptions that undergird our practice through participation in constructive discourse with our colleagues (Mezirow, 2000). It is about examining and revising our practice in fundamental ways as opposed to merely adding on to it. To be sure, transformation, deep learning and substantive change are complex endeavours. Therefore, we must support educators in embracing this complexity by providing opportunities to inquire into their teaching practise within a rigorous, challenging, and nurturing community of professionals, professionals who are willing to take risks and question the status quo themselves. Such inquiry communities move beyond a soft collegiality in which care is taken not cause offence and toward the tough collegiality that allows for hard questioning of our collective practice and is grounded in a willingness to explore other perspectives (Humes, 2007).
>
> (Ritchhart, 2023, p. 4)

Both Sachs and Ritchhart offer a very empowering and empowered vision of the teaching profession. It assumes an intelligent, resourceful, creative orientation and a commitment to robust critique and ongoing development for the benefits of students. Those of us who work in and around schools and pay attention to teachers know that these assumptions are not far-fetched. The question then becomes, given the current bent on a broad level towards more conservative and risk-averse practice, how we support the profession, both from within and without, in this quest.

FOSTERING CULTURES OF THINKING IN AUSTRALIAN SCHOOLS

So what does this mean for how we might go about ensuring that Richhart's ideas about cultures of thinking both take root and thrive in Australian schools, particularly at a time when pushing back against standardised and 'low variance' education cuts against the grain? I don't want to suggest that there's a recipe that school leaders and teachers should follow to get there – there's no standardised, low variance pathway to transformative education – but I do want to suggest three principles that we would do well to work with in what I consider to be troubled times.

The first is around supporting teachers to cultivate their own professional curiosity and to use it to interrogate their own problems of practice. Lytle and Cochran-Smith long ago made a case for practitioner inquiry as a means by which teachers could individually and collectively come to "know their own knowledge" (1992, p. 452). They were referring here to the capacity for inquiry-based professional learning, such as that advocated for by Ron Ritchhart in the quotation above, to support teachers in developing a rich understanding of 'evidence' grounded in their practice, that pushes back on narrow conceptualisations of "evidence-based practice" and "what works" in education, an approach resonant with that of Church (2015) in relation to supporting cultures of thinking in schools and classrooms. Dylan Wiliam makes a powerful comment on the nature of teachers' expertise and the questions we need to continue to ask in the classroom:

> In education, "what works?" is not the right question because everything works somewhere and nothing works everywhere, so what's... important in education is: "Under what conditions does this work?"... Teaching is all about knowing the conditions under which a particular technique is likely to work. *That is why I say that you can't tell teachers what to do... because the nature of expertise in teaching is not the kind of expertise you can communicate by telling people.*
>
> (Wiliam, 2006, p. 11, my emphasis)

Recalibrating professional learning within school communities away from "spray on" (Mockler, 2005) or "drive by" (Senge, Cambron-McCabe and Lucas, 2000) professional development, such that supporting teachers to question their practice, "within a rigorous, challenging, and nurturing community of professionals" (Ritchhart, 2023, p. 4) becomes the default mode can be a powerful pathway here.

The second is around the cultivation of trust and risk-taking. I mention these together because they are intrinsically linked. Much of the sociological literature around social trust observes that low-trust environments and organisations tend to be places where people are reluctant to take risks (see, for example, Misztal, 2019). It's important for schools to be communities in which people, both teachers and students, are willing to be vulnerable to each other in their learning, open to innovation and willing to try new things and engage with new ideas. Prioritising the cultivation of trust within schools may require leaders to carefully interrogate accountability mechanisms and processes in place for teachers, and to critically question how far these represent apparatuses of performative accountability, which deplete trust (Avis, 2003), and how they might be shifted towards more 'intelligent' forms of accountability, which seek to build trust and a sense of joint enterprise (O'Neill, 2013).

The third is around the embrace of creativity, particularly in relation to teachers' curriculum work. Supporting teachers to understand and reclaim the 'discretionary space' (Weaven and Clark, 2015) in which to put their professional judgement to work in the development of learning experiences for their students is enormously important in these times of standardisation. Fostering cultures of thinking in classrooms relies on teachers feeling equipped, motivated and supported to create the conditions for those cultures to flourish. Cultivating spaces for teachers to engage in the intellectual and creative work of curriculum and learning design, and to collaboratively engage with each other in this work is critical.

Of course, these three principles are deeply interrelated. They speak to creating particular kinds of school cultures where learning is valued beyond testing and performance and where the social and intellectual heart of education is privileged. They to some extent rely on each other, and to a great extent they rely on the kind of courageous leadership, from both school leaders and teachers, that is not afraid to swim against the tide. I doubt very much that history will be kind to the prevailing orthodoxies of schooling in the early 21st century: there are many aspects of our systems, structures and cultures that undermine the ongoing connection of both students and teachers into the project of education. Cultures of thinking offer an alternative possibility for both our schools and our broad educational goals, and it is my hope that this essay has offered some provocations as to pathways in troubled times.

REFERENCES

Avis, J. (2003) 'Rethinking trust in a performative culture: the case of education', *Journal of Education Policy*, 18(3), pp. 315–332.

Carroll, L. (2024a) NSW teacher training rules overhauled as accreditation process scrapped. *Sydney Morning Herald*. August 20, p. 5.

Carroll, L. (2024b) The teaching style behind the state's top-performing schools. *Sydney Morning Herald*. March 1.

Carroll, L. and Heffernan, M. (2022) Schools need shared lesson plans for teachers to stop learning 'lottery'. *Sydney Morning Herald*. October 16.

Church, M. (2015) 'Using inquiry-action projects to go deeper', in Ritchhart, R. (ed.) *Creating cultures of thinking*. San Francisco: Jossey Bass, pp. 298–302.

Cochran-Smith, M. and Lytle, S.L. (2009) *Inquiry as stance: practitioner research for the next generation*. New York: Teachers College Press.

Connell, R. (2009) 'Good teachers on dangerous ground: towards a new view of teacher quality and professionalism', *Critical Studies in Education*, 50(3), pp. 213–229.

Connell, R. (2013) 'The neoliberal cascade and education: an essay on the market agenda and its consequences', *Critical Studies in Education*, 54(2), pp. 99–112.

Day, C. and Sachs, J. (2004) 'Professionalism, performativity and empowerment: discourses in the politics, policies and purposes of continuing professional development', in Day, C. and Sachs, J. (eds.) *International handbook of continuing professional development of teachers*. Maidenhead: Open University Press.

Del Rio, J., Noura, H., Jones, K. and Sukkarieh, A. (2023) *Raising the grade: how schools in the Australian capital territory can lift literacy outcomes for students and the economy*. Canberra: Equity Economics.

Education Council. (2019) *Alice Springs (Mparntwe) education declaration*. South Carlton: Council of Australian Governments Education Council.

Fullan, M. (1993) 'Why teachers must become change agents', *Educational Leadership*, 50(6), pp. 12–17.

Heffernan, M. (2022) Push for shared lesson plans to help teachers. *The Age*. October 17, p. 14.

Humes, W. (2007) 'The meaning of colleagiality', *TES Magazine*.

Hunter, J., Haywood, A. and Parkinson, N. (2022) *Ending the lesson lottery: how to improve curriculum planning in schools*. Melbourne: Grattan Institute.

Jenkins, O. (2022) Lesson plans don't click. *Courier Mail*. October 17, p. 3.

Lingard, B., Sellar, S. and Lewis, S. (2017) 'Accountabilities in schools and school systems', in *Oxford research encyclopedia of education*. Oxford: Oxford University Press.

Lytle, S.L. and Cochran-Smith, M. (1992) 'Teacher research as a way of knowing', *Harvard Educational Review*, 62(4), pp. 447–475.

Mezirow, J. (2000) 'Learning to think like an adult: core concepts of transformation theory', in Mezirow, J. and Associates (eds.) *Learning as transformation: critical perspectives on a theory in progress*. San Francisco: Jossey Bass, pp. 3–33.

Misztal, B.A. (2019) 'Trust in habit: a way of coping in unsettled times', in *Trust in contemporary society*. Leiden: Brill, pp. 41–59.

Mockler, N. (2005) 'Trans/Forming teachers: new professional learning and transformative teacher professionalism', *Journal of In-Service Education*, 31(4), pp. 733–746.

Mockler, N. (2023) 'Dr Paul Brock memorial medal address: educational leadership: when what is necessary is not sufficient', *Australian Educational Leader*, 45(3), pp. 16–17.

Mockler, N. and Stacey, M. (2024) 'Outsourced curriculum planning to reduce teacher workload: tracing the evolution of a policy solution', *Curriculum Perspectives*, 44, pp. 567–571.

O'Neill, O. (2013) 'Intelligent accountability in education', *Oxford Review of Education*, 39(1), pp. 4–16.

Poulton, P. and Mockler, N. (2024) 'Early career teachers' curriculum realities: implications of school context on a continuum of curriculum-making possibilities', *Journal of Curriculum Studies*.

Pring, R. (2005) 'Education as a moral practice', in Carr, W. (ed.) *The RoutledgeFalmer reader in the philosophy of education*. Abingdon: Routledge, pp. 195–205.

Ravitch, D. (2009) How to remake education: beyond testing. *The New York Times Magazine*. September 25, p. 5.

Ritchhart, R. (2015) *Creating cultures of thinking: the 8 forces we must master to truly transform our schools*. San Francisco: Jossey-Bass.

Ritchhart, R. (2023) *Cultures of thinking in action*. Hoboken: Jossey-Bass.

Sachs, J. (2001) 'Teacher professional identity: competing discourses, competing outcomes', *Journal of Educational Policy*, 16(2), pp. 149–161.

Sachs, J. (2003) *The activist teaching profession*. Buckingham: Open University Press.

Sachs, J. (2016) 'Teacher professionalism: why are we still talking about it?', *Teachers and Teaching*, 22(4), pp. 413–425.

Sahlberg, P. (2016) 'The global education reform movement and its impact on schooling', in Mundy, K., Green, A., Lingard, B. and Verger, A. (eds.) *The handbook of global education policy*. New Jersey: John Wiley & Sons, pp. 128–144.

Santoro, D.A. and Hazel, J. (2022) 'Demoralization and remoralization: the power of creating space for Teachers' moral centres', *Philosophical Inquiry in Education*, 29(1), pp. 16–21.

Senge, P., Cambron-McCabe, N. and Lucas, T. (2000) *Schools that learn: a fifth discipline handbook*. New York: Doubleday.

Sizer, T.R. (1984) *Horace's compromise: the dilemma of the American high school*. Boston & New York: Houghton Mifflin.

The Australian. (2022) Help struggling students catch up [Editorial]. *The Australian*. May 30.

Thomson, P. (2002) *Schooling the rustbelt kids: making the difference in changing times*. Sydney: Allen & Unwin.

Weaven, M. and Clark, T. (2015) 'Discretionary space: English Teachers discuss curriculum agency', *Australian Journal of Language and Literacy, The*, 38(3), p. 162.

Wiggins, G. and McTighe, J. (1998) *Understanding by design*. Alexandria: ASCD.

Wiliam, D. (2006) 'Assessment for learning: why, what and how?', in *Cambridge assessment network conference, faculty of education*. Cambridge: University of Cambridge.

Cultivating a Culture of Thinking at Masada College:
Something We Are, Rather Than Something We Do

Ryan Gill and Carla Gagliano

Ten

IMAGINE A SAFE, SUPPORTIVE AND THOUGHTFUL ENVIRONMENT

Imagine if teachers had time and support to reflect and wonder, both individually and with their colleagues, in a nurturing environment. Imagine if schools were committed to developing a culture of thinking for their students, and also thought about how they could create the same authentic culture for their teachers too? Imagine how leaders might leverage existing and new structures within our schools to develop and enrich this culture? At Masada College, we envision a safe, supportive and thoughtful environment where teachers are free to investigate personalised areas of inquiry. Here, educators explore new ideas and perspectives on the big questions and dilemmas in their practice, relevant to all in the education sector. In this chapter, we share insights into the journey of our students and educators over more than a decade, where a personalised stance has been adopted and placed at the heart of our professional learning culture.

FOUNDATIONS OF LEARNING AT MASADA COLLEGE

Educators at Masada College have worked to cultivate and promote rich cultures of thinking, guided by Project Zero researchers from the Harvard University Graduate School of Education, notably Mark Church and Ron Ritchhart. Initially, efforts to build a culture of thinking involved using thinking routines (Ritchhart, Church and Morrison, 2011), but it became clear that more was needed to achieve the desired school-wide cultural change. Previously, professional learning was something done to our colleagues, who passively received practices that sometimes landed in their classroom toolbox. Other times, these sessions often focused on logistics and management within the day-to-day busyness of the school, leading to entrenched silos within departments and grade teams with little interaction among teachers. This led us to wonder: What else might we do to create an atmosphere hospitable to good thinking and

DOI: 10.4324/9781003541745-15

learning – not just for our students, but for our teachers too? How might we create opportunities for rich, valued and meaningful conversations to move our culture of thinking to the next stage? What if the focus of our professional learning was devolved to our educators themselves?

BUILDING A CULTURE OF THINKING

Building a culture of thinking is not just something you do; it is an ongoing process. It is never complete and it is not a one-off professional learning day. Building a culture of thinking is not a programme off the shelf or about faithfully executing a set of practices. There will always be early adopters, others stepping in for some of the time and some stepping out, but institutional change occurs when we recognise that building a culture is never 'done'. It's never about having everyone 'doing' this all the time, nor is it mandated. The impact is measured through reflective opportunities and what we might see on a subtler, nuanced level. Building a culture of thinking is about creating ongoing, authentic opportunities for reflection and communal growth around shared ideas and practices (Ritchhart, 2015a). For teachers to create a classroom culture where students think, inquire, collaborate, discuss, take risks and learn from mistakes, they need to experience such learning for themselves. Teachers respond to the way they are treated as learners by those that surround them. If teachers are controlled and dictated to, they may be inclined to control and dictate to their students. Conversely, if teachers are encouraged to innovate, collaborate and inquire, they will promote these processes in their classrooms (Ritchhart, 2015a). The notion is that in any school or institution people respond and generally mirror the conditions, beliefs and attitudes as well as the practices and behaviours they experience when interacting with others, so-called institutional mirroring (Ritchhart, 2023).

Risk-taking is necessary to drive innovation and create a new story of learning in schools. To build a classroom culture that encourages student risk-taking, teachers need to demonstrate their own willingness to try new things and be learners (Fullan, 2011). However, teachers may be risk-averse for various reasons, including the fear of being ostracised and the fear of public failure. Therefore, a supportive learning culture that embraces inquiry and innovation is important in supporting teachers to feel safe enough to take risks (Dweck, 2006; Le Fevre, 2014). When teachers explore and experiment with new ideas that may not always work, students observe how their teachers react and adapt. This helps students learn the value of failure, to understand that learning is a lifelong process and that mistakes are a natural part of the journey. Deepening our understanding of what it means to *become* a culture of thinking, rather than just *doing* culture of thinking, is at the heart of our goal for initiating this practice. Teachers begin to see beyond thinking routines, considering a broader range of interactive cultural forces, such as opportunities, language, time and expectations (Ritchhart, 2015a). This understanding, combined with routines supporting these endeavours, allows for a shift from a top-down approach to something fundamentally different.

By flipping the locus of control into the hands of those who needed it most – our passionate teachers within our school, who knew their students and classroom contexts best – we created an environment where professional learning was driven by those on the front lines of education.

GENERATING AND REFINING A PUZZLE OF PRACTICE

We began our journey to develop a culture of thinking with a volunteer group of teachers, aiming to establish a supportive, safe and thought-provoking space where we could commune around a personally generated puzzle of practice. There were four simple criteria: the puzzles had to be important to them, relevant to other educators, related to student learning and the right size. This stage was challenging for some, as many puzzles were generated during the initial brainstorming mode. However, as we sorted them, using the Question Sorts thinking routine (Ritchhart and Church, 2020), it became apparent that some puzzles were too specific, required large-scale institutional change, or would not be relevant when sharing and discussing with other educators beyond specific contexts. These were discarded in the initial phase, while others evolved or remained. The process was inspiring, as our teachers began to consider how they could foster a greater sense of curiosity in their learners, develop critical friends and questioners, nurture a growth mindset for our Kindergarteners, or create opportunities for independent learning for our Higher School Certificate students. In doing so, they began to shift their understanding of what nurturing a culture of thinking might be and what it may look like in their classroom context.

ESTABLISHING OUR STUDY GROUPS AND FACILITATING LEARNING

Generating and refining the puzzles was just the beginning. Ongoing and generative discussion of ways forward with their inquiry questions was needed, with something real on the table to anchor the conversation

(Ritchhart, 2015b). Coaching our facilitators was the next simultaneous step, distributing the leadership from the leadership team to passionate educators within the school who could shepherd small groups of fellow educators. In Study Groups, facilitators assisted participants to brainstorm through dilemmas, tune 'plans in the making' and reflect on classroom practice (in the form of student work samples) to help them develop their understanding and next steps towards their inquiry question (McDonald et al., 2013). Using protocols (sourced from the National School Reform Faculty), such as the Descriptive Consultancy, Tuning protocol or Looking at Students' Thinking (LAST) protocol, guided the conversation (McDonald et al., 2013). Regardless of what was on the table – even when a Kindy teacher shared their classroom experiments with a group of Year 9 teachers – there were opportunities to learn, reflect and apply to their own context and inquiry. It provided a reflective moment for all participants, keeping the business of teaching and learning firmly on the table in a real and substantive conversation within a non-confrontational, non-judgemental space. Sharing dilemmas, rather than polished pieces, was a welcomed move, as problems were just as valued as solutions. We learned that when teachers have the opportunity to actively engage in meaningful discussion, planning and practice, their teaching and student outcomes have the capacity to improve.

NAVIGATING CONCERNS AND EMPOWERING TEACHERS

There were moments of concern for some, with questions like: *Are we really going to be able to change this? What can I do when I'm just a Year 10 Geography teacher? What if parents don't agree with what we're doing? How can I do this when I'm trying to get through a packed syllabus?* While pertinent, we ensured these concerns did not leave our colleagues feeling paralysed. By engaging in a Realm of Concern/Realm of Influence protocol, participants became more empowered when they laid out their roadblocks and identified which concerns were within their realm of influence. This process led to breakthroughs and forward actions. When a culture of thinking is viewed as a community that supports teachers' growth, teachers begin to feel safe to be vulnerable, to admit failings or mistakes and to trust that their colleagues are giving feedback in order to help them improve. Our experiences showed us that when teachers are part of a culture of thinking, they are more likely to engage in rich conversations about learning, including the discussion of challenges, strategies and solutions. Learning then became an ongoing, collective responsibility rather than an individual one. This kind of authentic collaboration had a positive effect on student learning. Through collaboration, teachers have been able to better reflect on their teaching practice, allowing them to assess the impact of choices they make in their classrooms. We saw in a collaborative culture, morale improved, teachers reported higher job satisfaction, which in turn contributed to increased gains in student engagement (Fullan, 2011). While this has been our experience, we also understand that meaningful and sustained collaboration among teachers is not always found in schools. Without time and opportunities to collaborate, discussions centred around student learning cannot occur, leading to less teacher learning and the potential for a decline in openness to innovate.

CELEBRATION AND REFLECTION

With palpable engagement and connection to their professional learning throughout the year, a celebration was inevitable. Our final gathering for the year was a reflection and celebration of learning, culminating in insights and new questions generated as a result of the areas of inquiry. Colleagues shared artefacts of students' thinking, quotations from students and teacher colleagues, and anything else they felt worthy of sharing with others. This was an honest, genuine representation of the journey of their learning, with everyone participating in a gallery walk and conversation of what was on display (Church, 2015, cited in Ritchhart, 2015a, p. 301).

EVOLVING THE PROCESS

Fast-forward several years and as we continue to tweak and evolve the process, a personalised approach and a culture of thinking remain at the heart of our professional learning, with ongoing opportunities to share and commune with others. Our teachers observe their peers in action in their classrooms – stopping by for unannounced visits to observe and work in service of the teacher, by noticing and describing what they see without evaluating the practice. Once collated, this evidence can be shared and discussions can commence on how to enhance that practice. While protocols such as Snapshot Observation Protocol, Lesson Study or Learning Labs (Ritchhart and Church, 2020) may be useful tools for schools to support the reflection of practice, in our experience, providing teachers with time and just a little structure enabled them to make their own choices on what to prioritise and bump up. For some colleagues, the most powerful realisations came from a colleague observing specific actions in relation their puzzle of practice and reflecting and acting upon the documented evidence. This approach provides further opportunities to model practice and, importantly, anchor the conversation in evidence collected by peers and discussed with peers.

Since a culture of thinking is something that we are rather than something we do, the structures of our professional learning practices have evolved over time, but the underlying principles remain the same. We continue to consider the purpose for bringing our educators together, using a lens of a culture of thinking, ensuring that learning and teaching is the anchor for our conversations. No matter the initiative or project, our decision-making is driven by our commitment to all learning experiences being underpinned by our desire to continue to develop our culture of thinking at Masada College.

LIVING HISTORIANS: A SHOWCASE OF A CULTURE OF THINKING IN ACTION

What if students were given an opportunity to represent a narrative of history and create their own story? What if these stories were not just read about in a History textbook but they were able to bring meaning to a learner's inquiry? What if students had the opportunity to share their learning with a genuine audience, representing the story of a Living Historian, and communicated this learning with empathy and respect? One such opportunity is seen when our Year 6 and Year 10 students have the privilege of participating in the Living Historians Program, a unique initiative offered by the College.

This experience speaks to Ritchhart's (2015a) four design principles that can serve to create powerful learning opportunities: novel application, meaningful inquiry, effective communication and perceived worth. The Program provides students with a rare opportunity to connect with Holocaust survivors, two of whom being Mimi Wise (aged 88) and Egon Sonnenschein (aged 93). The students, aged 11 and 15, respectively, listen to their stories, conduct group interviews, undertake research and finally, present their own novel depiction of these survivors' remarkable tales through various artistic mediums, including script, drama, visual presentations, artwork and music. Students inquire into the profound notion that each survivor holds a name, an identity and an entire universe within them. The culmination of the students' efforts is showcased in a special assembly where survivors and their families are present to hear the representations of their learning, with an audience witnessing the personal connection established by the students in communicating the survivors' stories. The experience also profoundly affected the survivors themselves. Egon, visibly emotional, emphasised the significance of sharing these stories to prevent history from repeating itself. Mimi, too, was moved and stressed the need to acknowledge the reality of the Holocaust, ensuring that its memory endures as a stark reminder for generations to come. Ultimately, the Living Historians Program leaves an indelible mark on the students, empowering them to carry the responsibility of being witness to the witnesses. Armed with the candle of knowledge, they are now entrusted with enlightening the next generation, ensuring that the stories of the Holocaust survivors live on and we learn with and from the past rather than merely *about* the past.

Scan the QR code below for more insights into the Living Historians Program at Masada College.

Figure 10.1 Living Historians Program 2023 at Masada College.

BREAKING WITH THE ESTABLISHED MODELS OF PROFESSIONAL LEARNING

While school leaders need to be at the forefront of creating a culture of thinking in schools and break with old models of professional learning, teachers themselves must take an active role by respecting their colleagues, being open to new ideas and approaching the act of teaching as inquirers. When both leaders and teachers see the creation of a culture of thinking as a mutual goal for themselves, then the adults in the school can grow, innovate, question, take risks, reflect, examine, inquire, learn from and learn with one another (Ritchhart, 2020). Teachers are then able to create those same conditions for the students in their classrooms. By fostering such a dynamic and supportive environment for educators, we have the capacity to ultimately enrich the learning experiences of our students, ensuring they develop the dispositions and mindset needed to thrive in an ever-changing world.

As we continue to evolve our professional learning practices, it is crucial to recognise that this transformation is an ongoing journey rather than a destination. Continuous reflection, adaptation and commitment to fostering a culture of thinking among educators will ensure that we remain responsive to the needs of our students. This journey involves not only embedding new strategies and protocols but also nurturing a mindset that values curiosity, collaboration, reflection and a willingness to embrace change. By doing so, we can create an environment where professional growth is not a series of isolated events but a continuous and integrated story of our educational landscape.

A VISION FOR THE FUTURE

The journey of cultivating a culture of thinking at Masada College has been transformative, not only for our teachers but also for our entire school community. By fostering an environment where educators are encouraged to explore, reflect and collaborate, we have created a dynamic and supportive space that values continuous learning and innovation. We believe it is crucial to create a culture where teachers are valued as professionals and encouraged to take risks, be curious and collaborate. By creating opportunities for ongoing professional learning that is relevant to teachers' own practice and grounded in their own classroom experiences, schools can cultivate a culture of thinking that supports both teachers and students. A focus on creating a safe, supportive and thoughtful environment where teachers can engage in reflective inquiry not only benefits their own professional growth but also contributes to the overall success of their students. As we continue on this journey at Masada College, we are committed to constant reflection, inquiry and growth, recognising that building a culture of thinking is an ongoing process, rather than a finite goal. As we look to the future, our commitment to deepening and enriching this culture remains steadfast. Professional growth for and with our teachers is key as we envision a place where a culture of thinking is woven into the fabric of our daily practices, guiding both teachers and students towards a shared goal of lifelong learning and growth.

REFERENCES

Dweck, C.S. (2006) *Mindset: the new psychology of success.* New York: Random House.
Fullan, M. (2011) *The six secrets of change: what the best leaders do to help their organizations survive and thrive.* London: Jossey-Bass.

Le Fevre, D.M. (2014) 'Barriers to implementing pedagogical change: the role of teachers' perceptions of risk', *Teaching and Teacher Education*, 38, pp. 56–64. [Accessed 14 November 2024] Available from: https://doi.org/10.1016/j.tate.2013.11.007

McDonald, J.P., Mohr, N., Dichter, A. and McDonald, E.C. (2013) *The power of protocols: an educator's guide to better practice*. 2nd edn. New York: Teachers' College Press.

National School Reform Faculty. (2024) *NSRF protocols and activities… from A to Z*. [Accessed 10 November 2024]. Available from: https://nsrfharmony.org/protocols/

Ritchhart, R. (2015a) *Creating cultures of thinking: the 8 forces we must master to truly transform our schools*. San Francisco: Jossey-Bass.

Ritchhart, R. 2015b. 'Foreword', in Allen, D. and Blythe, T. (eds.) *Facilitating for learning: tools for teacher group of all kinds*. New York: Teachers College Press, pp. vii–x.

Ritchhart, R. (2023) *Cultures of thinking in action: 10 mindsets to transform our teaching and students' learning*. New Jersey: Jossey-Bass.

Ritchhart, R. and Church, M. (2020) *The power of making thinking visible: practices to engage and empower all learners*. London: Jossey-Bass.

Ritchhart, R., Church, M. and Morrison, K. (2011) *Making thinking visible: how to promote engagement, understanding, and independence for all learners*. San Francisco: Jossey Bass.

Principles of Adult Learning in Cultures of Thinking: Challenges, Calls to Action and Triumphs

Samantha Gooch

Eleven

A NOTE FROM THE AUTHOR, AN ADULT LEARNER

Most teachers get to know the parents within their school by talking to them about their child's learning and progress. My unique experience saw me spend just as much time with parents from my school talking about my own opportunity for learning. No, this does not mean what you might think.

In 2018, I was fortunate enough to sit across from two parents who had learnt that our teachers had been busily diving into the work of Ron Ritchhart in his thought leadership and research surrounding Cultures of Thinking. Their passion and intrigue were so strong that their vision was to support our school by sending teachers to the renowned Project Zero Classroom.

As a very fortunate recipient of their philanthropy, I travelled to Boston USA to attend Project Zero's renowned week-long institute. I returned a changed educator and, I believe, person.

This chapter details how my school, Kambala, has similarly pulled strong focus to the adult learners within its walls to grow its culture of thinking and excellence in teaching. It will recount my experience as a school leader leading this professional learning, one who has been fortunate enough to work alongside a Principal with a strong vision for fostering a thriving, collaborative learning environment.

INTRODUCTION

Understanding the Adult Learner for Professional Learning in a Culture of Thinking

School leaders responsible for professional learning in schools, in the most part, have a significant amount of classroom experience. While this depth of understanding about learning is undoubtedly valuable in planning learning for teachers, pedagogy (broadly, the study of teaching and learning processes), can differ to andragogy, "the art and science of helping adults learn" (Knowles, 1990, p. 54).

DOI: 10.4324/9781003541745-16

This chapter invites you to explore the intersection of adult learning principles and cultures of thinking. Moments of triumph that respond to key challenges and calls to action are recounted with the hope of sharing practices that might inspire and guide those committed to fostering a thriving culture of thinking in their own educational settings. The examples of practice shared come from Kambala, an independent early learning – Year 12 girls' school in Sydney, Australia.

In synthesising understandings about andragogy (Knowles, 1990; Knowles, Holton and Swanson, 2015) with two overarching descriptions of the adult learner, the essence of how teachers and school leaders might go about adult learning is offered. A considered approach, that goes beyond merely detailing what teachers need to learn, but how, is proposed.

ABOUT THE ADULT LEARNER, PART 1

Adults thrive in professional learning when they can actively participate in shaping their learning, when their prior experiences and knowledge are used as the basis for all learning and when they can reflect and derive meaning through collaboration.

Challenges & Calls to Action

While harnessing prior learning and experience is important for good pedagogy, and while both children and adults learn from experience, adult learning theory emphasises that individuals amass a wealth of experience throughout their lives, shaping their identity and self-perception (Forrest and Peterson, 2006). From an andragogical perspective, successful teacher education capitalises on this foundation, delving into teachers' existing knowledge base in order to broaden understanding, and sometimes to challenge it.

Striving to cultivate a culture of thinking has provided many ways to examine current practice through the lens of the eight cultural forces (Ritchhart, 2015), and even the mindsets for transformative teaching and student learning (Ritchhart, 2023). Ritchhart and his colleagues propose a variety of opportunities to support teachers to reflect within these frames (Ritchhart, 2015; 2023; Ritchhart, Church and Morrison, 2011).

Reflecting-upon, analysing and sharing lived experiences alongside one another can provide teachers with the chance to gain new insights, question assumptions and collaboratively construct knowledge that can be translated into improved instructional strategies. This type of learning places the professional learning experiences for teachers within the daily work of teachers, rather than separate to or outside of it (Putnam and Borko, 2000) and is a key principle of adult learning (Knowles, 1990).

Such collaborative approaches, prioritising learning as a collective endeavour (Ritchhart, 2023), serve as a call to action for school leaders to provide opportunities for dialogue and shared learning amongst teachers.

The examples below illustrate how Kambala has gone about harnessing the experiences of their adult learners and promoting opportunities for collective learning.

Triumph: Using Activations to Access Prior Experience & Build the Collective

Activations, otherwise known as 'warm-ups', link strongly to adult learning theory by placing immediate focus on adults' experience as a starting point for the learning or collaboration. Principal of Kambala, Jane Danvers, an experienced school principal in Australia, uses activations in almost all of her team gatherings, from leadership meetings to whole staff professional development workshops. She says, "commencing a meeting with purposeful activation is key to focusing attention and grounding everyone in the present moment. It draws people into the room, both physically and mentally, ensuring they are ready to engage fully and contribute meaningfully" (Danvers, 2024).

Activations can set the tone for intentional learning within a culture of learning, by placing thinking at the forefront of the experience.

Here are some examples.

- "Activations – Dispositions for learning"

Kambala embarked on a project by which they investigated the answer to a renowned question posed by Ron Ritchhart: "Who are our students becoming as thinkers and learners as a result of their time with us?" (Ritchhart, 2023, p. 31). This involved exploration into future competencies, with a deep examination of research, and a long-ranging consultation with community, including parents, teachers and students. The School was able to determine and conceptualise key dispositions, aligned with their existing School Values, to define the residuals of a Kambala education; that is, the enduring qualities and skills that students carry forward into their future as a result of their experiences at the school (Sizer, 1984, cited in Ritchhart, 2015).

When conducting professional learning to support how teachers might design learning around these dispositional traits, sessions began by asking teachers to connect to their lived experience. Here are some examples of Activations:

What quality or trait are you best known for? What might have influenced your pattern of behaviour? Was it something that you saw modelled, promoted or adopted to adapt?

Think of a person you admire. What specific quality or trait do you admire them for? How do you know they hold this characteristic and where do you notice evidence of this disposition in their actions and behaviours?

Activations can also be quick and might not require any discussion. For example, the teachers at Kambala were provided a Bingo chart with a set of dispositions listed. They were invited to choose a disposition that they would need to draw-upon in a variety of situations provided. This was a fun, low-stakes Activation that still leveraged adults' prior knowledge in order to prompt thinking in a specific area.

From these simple Activation exercises, the teachers were able to use their personal experiences to form a deeper understanding about dispositions as motivating behaviours. By reflecting on why they, or someone they know, might have developed a certain disposition, they could then think about and derive **ways they might create the conditions necessary** for dispositional development in their own learning environments. Some of these included modelling (demonstrating desired behaviours and attitudes through their own actions), naming (explicitly identifying and articulating specific dispositions to bring awareness to them), espousing (actively promoting and advocating for the importance of certain dispositions within the learning community) and expecting (setting clear expectations for students to embody these dispositions in their learning and interactions).

- "Activations – Culture Building"

Other Activations might fulfil different purposes, such as assisting teachers to keep focus on the impact of their roles as educators in a Culture of Thinking:*"Who is someone in your class that you are proud of this week?"*, or *"Where did your students experience challenge today?"*

As a buy-product, activations can be culture-building and joyful. For example, an Activation to close the academic year might be: "*The Season of Giving:What do you hope to 'gift' to others and what do you hope to receive?*"

Triumph: Making Thinking Visible to Promote Prior Knowledge & New Knowledge

Reflection is "thinking and [a] cognitive process" (Leitch and Day, 2000, p. 180) that is rooted in learning from experience (Dewey, 1938). Making thinking visible can be a useful way to leverage adult learners' experiences by documenting their reflection, thinking and new learning.

Schools committed to making thinking visible, valued and actively promoted (Ritchhart, Church and Morrison, 2011) are accustomed to finding spaces and embedding routines within their learning environments for their students to do so. Why should this be any different for the adult learning in our schools? Here are some examples:

- "One Word"

As a key concept within their new learning framework, Kambala identified *Global Mindedness* as a disposition they hoped to foster within their students. In launching the framework, it was important to create a shared sense of understanding and appreciation about *Global Mindedness*. Over the school term, a series of professional development workshops occurred and were led by teachers identified as passionate innovators of practice who strive to foster global mindedness within their students.

Before these workshops began, all teachers recorded 'one word' that they believed captured their understanding of the concept *Global Mindedness*. Words were kept for display. Digitally, they were documented using an App that instantly captures and can distribute notes with teams, via a PowerPoint, PDF or other formats. Post-it® is one such App that can do this (3M, 2024).

At the end of the term and during the final professional development sessions, teachers were again asked to record 'one word' that they believed captured their thinking about this disposition. The differences and shifts in thinking were remarkable.

An important step in this thinking exercise was not the 'one word' displayed on each Post-it; it was the learning that occurred due to the teachers' **reflection** on their initial response and what might have occurred to result in a shift in their outlook. This was possible due to the thinking that was made visible at all stages of the learning, and the spaces and forums designed to make it possible.

- "Graphic Recording"

In the context of professional learning sessions, graphic recording can visually document the journey to shared understanding, highlighting shifts in perspectives and evolution of ideas. To capture the collective thinking of Kambala teachers about *Global Mindedness*, a graphic illustrator listened intently and translated their spoken words and key ideas into a real-time illustration, using diagrams, symbols, texts and metaphors on a large canvas. This visual representation enhanced understanding and fostered engagement during the collective learning experience, creating a lasting record of group thinking and the learning process.

Triumph: Encouraging The Collective

Theory associated with andragogy emphasises that learning is inherently a social phenomenon for adults (Brookfield, 2013). The placement of the teacher as a lone learner through more transmissive forms of professional development (Knowles, 1990) is one of many reasons why these approaches are not conducive to effective adult learning.

Schools striving to cultivate a school-wide culture of thinking acknowledge this by prioritising learning for teachers as a collective endeavour, not an individual enterprise (Ritchhart, 2023). To assist teachers in reaping the benefits of learning as a collective, moments of togetherness can be organised carefully. Here are two examples that have influenced the success of these opportunities at Kambala.

- "Norms of Collaboration"

Inspired by the Norms of Collaboration proposed by Garmston & Wellman (2016), Principal Jane Danvers leads her Executive Team through an exercise to create working agreements at the start of each year. She poses the following question: How will we 'show up' when collaborating?

Individuals are encouraged to record their responses on Post-it notes and are guided to contribute positive assertions, such as "we listen with intent to understand" (rather than deficit phrases like "we don't interrupt when someone is sharing"). Team members work together to group the themes and ultimately derive a set of 'norms' to which each member will hold themselves, and one another, accountable.

Following Jane's Executive Team meeting, the Middle Management Team derived the following Norms for their collaborative time, and these are documented on their meeting agenda. Norms of Collaboration then transitioned seamlessly into the classroom for many of these teachers after participating in the activity with their own peers.

Working Agreement:

To maintain respectful interactions and enhance our professional goals, we will:

- *respect all voices to recognise the strengths and skills in the room.*
- *ensure that this remains a confidential space.*
- *model respect through professional language, punctuality and preparedness.*

Above: Some 'Norms' listed in the Kambala Academic Leaders' Working Agreement.

- "Routines for Grouping"

It has been valuable to consider the different ways to organise adults together in order to make their thinking visible, valued and actively promoted. Beginning with the **purpose** of the collaborative exercise has proven to be an effective approach.

Random groupings can assist perspective, empathy and understanding across the school as a whole. As with our students, we do not assume that it is comfortable for adults to group themselves at random. Some strategies might include:

- Shoulder Buddies: group with the person/people either side of you.
- Eyebrow Buddies: group with a person you connect with across the room.
- Number Buddies: group with a person who is holding up the same number on their fingers. This can be done with numbers 1–3, 1–5 or 1–10 depending on the size of the group.

Intentional groupings can serve to fulfil a more direct purpose for collaboration:

- Jigsaw Groups: group with people who have the same coloured Post-it note in-front of them, then regroup with people who have different coloured Post-it notes to share understanding.

- Affinity Groups: group with people who have the same (or a different) learning preferences based on those provided by the facilitator (for example, auditory, visual learning styles or, preferred ways to document learning).

ABOUT THE ADULT LEARNER, PART 2

Adults are more highly motivated when their professional learning is entwined with a clear purpose, when they see the direct relevance to their daily practice, and when they have opportunities to apply knowledge and skills in their classroom to benefit their students.

Challenges & Calls to Action

Adult learning is fuelled by purpose (Knowles, 1990). Having a clear sense of purpose motivates adults, influencing their decisions and boosting their engagement. Ultimately, for teachers, this means that they are interested in learning opportunities that apply directly to their daily experience and the goals, tasks or objectives they wish to fulfil in the classroom. School leaders therefore face the challenge of offering job-embedded professional learning experiences that align with teachers' sense of purpose.

The triumphs below illustrate how professional learning opportunities can integrate seamlessly into teachers' daily responsibilities. Here, a culture of thinking has been fostered by facilitation of thinking and discussions about practice, enabling teachers to apply insights born from reflection into their work. Enabling immediate transference to lived experience, as done in these instances, is a key feature of effective adult learning (Zepeda, 2019).

Triumph: Using Protocols and Thinking Routines for Curriculum Planning

If you ask teachers, they will say that one of the most significant challenges they face is lack of sufficient time to adequately fulfil the multifaceted demands of their roles. Often, pressures exist to complete tasks that conflict with what they value as important, often citing increased administrative burdens being placed upon them (AITSL, 2020).

Being part of a genuine culture of thinking allows for the collective use of ideas to build unity, tackle problems and foster collaborative support among teachers. Leaders can harness a variety of thinking structures that serve as productive mechanisms for collaboration, idea generation and problem-solving to support teachers in their daily work.

These examples illustrate how thinking routines and protocols have been used in a task-oriented manner, supporting teachers to carry-out their responsibilities and achieve their goals, while also supporting their professional knowledge and development.

- "Thinking Routines to Deepen Curriculum Knowledge"

As is the case for most states, territories and jurisdictions, governments publish new curriculum syllabus documents regularly. While providing opportunities for reflection and reinvigoration, syllabus-familiarisation and program writing can be a time-consuming endeavour.

Further, planning for teaching involves a well-informed knowledge of curriculum. Devoting time to this not only builds teacher confidence but can empower the design of effective and engaging learning experiences. Structured thinking activities can assist teachers in deepening understanding of new curriculum and thinking about the pedagogies that will best serve their students.

For example:

- Headlines Thinking Routine (Harvard Project Zero, 2022): Dig deeper into a syllabus rationale and summarise it using a Headline relevant to your learners and context.
- Step In, Step Out, Step Back Thinking Routine (Harvard Project Zero, 2022): Position yourself as one of your students to assume their existing skills, feelings, beliefs and knowledge. This assists teachers to plan learning with greater awareness of what their students might need in order to develop understanding.
- Peel the Fruit Thinking Routine (Harvard Project Zero, 2022): Examine different parts of a new syllabus, deconstructing elements to understand what new approaches or knowledge might need to be sought to facilitate learning. In particular, what new or innovative angles could be taken to move past the content-knowledge provided in the syllabus?
- "Visual Scope and Sequence"

Curriculum planning also requires teachers to make inquiries into, and construct plans for, the content and skill progression for students over years within their subject areas. For a new curriculum in Health and Personal Development, Junior School teachers at Kambala were guided to create a "Visual Scope and Sequence". Year Group Teachers created a one-page digital vision board to illustrate what a year of learning that matters (Perkins and Chua, 2012) would look like for their students.

The shared Google Slideshow was distributed to the Group to document thinking and facilitate collective planning. Year Group Teachers presented their initial Vision Boards. With this visual representation, the Junior School Teachers were able to reflect and analyse the choices being made for student learning, and identify salient themes and key skills and knowledge that might be missing.

Triumph: Defining Purpose and Crafting Our Learning Story

For collective efficacy to work in the way in which it has been proven (Eells, 2011), teachers should work towards analysing their impact on the things that have been identified to matter. In a true culture of thinking, this means unpacking the story of learning that is being told (Ritchhart, 2015) through examination of the espoused beliefs, values, traditions and routines at play within the classroom or school.

Clear communication of the school's purpose helps align all members of the learning community around what matters, guiding the collective shaping of the learning story. In this way, the school's purpose serves as a valuable 'north star'.

Encouraging teachers to explore the school's purpose deeply and to reflect on how their own practices contribute to the learning story can foster collective efficacy.

Here are a few ways the story of learning can be explored; one at a whole-school level and the other at a smaller, faculty level.

- "Our Purpose and Story of Learning – Faculty Level"

Patricia Wong and Harriet Wilson are Co-Leaders of a Mathematics Faculty at Kambala. As new leaders to a team including long-serving and recently appointed members, they were eager to co-construct the core purpose of their Faculty, and bring focus to the culture needed to fulfil this purpose.

They began by reviewing current practice, thinking about what they might need to Amplify, Modify, Remove and Create (Ritchhart, 2023). On a classroom whiteboard, the Faculty listed current practices to amplify, modify, remove and suggested what might be missing in 'create'. They distilled the lists into key themes, for example, 'learning to learn'.

From this, two learning initiatives were born to align with what they had identified as the central purpose of their work with students. For senior school students, teachers designed an explicit teaching program about the science of learning to improve the way students were utilising independent study time. For middle school students, enrichment-styled opportunities were changed to better promote engagement in Mathematics for girls and a culture of normalising challenge for learning.

To understand their collective impact, street data (Safir and Dugan, 2021) was gathered and analysed in regard to new initiatives, allowing the team to assess their impact against their overall purpose and the ambitions they had set for themselves.

The exercise also proves to be helpful in removing long-standing practices and programs that did not align with their current vision.

- "Our Purpose and Story of Learning – Whole School Level"

The Kambala Executive Team is intentional in using staff professional development days to affirm a clear and compelling school purpose, fundamental to a healthy and successful organisation (Lencioni, 2012).

Each year, the School holds a 'Culture Day'. This day marks the start of the academic year for all teaching and non-teaching staff, and sees the Principal re-establish a sense of shared meaning and direction.

On one of the Culture Days in 2024, Faculties and Department reflected using "The Six Questions":

1. Why do we exist?
2. How do we behave?
3. What do we do?
4. How will we succeed?
5. What is most important, right now?
6. Who must do what?
 (Lencioni, 2012)

Faculties/Departments made their thinking visible by producing an artefact to represent their responses. Teams accessed a room of resources, having autonomy and creative freedom in making their thinking visible. Artefacts arrived in the form of sculptures, videos and large canvases, which were shared during a gallery walk (Ritchhart, 2015) at the end of the day.

In the context of adult learning, this documentation of purpose has been instrumental in clarifying the reasons behind decision-making, inspiring and motivating all staff to engage with collective goals.

Triumph: Normalising Inquiry, Risk Taking and Innovation

Collaborative dialogues, where teachers engage in joint inquiry, can significantly contribute to adult learning. Such conversations can serve teachers by assisting them to understand their daily work by providing them the opportunity to question assumptions, and modify and create practices that live truer to their mindsets and goals for students. These are the hallmarks of the transformational learning practices that Ritchhart espouses (2023).

In appreciating that more powerful forms of learning for teachers within a culture of thinking occur when teachers are called upon to participate in such constructive dialogue (Ritchhart, 2023), school leaders might consider how they could go about creating these conditions.

The following are some examples of how risk taking and innovation have been promoted within a school context. It is important to note that these practices do not exist in isolation and are supplementary initiatives that aim to support, rather than define, a school's attempts to foster the trust, respect, vulnerability and authenticity so needed for transformative learning to occur (Ritchhart, 2023).

- "Memory Boards"

In order to set goals for the new academic year, Faculty Groups at Kambala were encouraged to make a "Memory Board". The focus of these boards was to highlight instances of experimentation, trial and joy in learning. Groups were encouraged to bring attention to notions of exploration and inquiry and even moments where 'mistakes' were made but learning was achieved. These boards served as a celebration of learning and all Faculty Groups shared their Memory Board during a Whole School gathering. During the sharing exercise, a forum of openness amongst teachers as a community of learners was fostered.

- "Puzzles over Products: Pictures of Practice Presentations"

Normalising the messiness of teaching and learning is highlighted at Kambala through regular opportunities for teachers to share their lived experiences. Teachers are encouraged to speak to the tensions, challenges and personal learning that might occur as a result of their own attempts to innovate their practice. During one Puzzles over Products session, Junior School Drama teacher Anna Derrig spoke of her attempts to improve student agency during Readers' Theatre. After sharing her noticings, Anna explained her idea to use peer feedback for formative assessment. She concluded her presentation with an invitation to colleagues to share any suggestions or knowledge they might have to support her with her classroom initiative… they were eager to assist.

CONCLUSION – A FINAL NOTE FROM THE AUTHOR

The parents mentioned at the start of this chapter had high expectations for the learning of their daughters. Above all, they recognised thinking as fundamental to learning and supported the school's vision of a learning community with a culture of thinking at its core.

They were also insightful enough to understand that for a culture of thinking to thrive for students, it must first exist for teachers (Ritchhart, 2015).

By focusing on the adult learners within our organisations, taking time to truly understand how they learn and the learning for them that actually matters, we honour the hopes of those parents who knew that the future of their daughters' education could only be as strong as the thinking and learning cultivated in the adults who guide them.

REFERENCES

3M. (2024) Introducing the new post-it® app. [Accessed 30 April 2024]. Available from: https://post-it.3m.co.uk/3M/en_GB/post-it-notes/ideas/app/

Australian Institute for Teaching and School Leadership (AITSL). (2020) *Shifting the balance: increasing the focus on teaching and learning by reducing the burden of compliance and administration: Review to reduce red tape for teachers and school leaders.* [Accessed 30 August 2024]. Available from: https://www.aitsl.edu.au/docs/default-source/red-tape/review-to-reduce-red-tape-for-teachers-and-school-leaders.pdf

Brookfield, S.D. (2013) *Powerful techniques for teaching adults.* San Francisco: Jossey-Bass.

Danvers, J. (2024) *Interview with S. Gooch.* 13 August, Sydney.

Dewey, J. (1938) *Experience and education.* New York: Macmillan.

Eells, R.J. (2011) *Meta-analysis of the relationship between collective efficacy and student achievement,* Ph.D. thesis, Loyola University of Chicago.

Forrest, S.P. and Peterson, T.O. (2006) 'It's called andragogy', *Academy of Management Learning and Education,* 5(1), pp. 113–122. [Accessed 26 June 2024]. Available from: http://www.jstor.org/stable/40212539

Garmston, R.J. and Wellman, B.M. (2016) *The adaptive school: a sourcebook for developing collaborative groups.* Lanham: Rowman and Littlefield.

Harvard Project Zero. (2022) *Project zero's thinking routine toolbox*. [Accessed 30 August 2024]. Available from: https://pz.harvard.edu/thinking-routines

Knowles, M.S. (1990) *The adult learner: a neglected species*. 4th edn. Houston: Gulf Publishing.

Knowles, M.S., Holton, E.F. and Swanson, R.A. (2015) *The adult learner: the definitive classic in adult education and human resource development*. 8th edn. New York: Routledge.

Leitch, R. and Day, C. (2000) 'Action research and reflective practice: towards a holistic view', *Educational Action Research*, 8(1), pp. 179–193. [Accessed 26 June 2024]. Available from: https://doi.org/10.1080/09650790000200108

Lencioni, P. (2012) *The advantage*. San Francisco: Wiley.

Perkins, D. and Chua, F. (2012) *Learning that matters: an expanding universe*. [Accessed 30 August 2024]. Available from: https://pz.harvard.edu/resources/learning-that-matters-an-expanding-universe

Putnam, R. and Borko, H. (2000) 'What do new views of knowledge and thinking have to say about research on teacher learning?', *Educational Researcher*, 39(1), pp. 4–15. [Accessed 30 August 2024]. Available from: https://doi.org/10.3102/0013189X029001004

Ritchhart, R. (2015) *Creating cultures of thinking: the 8 forces we must master to truly transform our schools*. San Francisco: Jossey-Bass.

Ritchhart, R. (2023) *Cultures of thinking in action: 10 mindsets to transform our teaching and students' learning*. New Jersey: Jossey-Bass.

Ritchhart, R., Church, M. and Morrison, K. (2011) *Making thinking visible: how to promote engagement, understanding and independence in all learners*. San Francisco: Jossey-Bass.

Safir, S. and Dugan, J. (2021) *Street data: a next-generation model for equity, pedagogy, and school transformation*. Thousand Oaks: Corwin.

Zepeda, S.J. (2019) *Professional development: what works*. New York: Routledge.

Empowering Educators: Using Professional Learning
Communities to Embed Cultures of Thinking
Kara Baxter

Twelve

INTRODUCTION

In the current and fast-changing educational landscape, adaptive approaches to teaching and learning are increasingly required to help prepare learners more effectively for the realities they will face. As technological changes continue to evolve and cultural and social norms change, critical and creative thinking skills, collaboration, and lifelong learning capabilities have become focal points for teachers in their classrooms. It is within this context that Cultures of Thinking (CoT) should be fostered within schools. CoT focuses on the development of students' critical thinking dispositions, which enables them to approach challenges with confidence.

To effectively incorporate CoT practices into schools, it is important to develop a professional learning strategy for teachers to model and share these practices. Professional Learning Communities (PLCs) and peer observation play effective roles in embedding CoT as well as developing the dispositions in both teachers and students. PLCs allow for teachers to be given the time and shared focus to develop their pedagogy with the support of other teachers. Dylan Wiliam emphasises the importance of Professional Learning Communities or Teacher Learning Communities (TLCs) in enhancing teaching and learning effectiveness in schools (2016).

This chapter explores how CoT mindsets and thinking routines are being embedded in classrooms using PLCs at Strathcona Girls Grammar. Teachers sharing their knowledge of CoT and supporting each other through peer observation enables growth in teacher development and shared pedagogical practices, which positively impacts student outcomes.

CORE PRINCIPLES OF CULTURES OF THINKING

According to Ron Ritchhart (2015), fostering a Culture of Thinking and reflection should not be an added task but a fundamental part of school life. CoT is anchored on principles that aim to create a classroom

DOI: 10.4324/9781003541745-17

environment where critical thinking is not just encouraged but celebrated. These principles include fostering curiosity, inquiry, and the development of habits that nurture an inquiring mindset. This involves cultivating traits such as open-mindedness, intellectual humility, and a willingness to engage with new ideas.

A key feature of CoT is the use of thinking routines – structured practices that help students make their thinking visible. These routines provide opportunities for both students and teachers to articulate, analyse, and refine their thought processes. For example, the routine See-Think-Wonder (Ritchhart, Church and Morrison, 2011) is widely used to spark curiosity and promote deeper exploration.

Another hallmark of CoT is the development of a shared language of thinking. When teachers and students use consistent thinking routines across year levels and disciplines, they create a common vocabulary that fosters reflection and critical thought. At Strathcona Girls Grammar, for instance, the question *"What makes you say that?"* is frequently used across the Junior School, Middle School, and Victorian Certificate of Education (VCE) classrooms to encourage students to justify and elaborate on their ideas. This shared approach is applied across subjects such as Humanities, English, and Mathematics, helping to embed a culture of thinking throughout the school. By integrating these principles, CoT transforms classrooms into vibrant spaces where thinking is a shared, celebrated, and continually refined process.

In a Culture of Thinking, there is a strong emphasis on fostering collaboration and teamwork within classrooms. Students are encouraged to actively listen and build upon each other's thinking, creating a sense of community and shared goals in learning. In Year 8 Humanities, students explored the causes and impacts of the feudal system and the church through collaborative debates. Using the Think-Pair-Share routine (Ritchhart, Church and Morrison, 2011), students first reflected individually on their assigned perspective, then discussed their ideas in pairs, and finally shared their arguments with their debate teams. Each group was responsible for presenting a cohesive argument based on historical evidence, requiring them to listen attentively to each other, integrate diverse viewpoints, and build upon their peers' contributions.

Another example of collaboration occurred through Year 11 Art with students engaging in a collaborative analysis process using the Connect-Extend-Challenge routine (Ritchhart, Church and Morrison, 2011) during a peer feedback session. After completing their artwork, students presented their pieces in small groups, where peers connected with elements they appreciated, suggested extensions for enhancing the work, and posed challenges or questions that encouraged the student to think deeper. This routine not only fostered critical reflection but also created a sense of collective ownership in the learning process, as students built on one another's insights to refine their work.

SUPPORTING TEACHERS IN EMBEDDING CORE PRINCIPLES OF CULTURES OF THINKING

To effectively embed thinking routines and foster CoT across classrooms, teachers need to be supported to intentionally embed the core principles of CoT into teaching practices. One of the most effective ways to achieve this is through PLCs. These communities provide a structured platform for teachers to collaborate, share insights, and engage in Action Research to refine their pedagogical practices.

At our school, we adopted PLCs to bring to life the first key mindset underpinning Cultures of Thinking: 'For classrooms to be cultures of thinking for students, schools must be cultures of thinking for teachers' (Ritchhart, 2023, p. 35). These PLCs emphasised Action Research, focusing on CoT practices, and facilitated collaboration between Junior School and Senior School teachers, fostering a cohesive and shared approach to teaching and learning.

However, embedding these principles is not without its difficulties. A key challenge for many schools is finding ways to encourage teachers to embrace CoT principles and routines. Teachers often have deeply ingrained habits and may require significant support and time to explore new methodologies. Like other schools, we also face competing demands that make it difficult to allocate sufficient time for teachers to meet, collaborate, and share their learning when exploring new strategies. Balancing lesson planning, marking assessments, co-curricular responsibilities, and administrative tasks can leave teachers feeling overwhelmed, reducing their capacity to fully engage in professional development. However, by redesigning our after-school Professional Learning time and focusing on a shared learning goal across the school we have been able to support teachers in their development.

Another challenge lies in managing the diverse needs and experiences of staff. Teachers at different stages of their careers require varying levels of support, and some may feel apprehensive about adopting unfamiliar practices. To support this, peer observation was crucial for teachers to reflect and feel supported in trialling new strategies. For example, experienced teachers sought guidance on aligning CoT with current curriculum goals, while newer teachers benefitted from peer observations to see thinking routines in action, such as See-Think-Wonder (Ritchhart, Church and Morrison, 2011) in Year 7 Science to spark curiosity, and Compass Points (Ritchhart, Church and Morrison, 2011) in Year 10 English to facilitate perspective-taking.

THE EFFECTIVENESS OF PROFESSIONAL LEARNING COMMUNITIES

According to Ritchhart's first mindset for Cultures of Thinking, fostering such a culture is not about one-off teacher training workshops (2023). Instead, it requires ongoing, embedded learning over time, with a focus on continuous reflection, shared learning, and collaboration among educators. Linda Darling Hammond also highlights the importance of learning communities by stating that, "Professional development models associated with gains in student learning frequently provide built-in time for teachers to think about, receive input on, and make changes to their practice" (Darling-Hammond, Hyler and Gardner, 2017, p. 14). She highlights the importance of deeply integrated professional development, within teacher's daily work. Dylan Wiliam (2016) agrees, singling out PLCs as a key part of effective teacher professional development.

At Strathcona Girls Grammar, PLC meetings are structured to have teachers use protocols and thinking routines such as the Tuning Protocol (National School Reform Faculty, 2024) and Think-Pair-Share (Ritchhart, Church and Morrison, 2011). These meetings support teachers in experimenting with the routines and exploring how changes in lesson planning might effectively embed these practices into their teaching. PLCs drive progress in implementing new pedagogical approaches by emphasising collaboration, collective accountability, and ongoing professional development. The time set aside for teachers to work in these groups each term allows for teachers to share their classroom experiences with embedding CoT practices. During these meetings, teachers have the opportunity to analyse student work – such as how students have shown their thinking in an assessment or classroom activity – and then devise strategies to enhance their teaching methods from what others have shared.

According to Wiliam (2012), the combined expertise within a PLC or TLC can result in problem-solving and innovative teaching approaches. The key features of TLCs include clear objectives and structure, collaboration, data, implementation, reflection on new learning, and time dedicated to the process. Integrating these features with CoT practices has empowered teachers to embed these approaches more effectively into their classrooms, creating meaningful opportunities to refine and enhance their teaching.

PROFESSIONAL LEARNING COMMUNITIES AND ACTION RESEARCH: DRIVERS OF A CULTURE OF THINKING

Action Research serves as a valuable tool within PLCs offering educators a systematic approach to examining and enhancing their instructional techniques. Action Research is also one example of a professional learning process that is designed to be an integrated part of the teachers' work. According to Timperley (2011), engaging in systematic inquiry into the effectiveness of practice enables teachers to take action that deepens their learning. Action Research involves a cycle of planning, taking action, observing outcomes, and reflecting on experiences. This process allows educators to continually enhance their teaching methods based on real-world evidence and practical knowledge.

At Strathcona, the integration of CoT principles through PLCs has been instrumental in refining teaching practices and fostering a collaborative learning environment. To promote the integration of CoT pedagogy and practice within PLCs, teachers can focus their inquiry by drawing on the 10 core mindsets of CoT (Ritchhart, 2023). To allow teachers choice and to foster exploration, teachers could choose to be a part of a PLC that focused on the following mindsets (Ritchhart, 2023):

- **Mindset 3**: *To create a new story of learning, we must change the role of the student and teacher.*
- **Mindset 4**: *Students learn best when they feel known, valued, and respected.*
- **Mindset 5**: *Learning is a consequence of thinking.*
- **Mindset 6**: *Learning and teaching are as much a collective enterprise as they are an individual endeavour.*
- **Mindset 7**: *Learning occurs at the point of challenge.*
- **Mindset 8**: *Questions drive thinking and learning.*

Teachers from across the Junior and Senior school were then placed into a PLC to unpack the mindset and then begin their Action Research Project to show how they would embed this mindset in their classrooms. Each PLC was guided by leaders experienced in the chosen mindset, ensuring that participants received expert insight into the application of these principles.

For example, to explore Mindset 4, two members of the PLC investigated how personalised feedback in Year 8 Music classes could help students feel more valued in their learning. They introduced individualised feedback sessions where each student discussed their progress and set personal goals for their musical pieces. This strategy was designed to foster a deeper connection between students and teachers, making students feel more recognised and appreciated, which positively impacted their engagement and performance.

For Mindset 5, Year 10 English teachers developed the Action Research question, "How does encouraging deeper questioning during text analysis improve student learning outcomes?" The teachers then trialled the Claim-Support-Question routine (Ritchhart, Church and Morrison, 2011), prompting students to critically engage with texts by making claims, supporting these with evidence from the text, and generating further questions. This routine emphasised that understanding and learning are rooted in thoughtful analysis and inquiry.

For an exploration of Mindset 6, a Year 7 Science teacher developed the question, "How can group investigations enhance collective thinking and learning?" The teacher then implemented collaborative experiments, where students worked in groups to design, conduct, and analyse their own investigations. This approach highlighted the importance of shared knowledge-building, as students not only deepened their understanding through individual thinking but also enriched their learning by drawing insights from their peers.

One of the most effective aspects of this initiative at Strathcona was providing all teachers with a step-by-step Action Research booklet. This resource was designed to help educators apply CoT practices in their classrooms by aligning them with their mindset and integrating them into lesson planning. The booklet included detailed instructions on conducting Action Research, reflecting on practice, and adjusting strategies based on findings. The feedback from teachers on the use of this resource was positive as it allowed them to continue their professional development independently while maintaining a sustained focus on CoT pedagogy and practice throughout their planning and instruction.

Another successful element was the formation of PLC groups comprising of both Junior and Senior School teachers. This structure enabled teachers from different grade levels to collaborate and share how thinking routines could be applied across various contexts. For example, a Junior School teacher working with Mindset 6 collaborated with Senior School teachers to explore how peer feedback could be adapted for different age groups in Health and Physical Education (PE). Junior teachers used Think-Pair-Share (Ritchhart, Church and Morrison, 2011) to facilitate group discussions on story themes, while Senior teachers applied the same routine to more complex VCE English activities, such as language analysis in different modes of text. The exchange of ideas between Junior and Senior teachers helped illustrate how thinking routines could be effectively adapted and scaled according to student needs and developmental stages.

However, some areas for improvement were identified. PLCs occasionally faced challenges with time constraints, such as different events impacting on Junior or Senior School teachers, which affected the depth of discussions and the implementation of Action Research. To address this, future PLCs could benefit from more streamlined agendas and additional dedicated meeting time in the term for discussing and analysing Action Research outcomes in greater detail.

The use of PLCs and Action Research enabled educators to leverage their colleagues' insights and experiences, facilitating a deeper understanding and application of CoT ideas. This collaborative approach not only improved individual teaching practices but also contributed to a more cohesive and effective school-wide culture of thinking.

PEER OBSERVATION: BOOSTING REFLECTIVE PRACTICES AND INSTRUCTIONAL ENHANCEMENT

In addition to utilising PLCs that focused on Action Research, teachers also used peer observation within their community of teachers. Peer observation involved educators observing their colleagues' teaching methods and giving feedback based on agreed criteria and objectives. Peer observation was structured to include a pre-observation planning session, the observation of the class, and a post-observation reflection.

Teachers were provided with a template for notetaking as part of a positive observation experience and examples of the difference between a descriptive observation comment, rather than being subjective and judgemental. Key prompts for the observation included: "How is the thinking routine introduced and scaffolded?", "How do students respond to and engage with the routine?", and "What evidence of student thinking is visible?"

For example, a teacher observing their colleague using the See-Think-Wonder routine (Ritchhart, Church and Morrison, 2011) in a Year 8 Humanities class on life in Medieval Europe would then document how students engaged with the thinking process, collaborated, and articulated their thoughts. Teachers would then meet after the observation class in a post-observation reflection meeting to discuss the observations and reflect on what worked well and if changes were needed.

This reflective process allowed teachers to explore new practices, receive valuable feedback, and refine their teaching methods. Students, particularly in the Senior School, appreciated seeing their teachers learn together and enjoyed the opportunity to have other teachers visit their classrooms.

The insights gained from these observations were then discussed during PLC meetings, where teachers collectively analysed the effectiveness of the thinking routines or new practices, as well as the students' engagement with them. This process fostered a culture of continuous growth and professional development.

One teacher shared, "Peer observation has exposed me to strategies and approaches. Observing my colleagues in action and discussing their methods has motivated me to experiment with techniques and refine my teaching practices. In this classroom students actively participate in thinking exercises that encouraged sharing and inquiry".

Another commented, "Peer observation has been incredibly beneficial as it is great to be able to receive supportive feedback on my practice and for the students to see that as teachers, we like to share strategies and support our learning like we expect of them. I could also see the change in students when I continued to implement different thinking routines".

Structured peer observations ensure that CoT approaches are not only embraced but also continuously refined through collaboration, reflection, and collective Action Research.

TEACHER REFLECTION ON PLCs AND CULTURES OF THINKING

Teachers who participate in PLCs often speak about development and a newfound passion for teaching. Reflecting on their experience of exploring Cultures of Thinking Mindsets and collaborating with others, many educators highlight the influence of learning and the integration of CoT pedagogy and practice into their teaching methods.

A Secondary English teacher at Strathcona expressed this sentiment by saying, "Being part of a PLC in which I could pick my own mindset has completely changed my approach to teaching VCE English. The collaborative conversations and peer feedback has allowed me to view my teaching from other teacher perspectives and from student feedback".

A Senior School Mathematics teacher highlighted the impact of Mindset 7 on her teaching methods. "By incorporating the *What Makes You Say That?* thinking routine (Ritchhart, Church and Morrison, 2011) during problem-solving activities, I found that students needed to articulate their reasoning and confront challenging problems without fear of failure, and it supported other students to reflect on how they were approaching the question". She also observed, "The shift towards embracing challenges has built resilience in my students. They are now more willing to engage with difficult problems and see mistakes as a valuable part of the learning process".

A Year 4 teacher exploring Mindset 4 made use of See-Think-Wonder (Ritchhart, Church and Morrison, 2011) to initiate an Inquiry Project on the Age of Exploration. This routine encouraged students to express their personal interpretations and connect with different parts of the topic. The teacher stated, "Using CoT principles has helped me connect with my students on a deeper level. They feel more comfortable sharing their thoughts and are more engaged in learning because they know their ideas are valued".

An English teacher noted a significant shift in her approach to text analysis after reflection on Mindset 8 and exploring the power of questions to drive thinking and learning (Ritchhart, 2023). She incorporated thinking routines like Claim-Support-Question (Ritchhart, Church and Morrison, 2011), which prompted students to generate their own questions about literary themes and character motivations in *The Giver*. This shift moved the classroom from a focus on teacher-led questioning to a more student-driven exploration, fostering deeper critical thinking and engagement with the text. The teacher observed, "I've seen my students move from passively receiving information to actively questioning and constructing their own understanding".

CONCLUSION

Creating Cultures of Thinking in educational settings requires a collaborative and reflective approach to teacher development. Professional Learning Communities and peer observation, guided by the research and insights of Dylan Wiliam, serve as powerful catalysts for transformative teacher development. PLCs offer structured opportunities for teachers to explore Cultures of Thinking mindsets collaboratively, share strategies, and reflect on their impact on practice. Defined protocols for peer observation also strengthen the use of CoT ideas as colleagues are able to see how other teachers and students use specific routines and practices and then adapt them for their own classrooms. The use of peer observation also led to rich discussions in PLC sessions.

By leveraging PLCs, Action Research, and peer observation, educators can deepen their understanding of CoT ideas, refine their instructional practices, and create vibrant learning environments where students thrive as critical thinkers and problem-solvers. Through structured collaboration, ongoing reflection, and meaningful student engagement with thinking routines, educators can cultivate a culture of thinking that empowers students to adapt, reflect, and succeed in a rapidly changing world.

TIPS FOR STRUCTURING EFFECTIVE PLCs AND ACTION RESEARCH

- PLCs should be included in meeting schedules two or three times a term to allow for planning, implementation, and sharing feedback.
- In order to enrich PLCs with CoT pedagogy and practice, educators can use protocols and templates that guide discussions and reflections.
- During PLC meetings, educators often begin discussions by following a protocol, such as the Tuning Protocol (National School Reform Faculty, 2024), which provides a structure for offering feedback on a colleague's lesson plan or teaching strategy (Wiliam, 2012). This protocol emphasises sharing feedback and fosters a culture of ongoing improvement within the PLC.
- To support a positive approach to peer feedback, teachers should be given guidelines that emphasise objective language, focusing on the roles of both the student and teacher in the classroom. Feedback should avoid judgemental statements, and the teacher being observed should keep notes for reflection.
- PLCs can make use of templates for Action Research planning and reflection to steer their work. These templates offer a framework for setting goals outlining action steps and evaluating progress towards creating CoT. For instance, teachers might use a template to detail the actions they plan to take to incorporate thinking routines into their teaching, monitor their progress over time, and assess how their efforts impact student learning outcomes.

REFERENCES

Darling-Hammond, L., Hyler, M.E. and Gardner, M. (2017) *Effective teacher professional development*. Palo Alto: Learning Policy Institute. [Accessed 13 December 2024]. Available from: https://learningpolicyinstitute.org/sites/default/files/product-files/Effective_Teacher_Professional_Development_REPORT.pdf

National School Reform Faculty. (2024) *Tuning protocol*. [Accessed 13 December 2024]. Available from: https://www.nsrfharmony.org/wp-content/uploads/2017/10/tuning_0.pdf

Ritchhart, R. (2015) *Creating cultures of thinking: the eight forces we must master to truly transform our schools*. San Francisco: Jossey-Bass.

Ritchhart, R. (2023) *Cultures of thinking in action: 10 mindsets to transform our teaching and students' learning*. New Jersey: Jossey-Bass.

Ritchhart, R., Church, M. and Morrison, K. (2011) *Making thinking visible*. San Francisco: Jossey-Bass.

Timperley, H. (2011) *Realizing the power of professional learning*. Berkshire, England: Open University Press.

Wiliam, D. (2012) *Embedded formative assessment*. Bloomington: Solution Tree Press.

Wiliam, D. (2012) *Sustaining formative assessment with teacher learning communities*. Seattle: Kindle Direct Publishing.

Wiliam, D. (2016) *Leadership for teacher learning: creating a culture where all teachers improve so that all students succeed*. West Palm Beach, FL: Learning Sciences International.

Why Are School Meetings So Bad? Some Reflections on Improving Collaboration in Schools

Doug Broadbent

Thirteen

Heidi, the new leader of learning, arrived early for the meeting. The rubbish was cleared, and the desks were moved into a circle. 'Much more collaborative', she mused. The meeting began soon after that, and the agenda was packed. ChatGPT was wreaking havoc with several assessment tasks, and Caleb, the Head of English, was desperate to come up with some ways of dealing with all the students who had used AI for their assessments. The Open Day was coming up, and the marketing team wanted to speak to the Heads of Department about putting on an impressive show for prospective parents. Just before the meeting, Patrica, the Director of Campus admin, asked for '1 minute' to quickly explain the new system for booking parent and teacher interviews.

The meeting began well. The instructions about the Open Day were clear. While there was some disquiet about coming into school on a Saturday, the proposal was generally well received. This was not the case with the '1-minute' discussion of the new Parent and Teacher Portal. The last event was problematic, and people were keen to make their frustrations known. After responding to complaints for 15 minutes, Patrica abruptly excused herself to 'attend another meeting'. Caleb was up next. He outlined all the challenges the English Department was having with hand-in assessments. As he spoke, Amber, the Head of Geography, rolled her eyes. They disagreed about many things, and the nature of effective assessment was one of them. Isaac knew how this would go and began checking his email as soon as Caleb began to speak. After 90 minutes, the meeting finally drew to a close. As Heidi started tidying the chairs, the Head of History came alongside her. 'Would it be okay to skip the next meeting?' she asked. 'I have so many other important things I need to do'.

Heidi sighed.

Sadly, many of the elements of this fictional meeting could be found in schools around the globe. Despite the best efforts of teachers and those who lead them, many of those in our schools have had a negative experience working with others. Meetings are often the cause of frustration for

DOI: 10.4324/9781003541745-18

the teachers. Sadly, this level of angst is not only directed at meetings, and many activities labelled 'collaboration' or 'collaborative' fail to live up to expectations. This short chapter will attempt to provide some insight into the experience of teacher collaboration. It will begin with a discussion of why collaboration has been such a challenge in schools. The chapter will then outline some ways that schools may begin to collaborate more effectively. At the end of each section, there will be some practical steps that can be taken to improve the quality of collaboration. While it is hoped that these suggestions can yield some improvement in the short term, this chapter is undergirded by the assumption that lasting change involves cultural change and not just the introduction of a few quick fixes (Ritchhart, 2015).

SO WHAT ARE THE ISSUES?

As Ritchhart has observed, "we are built to collaborate" (2023, p. 125). A quick search of any school or university website will quickly find a reference to collaboration in some form. While many departments, schools, or systems recognise the importance of collaboration, it is difficult to find clarity about what it means to collaborate. The literature about collaboration abounds with commentary about the challenges in defining the concept (Kelchtermans, 2006; Reeves, Pun and Chung, 2017). While there are numerous narrow definitions of collaboration, others are so broad as to encompass almost all interactions between teachers (Katz and Martin, 1997; Reeves, Pun and Chung, 2017). Lavié puts it simply when he suggests that collaboration is in a "semantic field that is broad" (Lavié, 2006, p. 774).

The ambiguity about collaboration is particularly evident when attempting to identify examples of collaboration. Several terms are often used as synonyms for collaboration, and it is often unclear if meaningful differences exist between the described activities. For example, activities like coaching are sometimes described as examples of collaboration (Levine and Marcus, 2010), but in other cases, this interaction seems to be excluded from concepts of collaboration (Kelchtermans, 2006). Therefore, despite all this scholarship, educators find themselves in a situation where the value of collaboration is assumed (Weddle, 2022), but teachers are not quite sure what they are being asked to do. The central contention of this chapter is that if educators are going to move forward in their attempts to 'collaborate', care needs to be taken to consider how we can clarify exactly what we mean by 'collaboration'.

WHAT IS THE WAY FORWARD?

Ritchhart has written extensively about developing positive school cultures (2015). The stories we tell about our beliefs and values (Ritchhart, 2023) are important in this process. If these stories remain vague and general, we are in danger of talking at cross purposes. It is, therefore, important to spend time surfacing assumptions about what it means to collaborate and engage in robust culture-defining conversations that move beyond the usual platitudes.

Recent research exploring conceptions of collaboration suggests there are two important ways in which teachers understand collaboration (Broadbent, 2020). Teachers have views about the purpose of collaboration and conceptions of how people collaborate. If teachers can begin to surface their assumptions about these two essential questions, we can have greater clarity about what it means to collaborate. With greater clarity about what it means to collaborate, it will also be possible to develop more effective collaboration.

CLARIFYING THE PURPOSE OF COLLABORATION

The first question that requires a response is, 'Why do we collaborate?' Simon Sinek's *Start with Why* (2011) captured the imagination of many with his call to focus on purpose. When it comes to schools, the most obvious claims about purpose relate to students. It is, therefore, not a surprise that many of the statements about the purpose of collaboration are connected to student outcomes. For many, collaboration aims to improve results in standardised testing (Goddard, Goddard and Tschannen-Moran, 2007; Levine and Marcus, 2007). Others take a broader view, and there are studies connecting collaboration to a range of desirable student outcomes, such as well-being (Borg and Drange, 2019) and dealing with emotional, behavioural, and learning problems (Allen-Meares, Montgomery and Kim, 2013).

While a focus on students is vital to the proper function of our schools, it is important to take a broader view of the cultural forces at work in our schools. If conceptions of collaboration are *entirely* based on improving student outcomes, the potential for building the capacity of teachers can be undermined. Professional learning is often left to a few events scattered throughout the year or a range of courses that draw teachers away from their colleagues to attend learning events run by a range of offsite providers. New practices may be learnt, but Ritchhart notes that what often happens is that "the practices being implemented will necessarily lack a strong footing" (Ritchhart, 2023, p. 3). If concepts of collaboration are expanded to include a more nuanced understanding of the professional growth of teachers, then it may be possible to develop the teacher's capacity and ensure that both the students *and* teachers can be the beneficiaries of collaborative activity.

One of the most potent expressions of the ambiguity about norms is found in the range of assumptions about what constitutes a 'good meeting'. In our opening story, poor Heidi was confronted by a group of people who were unclear about why they were meeting. Meeting agendas are often packed with items connected to the student experience. Assessments are discussed, special events planned, and items linked to improving student outcomes frequently dominate collaborative interactions between teachers. Without a clear understanding of the purposes of a meeting, those in attendance will inevitably be frustrated. While complete agreement about the nature of a good meeting may not be achieved, if the purpose of the gathering is discussed, those in attendance have a much greater chance of meeting their expectation. If, for example, people attend meetings because they believe they are the place where important information is communicated, then discussions about new pedagogy will appear irrelevant at best and quite possibly be resented as a waste of everyone's time.

PRACTICAL SUGGESTION: A ROUTINE TO CLARIFY 'NORMS'

At the heart of this chapter is the conviction that making assumptions explicit is essential to the effective functioning of schools. Difficulties inevitably follow if one teacher has a different conception of collaboration from their colleague's. The clarification of norms is a way of surfacing these assumptions (Troen and Boles, 2012). Clarifying norms seeks to express the 'way we do things here'. It is important to note that norms are not created. Everyone has assumptions about how and why things should be done (Richardson, 1999). You don't need to have a document called 'our norms' or a poster on the wall declaring your school's policy about collaboration to have norms. The point here is that it is important to discuss these norms and to make them explicit. It is only when these assumptions are openly discussed that teachers can develop a set of shared beliefs and practices about collaboration.

The idea of 'making things visible' lies at the heart of the approach of the appropriately titled *Making Thinking Visible* (Ritchhart, Church and

Morrison, 2011). This book contains several routines that can be used to surface all sorts of thinking. A particularly powerful way of organising ideas is a routine called Generate, Connect, Sort, Elaborate (Ritchhart, Church and Morrison, 2011). A form of this routine can be used to surface teachers' norms and make progress in developing a common language about collaboration.

For this exercise, the facilitator starts by asking group members to write down behaviours, actions, and postures they think the group should take on. Ideally, each idea is represented on a single Post-it note. After several ideas have been generated, the group can begin to sort the ideas into key themes. Connections are then explored, and the group can start elaborating on what has been outlined on paper. At the end of this process, the group members have been able to identify what they believe are the features of an effective group. These assumptions are what Troen and Boles refer to as norms, and it is important that these are made visible (Troen and Boles, 2012). This process does not guarantee a broader understanding of why we collaborate, but it does begin the discussion. If, for example, there is no mention of professional learning in the group's discussion of its norms, then it might be appropriate to ask, 'Is there any space for us to use our collaborative time to help each other grow as educators?'

CLARIFYING THE WAY WE COLLABORATE

Many teachers will have memories of creating a group project only to find students working individually shortly after the work has begun. After some questioning from the teacher, it is soon discovered that the task has been divided up with each group member given a fraction of the original task. 'I'll do the research', said one. 'I'll make the PowerPoint', says another, and 'I'll upload it', says the final member of the group who has successfully ensured that the task will now require minimal effort. For many teachers, the success (or failure) of collaboration can be measured by the effective division of labour. If there are four people in a group and each member does a quarter of the work, then the collaboration has been good. If one or more group members did less than their 'fair share', then collaboration is seen as negative. This conception of collaboration as cooperation was one of the most common assumptions emerging from recent research (Broadbent, 2020). This finding is not new, and Little's (1990) classic study of the types of collaboration outlines a spectrum of collaborative activity ranging from story-telling to joint work. The argument of both pieces of research is not that some forms of collaboration should be prohibited or perhaps renamed. Instead, both encourage readers to consider more sophisticated collaborative activities. Sometimes, it is appropriate for a group to divide up a task and delegate smaller packets of work to the group members. However, if that is all that groups do, an opportunity has been missed. In moving forward to develop the way we collaborate in schools, it is necessary to expand teachers' understanding of how they can collaborate. What follows is a discussion of a strategy for expanding how teachers understand how they collaborate.

PRACTICAL SUGGESTION: NEW METHODS OF COLLABORATION

In the same way that students can be encouraged to work more effectively through scaffolds, teacher collaboration can be enhanced through effective collaborative structures (Hargreaves, 1994; Vangrieken et al., 2015). Like the previous discussion of using protocols to surface assumptions about collaborative norms, protocols can help teachers discover alternative ways to collaborate. These can range from discussion protocols to professional learning activities that span many weeks.

One particularly useful protocol is the Tuning Protocol (Allen et al., 2018). This protocol moves teachers through a series of discrete stages and seeks to provide meaningful feedback to teachers about a specific problem or project. The Tuning Protocol begins with a short introduction, after which the 'presenter' provides some context to understand the work or project being presented. After this, the rest of the group is invited to ask clarifying questions before spending some time reviewing the work. Only then does the group move to providing 'warm and cool' feedback. The protocol ends with some reflection by the presenter before the group debriefs about the protocol. The power of the protocol lies in separating the discussion into discrete stages to ensure participants do not immediately jump to evaluation.

At the other end of the spectrum is Lesson Study. This form of collaborative activity has its origins in Japan but is practised around the world (Dudley, 2013). Many forms of Lesson Study are often quite involved, but simpler versions are available (AITSL, 2017b). There are also similar forms of this practice with other names. For example, Ritchhart has a practice called Learning Labs, which is similar to Lesson Study (Ritchhart, 2023). All of these practices involve teachers working through a series of clear stages. Teachers typically begin with identifying a particular problem and then work together to develop a lesson plan. One of the teachers delivers the lesson while the rest of the group observes. The group meets again to review what they have observed, and then another lesson is planned and delivered. After this lesson, there is a final discussion as the group reflects together on the problem of practice outlined at the beginning of the process. Like the Tuning Protocol, this collaborative activity works through a clear structure to encourage processes that might not emerge without the guidance of an explicit framework.

These structured approaches to teacher collaboration are only two examples of a range of collaborative activities available to teachers. There are many other resources that can help teachers identify other protocols and structures. For those looking for collaborative protocols, the work of Tina Blythe and her colleagues at Harvard is an excellent place to start (Allen et al., 2018; Blythe, Allen and Powell, 2015). There are also organisations such as the Centre for Leadership and Educational Equity, which publishes resources for teachers online (CLEE, 2024), and government organisations such as the Centre for Education Statistics and Evaluation, which produces material about different forms of collaboration (CESE, 2023). The point here is not that teachers must use the Tuning Protocol or implement Lesson Study; instead, the intention is to expand teachers' knowledge of ways to collaborate. For some schools, this may mean developing a suite of collaborative activities for teachers to explore. For others, it might mean introducing a single new programme of professional learning like Lesson Study. At the end of this process, if a teacher can emerge with at least one different way of collaborating with their peers, then progress has been made.

CONCLUSION

The central contention of this chapter is that concepts like collaboration are often encouraged but poorly understood. While professional bodies may mandate collaboration (AITSL, 2017a) and schools may extol the value of collaboration, too often, assumptions about collaboration vary. For schools to make progress in collaborating effectively, there must be clarity about why we collaborate and the ways that we collaborate. To broaden conceptions of collaboration, this chapter has identified some strategies for making teachers' assumptions more visible and inviting conversations about better ways to collaborate.

MEETING 2.0

With careful consideration of the purpose and nature of collaboration, let us consider how the meeting outlined at the beginning of the chapter may be recast.

Heidi began the meeting with a clear sense of how the group intended to function. The team had engaged in a conversation about their 'norms', which were now published at the top of the meeting agenda. There was some reluctance to introduce too many changes, but the group had conceded that it would be a good idea to use their meeting time to learn from each other. The group had gone through an article in the last meeting, and it seemed to go okay. Caleb had been encouraged to prepare a policy for using AI in English for this meeting. He was ready to roll it out, but Heidi has encouraged him to get feedback from the other Heads of Department. He was initially reluctant, particularly given his previous history with Amber, the Head of Geography. Amber had claimed her 'door was always open', but no one had ever accepted the offer. The Tuning Protocol was the first time that Amber had given any feedback to another department. Caleb was pleasantly surprised at Amber's perceptive questions and made notes as she offered him some useful suggestions about his AI policy. The rest of the meeting had some updates about the latest curriculum matters. These were similar to the items from previous meetings, but the group has agreed that these things needed to remain on the agenda. As the meeting ended, Patrica sidled up to Heidi. 'Thanks for that', she said, 'I really learnt a lot today.'

Heidi smiled.

REFERENCES

Aitsl. (2017a) *Australian professional standards for teachers.* [Accessed 1 September 2024]. Available from: https://www.aitsl.edu.au/standards

Aitsl. (2017b) *Lesson study.* [Accessed 31 August 2024]. Available from: https://www.aitsl.edu.au/tools-resources/resource/lesson-study

Allen, D., Blythe, T., Dichter, A. and Lynch, T. (2018) *Protocols in the classroom: tools to help students read, write, think, & collaborate.* New York: Teachers College Press.

Allen-Meares, P., Montgomery, K.L. and Kim, J.S. (2013) 'School-based social work interventions: a cross-national systematic review', *Social Work,* 58, pp. 253–262.

Blythe, T., Allen, D. and Powell, B.S. (2015) *Looking together at student work.* New York: Teachers College Press.

Borg, E. and Drange, I. (2019) 'Interprofessional collaboration in school: effects on teaching and learning', *Improving Schools,* 22, pp. 251–266.

Broadbent, D. (2020) *A Phenomenographic Study of Collaboration.* MA Thesis, University College London.

Cese. (2023) *Guide to Evidence Based Models of Collaborative Inquiry.* NSW Department of Education. [Accessed 4 July 2025]. Available from: https://www.scribd.com/document/704843246/2023-guide-to-models-of-collaborative-inquiry

CLEE. (2024) *Centre for Leadership and Educational Equity*. [Accessed 6 March 2025]. Available from: https://www.clee.org/

Dudley, P. (2013) 'Teacher learning in lesson study: what interaction-level discourse analysis revealed about how teachers utilised imagination, tacit knowledge of teaching and fresh evidence of pupils learning, to develop practice knowledge and so enhance their pupils' learning', *Teaching and Teacher Education*, 34, pp. 107–121.

Goddard, Y.L., Goddard, R.D. and Tschannen-Moran, M. (2007) 'A theoretical and empirical investigation of teacher collaboration for school improvement and student achievement in public elementary schools', *Teachers College Record*, 109, pp. 877–896.

Hargreaves, A. (1994) *Changing teachers, changing times: teachers work and culture in the postmodern age*. New York: Teachers College Press.

Katz, J.S. and Martin, B.R. (1997) 'What is research collaboration?', *Research Policy*, 26(1), pp. 1–18.

Kelchtermans, G. (2006) 'Teacher collaboration and collegiality as workplace conditions – A review', *Zeitschrift Fur Padagogik*, 52, pp. 220–237.

Lavié, J.M. (2006) 'Academic discourses on school–based teacher collaboration: revisiting the arguments', *Educational Administration Quarterly*, 42(5), pp. 773–805.

Levine, T.H. and Marcus, A.S. (2007) 'Closing the achievement gap through teacher collaboration: facilitating multiple trajectories of teacher learning', *Journal of Advanced Academics*, 19, pp. 116–138.

Levine, T.H. and Marcus, A.S. (2010) 'How the structure and focus of teachers' collaborative activities facilitate and constrain teacher learning', *Teaching and Teacher Education*, 26, pp. 389–398.

Little, J.W. (1990) 'The persistence of privacy – Autonomy and initiative in teachers professional relations', *Teachers College Record*, 91, pp. 509–536.

Reeves, P.M., Pun, W.H. and Chung, K.S. (2017) 'Influence of teacher collaboration on job satisfaction and student achievement', *Teaching and Teacher Education*, 67, pp. 227–236.

Richardson, J. (1999) *Norms Put the 'Golden Rule'into Practice for Groups*. [Accessed 4 July 2025]. Available from: https://learningteams.pbworks.com/f/Why+Norms_Golden+Rule+Article.pdf

Ritchhart, R. (2015) *Creating cultures of thinking: the 8 forces we must master to truly transform our classrooms*. San Francisco: Jossey-Bass.

Ritchhart, R. (2023) *Cultures of thinking in action: 10 mindsets to transform our teaching and students' learning*. New Jersey: Jossey-Bass.

Ritchhart, R., Church, M. and Morrison, K. (2011) *Making thinking visible*. San Francisco: Jossey-Bass.

Sinek, S. (2011) *Start with why: the inspiring million-copy bestseller that will help you find your purpose*. UK: Penguin.

Troen, V. and Boles, K. (2012) *The power of teacher teams: with cases, analyses, and strategies for success*. London: Corwin Press.

Vangrieken, K., Dochy, F., Raes, E. and Kyndt, E. (2015) 'Teacher collaboration: a systematic review', *Educational Research Review*, 15, pp. 17–40.

Weddle, H. (2022) 'Approaches to studying teacher collaboration for instructional improvement: a review of literature', *Educational Research Review*, 35, pp. 1–20.

Navigating Change
Section V

Modern education requires agile leadership capable of navigating an ever-changing landscape. Leaders must build relationships grounded in trust, create an inclusive, collaborative environment, and articulate a clear, compelling vision – cultivating an ecosystem that evolves organically, rather than following a rigid script. Building a culture of thinking in schools is not a quick fix but an ongoing, reflective journey. It demands patience and a long-term commitment to growth. Central to this is creating a shared dedication to thinking across the entire school community, ensuring that everyone feels invested in the process.

Mark Church emphasises that a true culture of thinking values thinking across the entire school community. He advocates for gradual, deep change, beginning with a core group of committed educators who model effective practices. School leaders should support ongoing professional learning, encouraging collaboration among teachers to enhance student thinking visibility. By investing in a long-term vision, schools can create lasting environments where thinking thrives.

Lani Brockwell notes the confusion stemming from national debates over teaching approaches. Her experience highlights that high-quality teaching blends traditional skills like literacy with dispositional or soft skills, essential for preparing students for academic and life success. Grounded in a Culture of Thinking, her teaching fosters environments where students feel heard and valued, nurturing both academic mastery and social justice.

Bruce Addison and Susan Garson explore the journey of building a culture of thinking at Brisbane Girls Grammar School. They address challenges such as changing a well-functioning culture and promoting cross-faculty collaboration. Bruce highlights the Principal's support and the Cultures of Thinking framework, emphasising a bottom-up approach that fosters collaboration and shared language. Susan expands on practical strategies for embedding this culture, such as the New Staff Immersion

DOI: 10.4324/9781003541745-19

program and Inquiry Action Projects. Both authors emphasise that change is complex and requires strategic planning and a supportive environment for teachers and students to thrive.

Martyn Anderson describes his school's transformative journey under Principal Kevin Richardson, who adopted the International Baccalaureate Middle Years Program. This shift emphasised holistic education and led to the formation of a 'Thinking Group' focused on classroom thinking routines. Collaboration with Ron Ritchhart highlighted the significance of classroom culture, prompting teachers to reflect on the 8 Cultural Forces. This initiative enhanced professional development, fostered collaboration, and shaped a school culture centred on thinking and transferable skills in response to societal and technological changes.

Pitfalls and Pathways: Transforming Culture and
Sustaining Change in a Culture of Thinking
Mark Church

Fourteen

One morning several years ago, I arrived early to a school where I was to meet with small groups of teachers throughout the day to engage in conversations focused on developing a Culture of Thinking. This school was somewhat new for me, and I was eager to meet the school leaders and teachers to begin our learning together. Outside the reception area windows where I waited, I could see young primary students arriving with their parents and running off towards their classrooms. Clusters of huddled teenagers, lost in their chatter, meandered off towards the senior school. And what appeared to be busy teachers passed by here and there, each looking as if they were on a critical mission to complete before the day could begin. There was vibrancy and life to the place, along with hints of laughter, and frenzy – the way schools typically feel as each new day begins.

Given my host was a bit delayed, I let my eyes wander around the reception area. The walls were adorned with awards and certifications, showcasing the school's commitment to safety, indigenous acknowledgements, and environmental care. A glossy magazine on the coffee table in front of me showcased various programmes and initiatives the school offers to families. Then I noticed a rather large poster – a 4 × 5 grid of student portraits showcasing the top 20 Year 12 students from the previous year's standardised exam scores. With the school logo emblazoned across its top and hearty congratulations to these high-achieving students, their faces beamed with pride.

At that very moment, I was reminded of a seminar I had attended some years prior at the International Conference on Thinking in Melbourne, Australia where thought-leaders from a variety of sectors gathered to share big ideas that hold significance in their fields. Specifically, I recalled a renowned culinary chef from the countryside whose interests and talk focused on the importance of community identity and sustainability. He argued that a community's identity is revealed in the signage that greets its visitors. A community is defined and ultimately sustained by being

DOI: 10.4324/9781003541745-20

known for what it produces and celebrates. So, I pondered: What messages could I gather about what this school community values, celebrates, and grows simply by its signage that greeted me that morning?

Looking at this rather prominent poster of portraits, the attention on these 20 students' exam results seemed to overshadow any celebration of their individual qualities, strengths, or intellectual character. All that was captured in this school's signage was a spotlight on high achievement, as framed in a very specific way: getting good results on external exams.

And whilst I would never want to take away a school ambition from its students to do well on all kinds of measures, I was left a bit disappointed by this poster. So much of these students' stories of learning remained hidden. There was no indication of how each of them accomplished what they did. There was no elaboration as to how the students went about learning content – presumably offered to all students, not just these 20 – in ways that allowed them to use what they knew in new, unseen, and unknown circumstances. What had these students done that set them apart?

I wondered if their success was simply a matter of them each doing more work. Had these students taken on more practice exercises and more assignments and in doing so, they earned the highest marks? Or had these students brought something significantly distinct in their thinking when approaching never seen exam scenarios? Did they respond to unknown exam scenarios with powerful thinking moves such as savvy connection-making and close and keen observation? Did these students bring strategic theorising with evidence and uncover complexities of ideas in unique and original ways? In this signage, the mysteries of just how these students learned and any powerful thinking moves they brought to their learning were unclear. I wondered: If the school could better illuminate the kinds of thinking moves these students brought to their learning that helped them achieve, might that put everyone in the school community in a better position to cultivate those very same thinking moves within more and more of the students? There had to be so much more to their stories of learning than simply smiles and test scores.

I begin this chapter with this story as it highlights the reality faced by many schools I've worked with: the desire to develop a Culture of Thinking while operating within an exam-focused, narrowly defined results-oriented system. This tension is felt deeply by many, and upon initial impression these two endeavours can very well feel at odds with one another. However, my experience has been that with some reframing and reflection, school leaders and teachers can come to see how investing in the types of thinkers students are becoming because of their time at school can not only help them achieve good results in the near term but can have long-lasting effect on how students move forward from school into their next ventures.

Yet, this reframing isn't without its challenges. In this chapter, I outline some common pitfalls I've seen schools struggle with in developing a Culture of Thinking and offer some pathways forward to transform and sustain change that supports a rich story of thinking and learning.

PITFALL #1: NOT HAVING A CLEAR VISION FOR WHAT A CULTURE OF THINKING IS AND ITS RELATIONSHIP TO LEARNING AND OUTCOMES ON VARIOUS LEVELS

For the past two decades, my colleague, Dr. Ron Ritchhart, and I have witnessed countless schools enthused by the idea of creating a Culture of Thinking. This enthusiasm is often heartfelt and genuine, yet there have been more than a few occasions where it seems that their conception of what a Culture of Thinking is and what it might do for their school feels rather misaligned. Over the years, I've heard statements such as "We've committed to do Cultures of Thinking for the next two years at our school." Or "We have agreed upon three thinking routines everybody will implement across all grade levels and vertical teams." Even "We'd like to have two days of training so that all staff can be exposed to Cultures of Thinking and then they can report back to their departments."

Statements like these raise grave concerns for me, as such language often reveals a conception of Cultures of Thinking as another programme to implement or another set of strategies to try. They frame a Culture of Thinking as something to be done – a remedy to fix certain issues, or practices with which to comply – rather than something to cultivate and become. To be clear, creating a Culture of Thinking is not about instituting a set of practices faithfully. Rather, it is about creating ongoing, sustained reflection on teaching and learning. Developing a Culture of Thinking involves close attention to examining how the cultural forces in classrooms and schools leverage the development of thinking dispositions within learners in service of deep subject-matter understanding (Ritchhart, 2015). This pitfall is problematic in so much as it is rather difficult for a school to cultivate a Culture of Thinking if they aren't entirely clear of the goal or purpose of doing so.

PATHWAY FORWARD: GET CLEAR ON HOW DEVELOPING STUDENTS' THINKING DISPOSITIONS SERVES LEARNING AND UNDERSTANDING

A key question we pose in our work around Cultures of Thinking is: *Just who do we wish the students we teach to be like as thinkers and learners as a result of their time with us?* And we ask such a question with both near-term and far-ranging goals in mind. Generally, responses to this question include educators expressing a desire for students to be curious, to be open-minded, to be collaborative, to exhibit empathy and compassion, to look for connections and meaning, to be healthy sceptics, to be strategic and creative problem solvers, etc. Looking over such a list, it is clear these habits are essential for thriving in our present world and will certainly be beneficial in the decades ahead. Fortunately, many of these very dispositions are also critical to achieving sophisticated responses on new and novel questions and problems posed on high stakes exams, should those exams require more than fill-in-the-blank or multiple-choice responses (Ritchhart and Church, 2020).

Achievement on tests ought not suffer when students become quite proficient at looking closely, making connections, developing theories, reasoning with evidence, uncovering complexity, considering viewpoints, etc. In fact, their investigations *should* become more sophisticated, their responses *should* become more elaborated, and their arguments *should* become more solid and well reasoned. By shifting conversation from a narrow focus on achieving high marks on test scores solely by "covering content" towards demystifying and nurturing the critical, high leverage thinking dispositions required to bring depth to students' grasp of the content, schools can create a more meaningful and impactful learning experience for them. This pathway forward requires being very clear and coalescing around a set of high leverage thinking moves that impact students' learning and understanding. When a school has clarity as to how cultivating a Culture of Thinking leverages their vision and mission, then developing a Culture of Thinking feels less like something to be done and more like something to become.

PITFALL #2: CONTENT VS. THINKING

"I like all this thinking stuff. But I've got a lot of content to teach." I've heard versions of this phrase on many occasions over the past two decades. Teachers tell me how interested they are in the ideas of Cultures of Thinking and even ponder what they might try here or there in their classroom. But their confessions generally reflect they were unable to get fully on board with Cultures of Thinking because, in their words, they "have a lot of content to teach."

When I encounter such exchanges, I empathise greatly. Indeed, teachers worldwide do have a lot of content to teach. And the pressures and mandates across so many systems seem to become greater more and more with each passing year. Even so, what fascinates me in this conversation is how the teachers themselves have framed the investment in students' thinking and its relationship to engagement with their course content. It's almost as if they're struggling with a dichotomous choice – either I pay attention to covering content or I pay attention to students' thinking.

The misstep here, I believe, is that these teachers, though quite enthused and desiring to do well, are approaching the teaching of content as if it exists in the absence of thinking. I've been waiting for the day when I hear something like: "I have a lot of content to teach. And therefore, the thinking moves I'll help students develop and engage in that will help them learn that content deeply shall be…" It's that last part of the previous sentence I'm eagerly listening for but haven't heard yet. Though, just because it isn't articulated does not mean that certain types of thinking are not being privileged within the content being covered. Unwittingly for many teachers, the dominant thinking move being privileged in "covering the content" is memory and recall. And while certainly memory and recall have their place in learning, what other thinking moves might a teacher also invest in and give attention to that would bump students' learning up even more? In other words, if it is content a teacher needs students to learn, is memory and recall alone the best move for students to be empowered with?

PATHWAY FORWARD: CLARIFY WHAT KINDS OF THINKING MOVES ARE CRITICAL FOR THE DEVELOPMENT OF DEEP CONTENT UNDERSTANDING. AND THEN BUILD A CULTURE THAT DEVELOPS SUCH MOVES

Years ago, a secondary school faculty I worked with brought samples of past exam papers of a variety of sorts to a staff development day I led. We decided to actually spend time combing over the exams, highlighting all the places where memory and recall alone would help the student get full marks. Once those sections of the exam were highlighted – which were rather sparse, challenging a lot of teachers' assumptions – we then began looking for other kinds of thinking moves beyond memory and recall. We used the thinking moves captured in The Understanding Map, a foundational idea in Making Thinking Visible (Ritchhart, Church and Morrison, 2011). We highlighted all sections of the mock exam requiring students to "look closely and describe what's there" to get the full marks. We asked ourselves which sections of the exam required students to build explanations and reason with evidence to score well? We identified parts of the exam that required making connections between ideas, considering perspectives, capturing the essence, or uncovering complexity to get the very best marks. While the process was meticulous, the conversations that emerged were quite rich. By undertaking this exercise, a more nuanced and interesting picture was revealed. In that moment, the teaching faculty began to have a clearer sense of the various types of thinking moves required for success in these exams. They also gained a sense of the degree of intensity in which that type of thinking came into play for that exam. This left us with a few important questions: How aware could we become of specific thinking moves essential for students to learn content and succeed in their exams? And given these essential thinking moves, what kind of learning environments and instructional practices ought we put in place throughout the school year to cultivate these thinking dispositions in students so they are empowered with the content they learn?

By gaining clarity about the kinds of high leverage thinking moves that strengthen content area understanding, no longer was the question, "Do I teach for thinking or do I teach for content?" Rather, the question became more of, "What kind of thinking dispositions to we wish to grow within students so routinely that they'll routinely bring it to all the content we study?" The pathway forward is to shift the conversation from "Content VS. Thinking" towards "Where does grappling with content create opportunities for thinking to develop? And what kinds of thinking moves create further opportunities to dig deeper into content?"

PITFALL #3: APPROACHING CULTURES OF THINKING AS IF IT IS A SET OF TOOLS TO TRAIN PEOPLE IN AND SCALE-UP AT ONCE

I've observed a recurring pattern in schools, particularly among school leadership, where a 'training mentality' prevails. This mindset, often rooted in past experiences, leads educators to adopt or reject making thinking visible practices without fully understanding the broader context of a Culture of Thinking and why this is important. This phenomenon is often linked to a 'roll-out mentality', a desire to involve everyone quickly and equitably. Yet, too often, it inadvertently creates a trap of superficial training about tools rather than deep-rooted dialogue about ideas and potential changes in beliefs and values.

I've seen so many examples of school leaders announcing their 'focus of the year' on this or that initiative. Indeed, roll-out initiatives could very well make sense from an efficiency perspective. School leaders may ask, "Why can't we just bring in the trainers on a professional development day so that everyone hears the same thing, and then we'll be off to a good start?" However, history has shown that these quick implementations often lead to superficial changes, focusing on surface-level activities rather than deep-rooted transformation (Ritchhart, 2015). The 'focus of the year' approach can easily imply a short-term commitment, leading to a flurry of activity without lasting impact. And teachers get fatigued. And leaders get frustrated. And then the cycle repeats.

PATHWAY FORWARD: BUILD AND GROW A CULTURE OF THINKING AS A LONG-TERM INVESTMENT

The tools and practices associated with creating a Culture of Thinking, such as thinking routines and other making thinking visible practices, have become integral components of classrooms where student thinking is valued and promoted (Ritchhart and Church, 2020). However, implementing these practices often falls into the trap of being viewed as a one-time training event, rather than an ongoing process of refinement and collaboration.

A Culture of Thinking emerges when everyone sees themselves as active participants in building a shared understanding of how thinking and learning are related. While individuals may initially struggle with tools, consistent practice and support can lead to deeper learning – for teachers and their students. The key is to view tools not as scripts to follow but as flexible and creative structures for developing thinking dispositions that increase students' knowledge, skills, and understanding. Good practices are good. But good practices in service of clear purposes are even better.

The pressure to involve everyone immediately can hinder genuine progress if a long-term view is not in place. School leaders generally encounter the dilemma of balancing the desire for rapid change with the need for meaningful impact. For example, while implementing thinking routines across all grade levels may seem like a quick win, without sustained reflection and conversation about student thinking and what educators gain insight on when looking and learning from this student thinking, these changes are unlikely to have a lasting impact.

Establishing a clear vision and direction for building a Culture of Thinking is essential. This involves consistently communicating the importance of this goal, modelling the desired changes, and prioritising the work of cultivating such a culture. Achieving a genuine Culture of Thinking requires a long-term commitment and a shared vision. It's not a quick fix but a fundamental stance. To foster this culture, it's essential to engage everyone in ongoing discussions about the vision for thinking and its implications to deep learning – offering them tools and structures to take action, but always bringing focus to purpose. By making the development of a Culture of Thinking a central focus, schools can create a more sustainable and impactful approach to lasting change (Ritchhart, 2023).

PITFALL #4: DEAR LEADERS, BEWARE OF MIXED MESSAGES

The actions of school leaders are instrumental in shaping the culture of a school community. A leader's behaviour sends a powerful message about what is truly valued. I once worked with a school director who had a vision of fostering a Culture of Thinking throughout her new school. She knew there was a lot of interest in Cultures of Thinking and believed this would be something cutting-edge that she could bring in. She provided substantial resources and support for teachers to engage in professional development related to this approach. And the teachers were enthusiastic about creating classrooms that encouraged active student voice and critical thinking.

However, the school director's own behaviour began to undermine her efforts. Despite her desire to join teacher study groups and be an active participant as a fellow-learner, her constant phone use during study sessions and classroom observations created a negative impression. Her presence was intended to demonstrate her commitment to the Culture of Thinking, yet her actions conveyed a lack of engagement and respect for the discussions. Her contributions, when they came, were not inherently wrong. But they lacked depth and relevance to the very classroom we'd observed and the very teacher who felt quite vulnerable in opening her classroom for others to use as a point of teacher reflection. While all the others who'd been a part of the observation offered insightful and reflective comments that came alongside the interests and needs of the presenting teacher, the director's contributions seemed superficial and disconnected from the collective thought process. It was clear that she was only half-heartedly part of these conversations, distracted by a myriad of other things. Had that been a single event, one might be a bit more understanding and empathetic of this busy school leader. Indeed, school leaders are often called into reacting to issues at a moment's notice. Unfortunately, this became a recurring pattern of behaviour over the months. Her actions sent mixed messages to teachers and raised questions about her genuine interest in fostering a Culture of Thinking. Teachers in these study groups realised that the director's words did not align with her actions.

Despite the abundant resources and a lot of 'talking the talk', this leader's commitment to developing a Culture of Thinking was superficial and fleeting. And indeed, over time the school's culture shifted towards a more perfunctory approach, characterised by a "let's just get it done" mentality. And they moved on to the next new thing as soon as the director spotted something else 'big' being talked about out there. This experience highlights the critical importance of leadership modelling. A leader's behaviour must align with their stated goals to effectively create a positive and productive school culture.

PATHWAY FORWARD: DEAR LEADERS, PLEASE BE AWARE OF AND INTENTIONAL ABOUT THE CULTURAL FORCES IN YOUR OWN LEADERSHIP – FOR THEY SEND HUGE MESSAGES ABOUT WHAT YOU TRULY VALUE

We've emphasised the importance of schools being Cultures of Thinking for teachers to foster Cultures of Thinking for students for decades (Ritchhart, 2023). However, realising this requires a significant shift in understanding and practice for many school leaders.

Developing a culture of reflective practice among educators, where they become students of their students and themselves, necessitates more than occasional professional development sessions with visiting experts. It involves investing in sustained opportunities for teachers to study together, experiment with ideas, and receive ongoing insight, reflection, and support. Additionally, it requires a deliberate shift in typical discourse about teaching and learning, focusing on close examination of classroom practices and challenging deeply held assumptions. Above all, school leaders play a pivotal role in fostering a culture of thinking by embodying the qualities of intellectual curiosity and a genuine commitment to promoting thinking in both students and teachers.

A key element of modelling a Culture of Thinking is communicating the importance of thinking as a foundational to learning. Leaders should explicitly convey to students, teachers, and parents that thinking is not an add-on luxury but an integral part of the learning process. This can be achieved through clear expectations, ongoing conversation, and a focus on intellectual development in all aspects of school life.

Furthermore, leaders must demonstrate their own commitment to professional learning and risk-taking. Inconsistent behaviour, such as claiming interest in Cultures of Thinking ideas while modelling superficial engagement, can undermine efforts to develop such a culture. By actively engaging in professional development and encouraging their team to do the same, leaders signal that growth and improvement are essential components of their teaching roles. This sends a powerful message that learning is an ongoing process and that educators should continuously strive to enhance their practices through collaboration with one another. By bringing keen self-awareness to their own use of language, time, modelling, expectations, and interactions with colleagues, leaders can ensure that the school's core mission remains central to their actions.

IN CONCLUSION

I still vividly recall the 20 students featured on the school poster that morning, their faces arranged in a neat grid. Years later, I wonder about their continued success, their journeys, and the joy they've found in life. But I also ponder the fate of the students who didn't make the poster – the next 20, and the next, and the next. I'm certain that, though they didn't grace the reception area poster, these additional students were equally cared for and supported by the school's dedicated educators.

Yet, I can't help but wonder if the school could have made a more profound impact on all students and families by making some of the mysteries of what accounts for deep learning more transparent. In fact, I wonder this for all schools desiring to create a Culture of Thinking. Of course, there are likely many reasons this school – and many schools – have such posters displayed. Perhaps it helps with marketing the school to prospective families. Perhaps it's just something that is part of their institutional history – they've done it for so long that it is simply a thing that they do. My intention is not to vilify this poster display in any way. However, I do wish to raise a point to consider for those wishing to become a Culture of Thinking: By demystifying the thinking processes students employ to achieve both short-term and long-term learning, could schools better communicate their story of learning and grow powerful thinking in students that will help them in the present and long into adulthood?

Instead of solely focusing on standardised test scores, schools could communicate the unique thinking dispositions they cultivate within their culture. By articulating both the content students learn and the thinking dispositions they develop within and through that content, schools could provide a more comprehensive picture of their educational outcomes – in ways that push beyond surface measures.

Furthermore, professional learning should shift away from simply training teachers in new tools. Instead, it should foster ongoing conversations that allow teachers to become true students of their students and of themselves. School leaders must also critically examine their own language, interactions, and modelling to ensure they consistently convey the values, growth, and achievements that define the school community.

Through sustained reflection and a commitment to ongoing improvement, schools can pave the way for a future where students are celebrated as thinkers and learners. By prioritising the development of thinking dispositions within their Culture of Thinking, schools can ensure that their legacy is one of intellectual growth and success. The pathways forward are many. And the signage along the way has the potential to be very promising.

REFERENCES

Ritchhart, R. (2015) *Creating cultures of thinking: the 8 forces we must master to truly transform our classrooms.* San Francisco: Jossey-Bass.

Ritchhart, R. (2023) *Cultures of thinking in action: 10 mindsets to transform our teaching and students' learning.* New Jersey: Jossey-Bass.

Ritchhart, R. and Church, M. (2020) *The power of making thinking visible.* New York: Jossey Bass.

Ritchhart, R., Church, M. and Morrison, K. (2011) *Making thinking visible.* San Francisco: Jossey-Bass.

Breakfast, Phonics and Cultures of Thinking: Modern Tools for An Education Renaissance
Lani Brockwell

Fifteen

Ritchhart's Cultures of Thinking provides educators, leaders and communities with a path to design excellence for their students in Australia's shifting educational landscape. As society changes, education adjusts to deliver the skills and knowledge demanded of our graduates. It is essential that our graduates can engage in high-quality thinking and are supported with practices that embed thinking in the fabric of their behaviour. In the same way that systematic synthetic phonics provides a best-practice pedagogy for teaching students to decode words, Cultures of Thinking offers teachers a pedagogical approach and practical strategies to ensure that a child's right to engage in high-quality thinking remains central to the purpose of our classrooms – no matter the curriculum we report to.

The newspaper is out this morning with the National Assessment Program – Literacy and Numeracy (NAPLAN) results again and I feel a collective wave of anxiety hit my profession. While NAPLAN holds a mirror up to traditional numeracy and literacy skills, where is the national point of reflection on what the children of our society are capable of thinking, analysing and creating? We are still worshipping and raging in response to a test, without acting on the results or asking why it is all we are measuring. It is well established that dispositional growth is a key indicator of success (OECD, 2024), yet there is no focus drawn to this through our national testing. To echo Ron Ritchhart, it makes me wonder how we are designing our schooling systems – is it with expectations of students? Or expectations for them? (Ritchhart, 2015).

During my education career, I have practised as a professional coach for pedagogical approaches to Systematic Synthetic Phonics (SSP) and for Cultures of Thinking. At first glance, these roles may seem at odds with each other. SSP focuses on biologically secondary skills, while Cultures of Thinking practices support biologically primary ones; one is necessarily concerned with explicit, direct instruction (EDI), the other tasked with the constructivist goal of surfacing, challenging and extending a

DOI: 10.4324/9781003541745-21

student's thinking. In reality, these disparate experiences have enriched and informed my understanding of high-quality teaching. It is not one or the other but rather which approach for which task. Committing to each and bringing forth their benefits has allowed my beliefs to bridge the traditional curriculum worlds of teacher-centred instructional methods v. constructionism. There has been an ongoing disagreement in our country (Vanderburg and Trotter, 2021) about which is a superior approach and the fuss it causes leaves teachers adrift in both curriculum and pedagogical choice. They are forced to adopt a single approach, rather than provided with the evidence they need to understand how to equip their students for excellence. My experience and expertise demonstrate a path forward for teachers, one that ensures students master traditional disciplinary skills so that they can share the depth and complexity of their thinking.

EDUCATION IS WHAT PEOPLE DO TO YOU. LEARNING IS WHAT YOU DO TO YOURSELF (ITO, 2014)

It may seem strange that I feel just as passionate about ensuring a child's right to think in our classroom as I do about ensuring their right to read and spell. Surely, kids just do both quite naturally – can't everyone read? Doesn't everyone think? In my home state of South Australia, the adult literacy rate was last measured in 2008 at 53% (Australian Bureau of Statistics, 2008). So, it's no secret that without explicit phonics, literacy is limited to the lucky. Not even socio-economic advantage can save you from poor phonics instruction. Similarly, multiple international measures of our students demonstrate that our national results have been slipping backwards since 2002 (De Bortoli, Underwood and Thomson, 2023). I would suggest that this demonstrates that the *culture* of a classroom is so powerful that children will identify and respond to what they expect will please the adult who is teaching them. Without Ritchhart's Cultures of Thinking providing a designed approach, teachers are left to design their own pedagogical path to support and extend student thinking. While we still require our graduates to have traditional skills of numeracy and literacy, we now more keenly understand that what creates ongoing success for them are the dispositional or 'soft' skills (Zhao, 2015). Traditional models of schooling asked, "what is it we need our students to know and do?"; modern schooling now has the opportunity to instead ask, "who is it we want our children to be?". It has never been more critical that we support our teachers in this quest, not only to ensure the child's right to high-quality thinking but a teacher's right to be supported in their desire to provide excellence.

PEOPLE ARE THE PRODUCT OF OUR LESSONS

In the classrooms where I built my culture as guided by Ritchhart's research, the little girls who were once my students are now adults. It has been a long time since they reached for my hand in the assembly line, explained their lost library books or shared their learning with me. However, I reached out to my former cohort to ask what they remembered of the classroom we shared and if they'd like to chat about the impact those experiences had. By focusing on the culture of my classroom, I was hoping to impact not just their skills and knowledge but the very fibre of how they learnt, how they interacted and understood themselves as students. So, it feels disingenuous to write about my work with them without asking my former students if they still feel the residue of our lessons together.

Mia was the first to reach out. She was always a naturally vivacious person and was excited to share with me about a time that she identified as one she loved. Her response however shared a general frustration. "Well, you'd never answer my questions properly. I would want you to say 'that's right or wrong' but you'd say 'why do you think that?' or 'that's interesting, explain it to me?' I still hear some of your questions in my head, particularly when I'm talking or working with people. I pause more, you make me rethink my words!" (Heywood-Smith, 2024). She laughs in frustration and shares something that makes me smile. "You were really good at having conversations with little people, it was always a class discussion. Everyone had time and I remember feeling very much heard and listened to. It really reduced the hierarchy of teacher and student and I think because you listened to us so carefully that it made us listen to each other and expect to be listened to. It made me wonder what I might have to say". I ask her one last thing – you've shared a lot about listening carefully, is that something you do now? do you listen deeply, do you try to make people feel heard? She cocks her head and thinks. "I think I'm getting better at it because now I know it's important to me". I find this comment humbling. As teachers, we can only really do our job of reporting to the curriculum if we are observing and recording our students, seeking out the verbs and nouns of an achievement standard in the artefacts of their learning. If modern curriculum would ask us to listen deeply and to model the importance of really hearing, I wonder what it is we might then be teaching. I wonder how transformative that might be for our communities and workplaces, for our sports fields and our parliaments. As Ritchhart says, we can't teach dispositions, we can only enculturate them (Ritchhart, 2023).

Evie responded soon after. No, she didn't remember talking about Cultures of Thinking, although she remembered some of the thinking routines. Yes, she had some memories of the language that we practised in our discussions, and she thinks she still uses some phrases. No, she had nothing for the structured learning journeys I planned so carefully. What she was emphatic about, however, was that she remembered the learning culture. She described the safety she felt and the way she was listened to during discussions. For me, this brought up memories of learning to hold my tongue, of using wait time one and two to provoke my students to explain their statements, rather than letting my anxiety fill in their learning gaps. "It was little things. It was that there were all these alternative ways you found to engage my interest and to make me feel interesting. It taught me that learning didn't have to mean 'sit at a desk and study'. I feel like as I got older teachers were saying, quick make flash cards but I knew from our class that learning didn't have to look like that, you just learnt with us" (Leathart, 2024). She spoke about how this changed understanding of engagement impacted her study practices later, designing her own methods that integrated banter with a study buddy, timed games and recording interactions rather than flash cards or repeated essay writing. She said her takeaway was that *learning didn't have to be boring*; mine is to wonder why it ever had been.

A BRIEF HISTORY OF SCHOOL

It amazed me to learn that the modern school system is a structure that is not so old, originating in Victorian England (Mitra, 2018). It was created as both an effort to support the vast colonial network and a solution to the large number of children no longer required in factories due to industrialisation (Mitra, 2018). That's not a very inspiring picture to have in your mind's eye when you are walking your five-year-old in for the first day of school. Sugata Mitra describes the purpose of schools as to produce people to work as part of the bureaucratic administrative machine. The graduates were required to do three things – read, write and do arithmetic in their head. Graduates should be interchangeable in regard to their skill set, so that they could be posted to any outpost and reproduce the work required to support the British Empire. As Mitra says, the modern school system is not broken, it's just outdated (2018). This is echoed by Ritchhart in his book *Intellectual Character*, as he attests that quality education is about much more than test scores, it is about who students become as thinkers and learners as a result of their time in schools (2002). This is a much warmer vision to walk your child towards on that first day of school. But how can we ensure it is embedded in the practices of Australian classrooms?

Unfortunately, few of the structures of education are built around the neurological needs of a child. I'm not sure if any of the structures look at the magic that a four-year-old child's brain is capable of and then ask, "what conditions does a four-year-old need to maintain their love of intellectual inquiry? What are the skills they require?" The structures of school have been consistent for hundreds of years now. Our children find themselves grouped in age-based classes. Teachers are handed content-heavy age-based curriculums and are asked to assess them against age-related outcomes. Any parent understands how impactful just a few months can be on a child's readiness. I suspect many of us have stood at a toddler's birthday party and admired one child's sure-footedness when they climb while worrying about our own child's gross motor skills. Or marvelled at another's eloquent vocabulary and felt a niggling concern at our own child's inability to articulate speech sounds. There is nothing of the industrial revolution in the being of a five-year-old. Foundation students are all energy, creativity and engagement but the structures of school are static, timed and levelled. It is in this space that Cultures of Thinking has the capacity to lift curriculum into the modern age. By providing teachers with an understanding of high-quality pedagogy, we ensure that we develop our children as citizens, as people and as learners while mastering the disciplinary skills of literacy and numeracy.

So much of our life is designed as fit for purpose: kitchen bench tops are fitted to your height, groceries are delivered to your door and my drink bottle is inscribed with my initials. Yet, the structures of modern schooling are no longer congruent with the graduates we hope to produce. If the purpose of school is learning, we need to recognise that learning is a consequence of thinking (Ritchhart, 2023). While teaching a child to read requires a very different pedagogical approach to supporting students to think, it is the exactly same passion that drives my work in both areas. Both are underpinned by a deep sense of social justice and the belief that every child has the right and responsibility to fully participate in society as they grow into adulthood. Without effective literacy teaching, a child may not have the opportunity to read freely and build their specific and technical vocabulary. Without specific and technical vocabulary, we may be denying a child the capacity to articulate and record their thoughts. Without the expectation to think in a classroom, we are not supporting children to challenge and change their understanding. We are not supporting them to become learners. One skill set feeds and develops the other and both are central to ensuring our children's capacity to forge their own way and build their own opportunities, no matter the socio-economic status of their parents.

When I began teaching under the South Australian Curriculum, Standards and Accountability framework, it did not occur to me that I would have adjusted to multiple curriculum frameworks, both federal and state based, just twelve years later. Waves of curriculum change create layers of recommended pedagogical approaches, asking teachers to switch their beliefs and practices to impact classroom outcomes with the change of a state or federal mandate. This means that not only are we required to adjust the content of what is being taught but also the approach of how best to share it. Ritchhart's Cultures of Thinking work is a layering of tools, pedagogy and the practice of a disposition that seamlessly enriches the learning of any curriculum framework. It lifts a student's existing knowledge and supports them to form new understanding. Thinking is not just an important tool in the role of education; it is a tool for social justice.

THOUGHT IS ENGAGEMENT AT PLAY (RITCHHART, 2023)

For many years, I worked in a school that had a high socio-economic community and it was in this space I began practising and developing my Cultures of Thinking pedagogy. Simultaneously, my husband taught in one of the state's most socioeconomically disadvantaged areas. We both taught the same year level and often over dinner we would fervently discuss what we had shared with our class that day. It was an ongoing point of contention that the Creating Cultures of Thinking pedagogy I was using to structure children's learning, the thinking routines I was embedding and the practices of language and timing I was rehearsing were only for high socio-economic classrooms. As I shared about the opportunities I'd crafted for my students and the subsequent rich debates that had unfolded, my husband would respond, "*Many of my students would* find it difficult to manage. They won't sit with a (seemingly) unstructured task for that amount of time".

His class had found great success in small group explicitly targeted learning, tightly designed numeracy learning and systematic synthetic phonics. He knew what was successful in developing their skills and he had the data to demonstrate their progress. We were at loggerheads, and so I offered to model a Cultures of Thinking lesson with his students. I'll be honest and declare this was less about generosity and more about winning a dinnertime argument. However, I was prepared to die on the hill declaring that it is the right of all students to think, so I'd also better be prepared to teach on it. My husband was seeing the needs of his students in response to Maslow's hierarchy (Maslow, 1958): it is their right to be fed and to rest, it is their right to learn to read, to write, to be numerate and to be connected to their community. However, I feel that Freire would agree with me that if we aren't embedding thinking practices in low socio-economic classrooms, we are complicit in their oppression (2018). It is important to acknowledge here that I have a deep respect for the community he was working within and that they provided their children with far more than just a classroom. However, if we are aiming for equity in education, I would suggest that providing students with a culture of thinking is just as important as providing them with the alphabetic code and spelling generalisations, and almost as essential as their breakfast.

I won't pretend my heart wasn't in my throat as I walked into the classroom that day, or that I didn't doubt my ability to ensure meaningful discussion and engagement. However, what we witnessed was that a lesson designed to ignite thinking brought a classroom to silence and then to life. Students whose literacy was at a reception level engaged in rich discussion with their peers. They offered up deeply thoughtful explanations with a vocabulary that may have been more limited than many of my own students but with a conviction and understanding that was no less impressive. We watched a class who understood the behaviour norms of a wellbeing programme adopt the behaviours of collaboration and work to connect their understandings to think together, to gently challenge each other and to evidence their beliefs. One of my husband's concerns was the range of literacy levels across his class, and that the activity would preclude and disengage some students. Education activities that offer students complexity are often wrapped in text. However, the beauty of facilitating thinking is that it has a remarkably low entry point and no academic ceiling.

Our lesson focused on the artwork, 'Pizarro Seizing the Inca of Peru', a powerful work riddled with the outcome of invasion and illustrating a power imbalance, a topic the children understood, identified and evidenced after their unit on colonisation had provided them with specific vocabulary. Often, we think of differentiation as multiple lessons or structured worksheets for a single experience. However, lessons designed with Cultures of Thinking practices provide multiple entry points for student understanding. Students practise their thinking together, riffing and building on each other's perspectives. It is a pedagogy that ignites collaboration and provides teachers with ample opportunity to document each child's astounding capacity to understand, reason and think. Cultures of Thinking practices are divorced from socio-economic background, from sex or gender, from curriculum. They lift the workload of teachers in schools to shine a light on learning as thinking; they play solely in the space of engagement.

The thing about developing your practice using Cultures of Thinking pedagogy and practice is that it transforms the way you are, not just as a teacher when in practice but as a thinking individual. It forces you to notice yourself, your language, your relationships and the space you create for others to grow. If you spend the time, then, like me, you might find the way you show up in a classroom changes. For me it was because I very quickly came to understand that children model from behaviour, language and thinking strategies more quickly and deeply than they would ever take up or mimic instructions. This was particularly pertinent for me in the way I learned to use language. As Ritchhart notes in *Creating Cultures of Thinking*, language "is at once ubiquitous, surrounding us constantly, yet we hardly take notice of its subtleties and power" (2015, p. 64). Students listen to us so closely that they soak up our undertones and our expectations. They notice and reflect the specificities of our terminology and by extension they rise to fill the empty air we leave them, with their voice.

TO EDUCATE IS AN OPPORTUNITY TO DEVELOP OUR COLLECTIVE HUMANITY

I had the privilege of sitting with Ritchhart during my early exploration of Cultures of Thinking practices and I remember taking an assessment I was designing to him. I was really stuck because the project was drawing on elements of the History and Social Science curriculum that felt dry to me. Essentially, it was asking me to assess students on their ability to compare statistics about countries and draw conclusions. I asked Ron how to make it engaging and if he knew a routine or project I could take inspiration from. I am not going to pretend he offered me a solution, instead he supported my thinking, asking what it was that I wanted my students to understand about the world by their ability to compare it. The answer is both simple and deeply complex. I wanted them to know that comparison should be used as a mirror to our humanity, not a tool for a race. I set about constructing the learning and drew on the 'the thinking moves' as the structure for the student journey. Just because the curriculum outcomes didn't identify thinking as important didn't mean that I wasn't going to bring it to the forefront of our learning. The final step asked students to capture the heart of the idea. To add depth to the learning I had asked students to choose a single custom from one country and attempt to identify why that culture valued that custom. It was my hope that in asking for their critical analysis of a cultural action they would recognise a similar motive within their own life.

To level with you, creating space for a child to practise their critical analysis and reflection can be scary as a teacher. My experience is that children don't shy away from complexity, their minds are as capable as any adult's, but most importantly, they crave to be in the mix. Our learning was during pre-covid days, AI only existed in The Terminator films and the fear being pedalled by the media at the time was about immigration. There was war in Iraq and in Afghanistan and the media particularly directed their campaign at women wearing hijabs. These all may be factors in why when choosing a cultural practice to *capture the heart of*, Amy chose the religious practice of women choosing to wear hijabs in Iran.

As a teacher, it can be tempting to want success for a child so much that you give them the answer and lead their thinking. Or to fear for our students so keenly that you make the appropriate thing to say plain to them and shore them up with useful terminology. However, I attempted to model independence and let Amy explore. I let her wrestle with the ideas and gave her time to learn. If you were to measure Amy by her NAPLAN scores or her Progressive Achievement Tests (PAT) data, you would have no concern about her academic progress, but they would also be unlikely to impress you. However, these scores would also share no hint of her humanity or her ability to reason with empathy and logic. I was humbled by her response. She deemed that the practice did not feel fair in the frame of her own life but that "by taking part in this practice, Iranian women were choosing to invest their beauty in their religion and in their beliefs rather than in the beliefs they held about their bodies". Given the time and space to reason, Amy chose to find a common understanding of a foreign practice. She suggested that as women we all invest in our beauty one way or another and she made space to find a commonality. It is in moments like this that I feel frustration with our outdated school model, one built with the colony in mind. I wonder what a redesign might change if it was designed around a child's astounding capacity to wonder and reason, their innate desire to connect and develop their humanity.

I'm back in the kitchen flicking through the newspaper as I watch my three-year-old, Freddy, practise stapling old bank statements together. My child will be learning to hold a pencil soon, but I no longer worry about his phonics education. The team I work with have spearheaded the South Australian Department for Education's efforts to develop phonics practice across this state, lifting the Year One reading rate by nearly 30% in just six years (Government of South Australia, 2023). He'll have the privilege of literacy. Tomorrow, NAPLAN results will have left the front page and there are plenty of things to replace them: climate change, international conflict, national reconciliation, teen technology addictions, the housing crisis and the possibility of another pandemic.

We all have a Freddy, a Mia, an Evie or an Amy in our lives. Whether they are our child, our student or our neighbour, they are the people we are leaving the future to. What is it we can cast a light on that might impact their future? While the Government works to ensure their ability to read and write is secure, what can we do to ensure their right to think?

As their teachers, we will be constantly asked to grow. We will be asked to adjust to curriculum change, to work through staffing shortages, to meet the needs of students who enter school with fewer language skills than the cohort before, to use both outdated technology and outdated schooling structures to produce the adults of the future.

It can feel overwhelming, but teachers have the power of pedagogy and Cultures of Thinking offers a map to support us to leverage the thinking of our students. It lights the path as they learn to develop their understanding, challenge and evidence their own perceptions and design the patterns of their behaviour. As teachers we have the advantage of being learners but before I ask you to take up another task, be assured that I know you already have enough to do. Instead, if you crave change, I'd encourage you to reflect that the culture you build is about who you choose to be. It might give you the opportunity to do less and be more.

You could start by asking yourself, who is doing the thinking in my classroom? Or do even less and take a moment to maintain the silence during a class' absent response and find out what beauty your students might fill that space with.

As a leader, your circle of influence is a lighthouse of your values. We are never actually free of the role of teacher. I would ask how your relationship with your staff impacts their relationship with their students. How might students' ability to evidence their thinking improve after you have modelled to your staff the importance of evidencing theirs? How might you lead so that your educational beliefs translate to enrich the integrity of your relationships?

We have the capacity to design the impact of our time with students and the responsibility to understand the residual mark we leave as their teachers. By applying Ritchhart's cultural forces we enculturate the dispositions that will support our children through the coming challenges of our future.

REFERENCES

Australian Bureau of Statistics. (2008) *Literacy of South Australians*. [Accessed 23 August 2024]. Available from: https://www.abs.gov.au/ausstats/abs@.nsf/featurearticlesbytitle/FF560D7BF1F50A5ACA2574B0001225CA

De Bortoli, L., Underwood, C. and Thomson, S. (2023) 'PISA In brief 2022: Student performance and equity in education', *Australian Council for Educational Research*. [Accessed 25 August 2024]. Available from: https://doi.org/10.37517/978-1-74286-727-4

Freire, P. (2018) *Pedagogy of the oppressed: 50th anniversary edition*. New York: Bloomsbury Academic.

Government of South Australia. (2023) *Primary school literacy skills on the rise*. [Accessed 31 August 2024]. Available from: https://www.premier.sa.gov.au/media-releases/news-items/primary-school-literacy-skills-on-the-rise#:~:text=Year%201%20students%20in%20South%20Australia%E2%80%99s%20public%20schools

Heywood-Smith, M. (2024) *Telephone conversation with Lani Brockwell*, 22 August.

Ito, J. (2014) *Want to innovate? Become a now-ist*. March, TED. [Accessed 31 August 2024)]. Available from: https://www.ted.com/talks/joi_ito_want_to_innovate_become_a_now_ist

Leathart, E. (2024) *Telephone conversation with Lani Brockwell*, 22 August.

Maslow, A.H. (1958) 'A dynamic theory of human motivation', in Stacey, C.L. and DeMartino, M. (eds.) *Understanding human motivation*. Cleveland: Howard Allen Publishers, pp. 26–47.

Mitra, S. (2018) *The future of learning*. October, TED. [Accessed: 26 August 2024]. Available from: https://www.ted.com/talks/sugata_mitra_the_future_of_learning?subtitle=en

OECD. (2024) *Skills summit 2024 – Issues for discussion paper*. Organisation for Economic Co-operation and Development. [Accessed 23 August 2024]. Available from: https://one.oecd.org/document/SKC(2024)1/en/pdf

Ritchhart, R. (2002) *Intellectual character: What is it, why it matters, and how to get it.* San Francisco: Jossey-Bass.

Ritchhart, R. (2015) *Creating cultures of thinking: The 8 forces we must master to truly transform our classrooms.* San Francisco: Jossey-Bass.

Ritchhart, R. (2023) *Cultures of thinking in action: 10 mindsets to transform our teaching and students' learning.* New Jersey: Jossey-Bass.

Vanderburg, R. and Trotter, P. (2021) 'How constructivist theories of development can be used to re-conceptualise NAPLAN as an opportunity to develop student resilience', *Australian Journal of Teacher Education*, 46(9), pp. 1–21. [Accessed 22 August 2024]. Available from: https://www.researchgate.net/publication/356255982_How_Constructivist_Theories_of_Development_can_be_used_to_Re-conceptualise_NAPLAN_as_an_Opportunity_to_Develop_Student_Resilience

Zhao, Y. (2015) 'A world at risk: An imperative for a paradigm shift to cultivate 21st century learners', *Society*, 52(2), pp. 129–135.

Seeping Upwards and Across: Embedding Cultures of Thinking at Brisbane Girls Grammar School

Bruce Addison and Susan Garson

Sixteen

We start this chapter with a few questions. Firstly, how do you change or pivot a culture that is performing very well according to a wide variety of metrics? Secondly, how can you break down apparent silos in a long established and purposefully constructed discipline-specific faculty structure? Thirdly, how have we used, developed, and inculcated Cultures of Thinking to achieve a cross-fertilisation of ideas across and within this faculty structure? These were the questions, with the benefit of hindsight, which our school faced when thinking expansively in an era in which Queensland's unique approach to school-based assessment was set to undergo significant change. This chapter uses a personal narrative lens emanating from the stories of two significant change agents involved in this project. It sheds light on not only how we have achieved change, but also highlights that change is seldom a linear or planned concept. Our stories are as follows.

BRUCE'S STORY

Change is clarifying as much as it is potentially jarring. This story commences with my decision to change schools at the end of 2009. The cultures of both schools, old and new, were strikingly different. When arriving at my new school, I was asked a relatively simple yet certainly not a benign question. "What was the learning framework at Brisbane Girls Grammar School (BGGS)"? I had worked at BGGS for 11 years, yet found it a very difficult question to answer. After much hesitation, I came up with the response 'deep learning'. Since making this statement, I have learned that 'deep learning' as an overarching term is frowned upon, unless it can be defended by clear and identifiable pointables (Wu, 2024). This question, little did I know, was to become fundamental to our change story.

Life went on and unexpectedly, four years later, after a variety of educational experiences and contexts, I would again be back at BGGS. Running counter-culturally to so much of the literature, BGGS has a highly discipline-based, if not siloed, faculty structure. Interestingly, silos are celebrated, and they do work in our context. Within these faculties, staff only teach in one subject area. This has a long history, is very much embedded in our organisational DNA, and is all about building a culture of concentrated expertise. The opportunity for our students to 'learn deeply' in this fashion is prized. We call it faculty-based discipline-specific deep learning. Fads have come and gone, yet we have remained determined to retain and build upon this much treasured disciplinarity. In many respects, this thinking is congruent with Howard Gardner's (1999) work relating to the notion of passionate disciplined minds. Reflecting on whether this is 'deep learning' or merely subject-specific deep disciplinarity is an organisational constant in all of our curriculum thinking.

My new appointment as Dean of Curriculum and Scholarship was a new position at the school. I was a member of the Senior Leadership Team and had no direct reports. My brief, amongst other things, was to 'think' and to investigate the possibility of introducing a learning framework. On one level, it was a dream job and on another it was a difficult brief. The question was where to start. For a number of reasons, the school had avoided any concept of a learning framework as unworkable. One of the reasons for this was the overtly siloed nature of our curriculum offerings. Over the years, we had seen both Dimensions of Learning and Habits of Minds do much to enrich both learning and teaching anecdotally and as reported in the literature (Tarleton, 1992; Boyes and Watts, 2009). When thinking about a potential learning framework, the 'deep learning' conversation was never far from my mind. We eventually chose Cultures of Thinking as the way to ignite visible thinking into our classroom practice. It has been a notable success. Interestingly, it is not a learning framework but rather a way of living that ignites the passions of both teacher and learner – the essential ingredients of the pedagogical compact.

With the benefit of hindsight, three seemingly unrelated factors led us to endorsing Cultures of Thinking so whole heartedly. The first was the extraordinary insight of our Principal to give me the space to think without distraction. The second was the discovery of Dr Ron Ritchhart's Cultures of Thinking concept itself. The third, the lens provided by Professor Frank Crowther AM whose scholarship gave us the courage to talk in terms of both personal pedagogical gifts (Crowther, 2016) as well as the concept of school-wide pedagogy (Crowther, Andrews and Conway, 2013). Crowther's concept of personal pedagogical gifts provided staff with a unique lens to interpret Ritchart's 8 Cultural Forces in the context of their own bespoke classroom environments. These three forces or 'change forces' occurred almost simultaneously and have infused our silos with a common language underpinning the concept of visible thinking.

The school's awakening to the concept of Cultures of Thinking can be traced back again to a couple of unrelated occurrences. Firstly, our then Head of Faculty – International Studies, Ms Susan Garson attended a Conference on Cultures of Thinking at Melbourne Grammar School in 2016. Susan was deeply encouraged and energised by what she had learned and the potential she could see. She presented her conclusions to her middle management peers as well as the attending Senior leaders at a Head of Faculty meeting shortly after her return. The next unrelated event also occurred in 2016 when I accompanied my wife to an educational conference in Singapore. She came back to our hotel room after a wonderful session led by Dr Ron Ritchhart. I did not know of Ritchhart's work intimately but remembered the wonderful presentation to our Heads of Faculty. These two events – my colleague's enthusiasm combined with my wife's evangelical-like zeal for the same methodology certainly tweaked my curiosity. Upon return to Australia, I read Ritchhart's book – *Creating Cultures of Thinking: The 8 Forces We Must Master to Truly Transform Our Schools* (2015). The question became how to introduce this thinking into a very successful, highly balkanised school structure.

The work of Professor Crowther is the third unrelated factor in this story. His courageous stewardship of the field of education and its soulfulness has been remarkable for decades, in a world in which more rationalist sentiments have held sway. His article in *The Australian Educational Leader* "Developing Teachers Pedagogical Gifts – the most important leadership challenge of our time" (Crowther, 2016) allowed us to view curriculum change as well as teaching and learning through a teacher 'friendly' relational lens. Professor Crowther eventually visited the school, generously sharing his insights and experiences. During our discussions, he introduced me to the work of Fred Newmann (Newmann and Wehlage, 1995). Reading and digesting this thinking was also pivotal, as it led us to the concept of school-wide pedagogy. Professor Crowther's thinking, albeit through our lens, directed us to embrace school-wide pedagogy as a means, in part, to introduce Cultures of Thinking not so much as a curriculum framework, but to best support our unique concept of faculty-based discipline-specific deep learning. This was a deliberate strategy to encourage interfaculty co-operation and learning. Utilising the concept of personal pedagogical gifts, in tandem with the organising thread of school-wide pedagogy, enabled us to think carefully about what Parker Palmer (1988) would call the 'interior' life of a teacher. Tapping into and celebrating the 'interior' lives of our teachers was a key factor central to the seep of change we wanted within and across our faculties with the introduction of Cultures of Thinking. If teachers understand that change is inclusive and not imposed or preordained, there is a greater chance of success.

We knew that through careful stewardship, this change could seep up and through the school. Such an approach had the possibility of working given our deeply balkanised faculty structure, as top-down insistence would have been a top-down and out initiative that was doomed to fail (Sabatier, 1986). Our mantra became 'not top down and out but rather bottom up, through and across'. This was all devised from the perspective that teachers want to be nourished as they go about their own learning and as they devise appropriate learning strategies for their students. Our key mission was how to nourish our teachers in the cause of a contemporary approach to both learning and classroom practice. The success of such initiatives requires careful planning, strategic focus, and implementation, a detailed understanding of organisational dynamics as well as key staff buy-in and support. In the case of introducing Cultures of Thinking at BGGS, the time was right for these conditions to emerge. Stewardship of change is all important. Concepts can be conceived, but if they are not guided by intricate organisational knowledge, slow looking, genuine belief, collegial care, and goodwill, change will fail and often horribly.

Our school-wide pedagogy was conceived as an umbrella to represent oversight rather than top-down insistence. Under this 'umbrella' would flourish a number of school-wide curriculum initiatives. On one side was our concept of 'noticing learning', much of which has been reported in the Oxford Review of Education (Adie, Addison and Lingard, 2021). On the far side were the cognitions representing the then systemic changes occurring in Queensland under the aegis of the Queensland Curriculum and Assessment Authority (QCAA). Most importantly and representing the handle of the umbrella was 'Cultures of Thinking'. We were on the way. The question then was how to make it work.

SUSAN'S STORY

This section of our chapter moves to some of the practical ways that we have developed silo seep through and across the school. Our journey towards a more cross-faculty collaborative culture follows from what seemed like an inevitable movement towards Cultures of Thinking as our common pedagogical language (*). This started in earnest with our staff conference of 2018. Two exceptional educators and Cultures of Thinking practitioners, Mr Simon Brooks and Mr Ryan Gill, both at one stage at Sydney's Masada College, led our academic staff across two days of learning. Both Mr Brooks and Mr Gill were founding members of the Project Zero Australia Network, which is a group of educators inspired by Project Zero ideas from the Harvard Graduate School of Education (HGSE). As advocates for Project Zero pedagogies and practice, Mr Brooks and Mr Gill educated our broader staff on learning as a consequence of thinking and that understanding is something you do rather than something you have. They prompted us to consider that intelligence can be learnt, and dispositions are required to develop thinking skills. Learning in collaboration was a taken-for-granted practice at this staff conference. The buy-in from staff, which at times can be a little cynical, was outstanding. As a result, three invaluable forms of internal professional learning were developed for our staff: new staff immersion, Inquiry Action Projects/Study Groups, and Cultures of Thinking coaching.

NEW STAFF IMMERSION

The development of our School-Wide Pedagogy model with Cultures of Thinking at its core enabled a common language to feature in our induction of new staff. Such a common thread had hitherto been elusive. Our strategy was to continue to use our expert consultants, Simon Brooks and Ryan Gill, in the delivery of what we framed as our new staff 'Thinking for Learning' days. During the first of such sessions, they masterfully folded the world of educational theory into various aspects of visible thinking. This role modelling creates an environment where new staff understand quickly what it is like to be a part of a culture where visible thinking is both valued and promoted. When teachers feel a culture of thinking in action, rather than being told about it or reading about it, it can be much more powerful. They start

---

* *My predecessor Dr Ann Farley worked with Dr Bruce Addison at the beginning of this journey, and we acknowledge her great contribution.*

to see how these methods can transform their classrooms and how they might adapt current practices to make student thinking front and centre. Creating a culture of thinking for teachers represents Mindset 1 in Ron Ritchhart's new book, *Cultures of Thinking in Action*. Ritchhart argues that if teachers are involved in learning opportunities that endorse visible thinking, they will be more likely to mirror this when teaching in their own classrooms (Ritchhart, 2023). They tend to be more open to innovation, collaboration, and trialing inquiry methods with their students, when they have been exposed to these ideas as learners. As a result, they become facilitators of learning, model their own thinking with students, and are arguably more effective at bringing the groups' ideas together to enable deep understanding. Furthermore, in the 'Thinking for Learning' days new staff are introduced to language moves and thinking routines that assist them in stretching their own as well as their students' thinking. The second session builds on the first and is more practice based, as teachers bring evidence from their own classrooms, results from a student survey, and reflections on their practice to share with colleagues.

Foundational to this new staff inculcation is the underlying power of the 8 Cultural Forces as a means by which to both guide and develop their practice. The development and discussion of mindsets and underlying dispositions, linked to a culture of thinking, are integral to our 'Thinking for Learning' days as well. Three foundational questions emerged when designing these professional learning days. Firstly, how can we encourage students to take ownership of their learning and develop their thinking, instead of guessing what is in the teacher's head? Secondly, how can we promote curiosity and collaboration? Thirdly, how can we make sure we plan learning opportunities that are deep and that really challenge our students to think in order to understand? Our consultants include a variety of media and stimulus materials to support this learning with staff. For example, they prioritise the use of complex visual prompts, unpack video excerpts of effective classroom practice where a culture of thinking is evident, and invite teachers to engage in thinking routines linked to this content. Our new staff learn by doing. They hear, see, and feel what it means to be part of a culture of thinking and no doubt have more confidence to trial different strategies in their classrooms to accomplish this. Through these learning experiences, our new staff get to understand our concept of inquiry, depth, and the expected form of pedagogical expression underlying our teaching and learning.

INQUIRY ACTION PROJECTS

As part of our Cultures of Thinking journey, we soon discovered that if we wanted powerful learning experiences for our students, we needed to offer them to our teachers on an ongoing basis. Teachers need opportunities to actively engage in meaningful discussion, planning, and practice, in order to be motivated in their work (Ritchhart, 2023). Inquiry Action Projects have formed an indispensable part of our suite of professional learning since 2018. Involvement in Inquiry Action encourages teachers to go beyond connected talk to develop a more exploratory and inquiry mindset linked to an aspect or aspects of their classroom practice (Ritchhart, 2023). Teachers are invited to take part at the start of each academic year in cross-faculty groupings. Inquiry Action is a very rich experience that not only invites individuals to set a focus for themselves, but also encourages learning in a supportive and collaborative environment. These regular collaborations with peers allow teachers to construct and re-construct their practice for the benefit of student learning beyond the narrow scope of assessment. Such groupings have done much to inject a cross-fertilisation of ideas across our faculty silos. For example, we have seen inquiry action projects undertaken with similar throughlines, such as valuing independence and risk-taking across the disciplines of drama and music and maths. Projects focusing on the cultural force of environment have been evident in both accounting and history. Therefore, staff have found that whilst they teach in different areas, they are attracted to similar areas of inquiry. Coming together to share learnings from these inquiries has caused teachers, who might never have conversed across a school year, to find commonality and to help each other.

Reflection and sharing in relation to an inquiry question happen within the context of a structured study group that meets twice per term. The benefit of teachers learning in study groups is that they are founded on agreed non-judgemental norms and respectful interactions. It is never about correcting or fixing the approach of the presenting teacher, but rather about growing collective practice by listening respectfully and learning from others. A presenting teacher invites others into their thinking, exploration, and active reflection where there is often more "problem posing than problem solving" (Paterson, 2019, p. 35). Study group members from a range of different faculty areas press each other's thinking using protocols, clarification and probing questions, and through offering possible suggestions for next steps. At the same time, group members gauge how classroom experiences or strategies from a presenting teacher might be useful to enrich their own practice. Professional vulnerability and openness are essential preconditions for successful study group learning. Messy thinking is encouraged.

For me, the beauty of Inquiry Action groups lies in the way in which they encourage cross-faculty learning amongst staff, enriching classroom experiences for both teachers and students. In a highly siloed environment, this cross-faculty fertilisation has provided much insight, discovery, and playful pedagogy. At the same time, these groups are a way to celebrate the power of teachers' personal pedagogical gifts and the way their practice is shaped by these. Staff participating in these groups are encouraged to make small but meaningful changes in their classrooms based on new thinking, strategies they have trialled, as well as through analysing evidence of student work they might collect. Students are expected to think deeply about the content they learn and are expected to share their ideas with others to build understanding. The key to it all is contribution – truly being a part of a culture of thinking.

A central component of Cultures of Thinking Inquiry Action has been to ensure that a variety of staff have engaged in professional learning around the art of facilitation, as well as gaining an in-depth knowledge of an array of protocols. Core qualities of artful facilitation include: curiosity, listening, recognising what is powerful and transformative, believing in the growth of others, and the willingness to disturb and be disturbed are at the very core of our approach (Allen and Blythe, 2004). Our facilitators support a genuine culture of participation as well as the important 'hierarchical blindfold' that goes a long way to enable genuine sharing, equity, and trust. The hope is that through this modelling, our teachers will then infuse their classrooms in much the same way.

Celebrations of learning conclude the Inquiry Action process. Participating teachers create a poster at the end of the year, to make their thinking visible about their chosen inquiry question. The poster is not a flashy, polished artefact, rather it documents 'messy' thinking about a teacher's year-long exploration of practice. The poster highlights both successes and challenges. These prompts are used as a guide:

My inquiry action question is …
Some actions I took were …
The payoffs were …
What is next …?

Inquiry Action Projects and study groups constitute communities of practice (Wenger, 1997; 2000) amongst and between staff. These have no doubt been pivotal in shifting culture, increasing collaboration, and developing if not transforming, aspects of classroom learning to push students to think beyond exams. Participating teachers have shared their reflections in the past:

> *I am flipping the focus from being about outcomes, to being more about process. (Teacher 1)*
> *I have learnt about modelling my own thinking to students – I started to say things like it's ok to get it wrong, please ask questions, I don't know the answer to that, what I might try is this. (Teacher 2)*
> *I liked being able to come together with other teachers from all different teaching areas and share ideas, and ... it was surprising to take things from what somebody was doing in French ... I can apply that in my discipline. (Teacher 3)*

Our aim for cross-faculty seep and learning has been achieved and continues to grow. Inquiry Action projects have blended well into our culture of discipline-specific deep learning.

CULTURES OF THINKING COACHING

In 2021, we embarked on a new coaching initiative for teachers, as an extension to the previous work with Inquiry Action projects. Coaching offers another avenue for staff to develop an inquiry mindset linked to pedagogy as well as cross-faculty pairing. Coaching not only creates opportunities for intentional conversations about pedagogy, ways of thinking and being, but also contributes greatly to our goal of silo seep.

Seepage of ideas often starts with an individual teacher pursing an inquiry and then sharing information or strategies with staff within faculties. Blended coaching invites the development of awareness and responsibility allowing teachers to unlock their potential and improve their teaching practice in pursuit of a goal (Whitmore, 2017). Encouraging autonomy and agency in teachers comes as a result of offering them opportunities to reflect on their practice – making time for thinking (Costa and Garmston, 1985; Peterson and Deal, 2009). Teachers are paired with a coach as a guide on the side, who acts in service of their learning. Meetings once per term serve as opportunities to engage in regular professional dialogue, based on the GROW Model – 'goal, reality, options, what next' (Whitmore, 2017, p. 95). Discussion usually involves talking through successes and challenges, sometimes looking through the lens of the 8 Cultural Forces for current realities, extending thinking about dispositional development, as well as trialling specific strategies. At the same time, coaches can offer strategies to coachees, based on their deep knowledge of Cultures of Thinking approaches to teaching and learning. For example, they might offer suggestions around questioning techniques or new Thinking Routines to enhance collaboration and visible thinking. These are the means to normalise cross-faculty dialogue, discussion, and learning. Teachers who work with coaches tend to practise new strategies more often and with greater skill than those who are not coached (Needham, no date). In addition, they tend to retain and increase their skill levels over time and demonstrate a clearer understanding of the purposes and uses of new teaching strategies (Joyce and Showers, 2002). When a teacher's toolkit expands and they are invigorated in the classroom, it is likely they will want to share ideas with colleagues, be it in meetings, incidental conversations or in the planning of new units of work.

Coaching has built a sense of trust amongst and between staff at the school, where teachers have been seen to increase their confidence and then share their pedagogy within both their faculties but most importantly across other faculties. This is unsurprising, as Cultures of Thinking coaching approaches reveal the making of meaning *together*. Professional dialogue becomes regular and feels natural and can easily expand beyond the coaching setting. Coaching has resulted in a sense of joy being brought back into pedagogical discussions as educators laugh together, work through frustrations, celebrate wins, and enjoy the collegiality. Thinking about practice with another is being less 'siloed' as a matter of course.

It is very helpful to have someone "outside" of me but beside me: someone who can sort the wheat from the chaff and zero in on ideas I am too close to see and then, gently turn my head to focus on the important stuff. (Teacher 1)

Each meeting is personalised and meaningful, provoking me to think about my classroom observations. The cordiality of coaching makes the process run smoothly and foregrounds the value of established classroom culture. (Teacher 2)

I have found that I've gone back to colleagues in my Language faculty and shared my learnings, or simply added new ideas to our programming. (Teacher 3)

One of the delights of being part of Cultures of Thinking coaching is hearing the rich narratives of experience that are shared. Rarely do teachers have the time to pause, reflect, plan, and discuss learning opportunities they attempt and the effects they see on student learning. Coaching provides this space and can have profound flow on effects.

CONCLUSION

We believe that cross-faculty collaboration and seeking to embed a culture of thinking has contributed a great deal to our discipline-specific faculty-based culture. Through investing in professional learning, exploring visible thinking as a worthwhile approach to invite curiosity and deeper understanding of ideas, we have strengthened our academic culture. We are excited for the next few years, to see this culture sustained and enhanced, as new staff and students become valued contributors to our learning community.

REFERENCES

Adie, L., Addison, B. and Lingard, B. (2021) 'Assessment And learning: an in-depth Analysis of change in one school's assessment culture', *Oxford Review of Education*, 47(3), pp. 404–422.

Allen, D. and Blythe, T. (2004) *The facilitator's book of questions*. New York: Teachers College Press.

Boyes, K. and Watts, G. (2009) *Developing habits of minds in secondary schools: an ASCD action tool*. Virginia: ASCD.

Costa, A.L. and Garmston, R. (1985) 'Supervision for intelligent teaching', *Educational Leadership*, 42(5), pp. 70–80.

Crowther, F. (2016) *Energising teaching: the power of your unique pedagogical gifts*. Camberwell: ACER Press.

Crowther, F., Andrews, D. and Conway, J. (2013) *School wide pedagogy: vibrant new meaning for teachers and principals*. Melbourne: Hawker Brownlow.

Gardner, H. (1999) *A disciplined mind: what all students should understand*. New York: Simon and Schuster.

Joyce, B. and Showers, B. (2002) *Student achievement through staff development*. Virginia: ASCD.

Needham, K. (no date) *Five conversations for professional growth*. [Accessed 7 March 2025]. Available from: https://www.growthcoaching.com.au/resource/5-conversations-for-professional-growth/

Newmann, F. and Wehlage, G. (1995) *Successful school restructuring: a report to the public and educators by the center on organization and restructuring of schools*. Madison, WI: National Association of Secondary School Principals.

Palmer, P. (1988) *The courage to teach: exploring the inner landscape of a teacher's life*. San Francisco: John Wiley and Sons.

Paterson, C. (2019) *Churchill fellowship report*. Available at: https://www.churchilltrust.com.au/fellow/cameron-paterson-nsw-2019/ [Accessed 14 November 2024].

Peterson, K.D. and Deal, T.E. (2009) *The sharping school culture fieldbook*. San Francisco: John Wiley & Sons, Inc.

Ritchhart, R. (2015) *Creating cultures of thinking: the 8 forces we must master to truly transform our schools*. San Francisco: John Wiley & Sons, Incorporated.

Ritchhart, R. (2023) *Cultures of thinking in action: 10 mindsets to transform our teaching and students' learning*. New Jersey: Jossey-Bass.

Sabatier, P. (1986) 'Top-down and Bottom-up approaches to implementation research: a critical analysis and suggested synthesis', Journal of Public Policy, 6(1), pp. 21–48.

Tarleton, D. (1992) Dimensions of learning: a model for enhancing student thinking and learning. Ed.D. research project, Nova University.

Wenger, E. (1997) 'Practice, learning, meaning, identity', Training, 34(2), pp. 38–39.

Wenger, E. (2000) 'Communities of practice and social learning systems', SAGE Social Science Collections, 7(2), pp. 225–246.

Whitmore, J. (2017) Coaching for performance: the principles and practice of coaching and leadership. 5th edn. Nicholas Brealey Publishing.

Wu, X.-Y. (2024) 'Exploring the effects of digital technology on deep learning: a meta-analysis', Education and Information Technologies, 29, pp. 425–458.

Thinking at the Forefront: Immanuel College's
Cultures of Thinking Journey

Martyn Anderson

Seventeen

INTRODUCTION

'Word, phrase, sentence.' Three simple words. This could not be that difficult, could it? A group of Immanuel staff in early 2012 sat down together at a Critical and Creative thinking workshop run by Janet Farrell from the Association of Independent Schools of South Australia. The workshop began with sharing some text and then having to think about a word that resonated with us, a phrase and then a sentence that we deemed important from the text (Harvard Project Zero, 2022). I was first struck by the simplicity of what was being asked and the accessibility. What followed this routine was 30 minutes of very rich dialogue between colleagues. I soon realised there were more of these routines that were simple and accessible and had the potential to be very powerful to make thinking visible.

These workshops with Janet started Immanuel on a journey that helped put thinking at the forefront of our approach to teaching and learning. It supported the development of clear learning principles and culminated in working with Ron Ritchhart on a three-year Cultures of Thinking project. This project was a significant turning point for teachers and students, standing out from numerous other educational initiatives. Cultures of Thinking has continued to be at the core of the Immanuel's educational journey. It was our experience that the importance of thinking deeply resonates with teachers, and we came to understand that all classrooms have a culture. The challenge for our school and for teachers was how to guide them to consider what to do with that culture. This was more than just improving academic outcomes but to encourage our students to become better people who listened, were curious, could understand different perspectives and express their views in a confident and articulate manner.

CONTEXT

Immanuel College (Years 7 to 12) is an independent school based in Adelaide, South Australia. It is a Christian school belonging to the

Lutheran Church of Australia and has a strong and rich history dating back to 1895. Its Novar Gardens campus is in the western suburbs of Adelaide near Glenelg. Due to strong and inspirational leadership by the newly appointed Principal, Kevin Richardson in 2002 the school became known for its innovation, contemporary learning spaces and forward-thinking approach.

Kevin's mantra was 'the heart of education is the education of the heart.' This was instilled into us as teachers. He would often say to prospective families, Immanuel is about finding your child's 'piece of sunshine.' His key message was that education was more than just excellent academic outcomes; education was about developing our young people into the best version of themselves.

As mentioned, in 2012 Immanuel had an enthusiastic group of teachers attend a Creative and Critical Thinking course with Janet Farrell. Janet was a former Director of Teaching and Learning at Wilderness School and later an Association of South Australian Independent Schools consultant. Janet understood the importance of thinking in the curriculum and was influenced by the work that had emerged with Ron Ritchhart, David Perkins and many others. She always talks about Immanuel College teachers being her loyal customers!

As a group, we were exposed to these thinking routines, and we were eager to share this with our colleagues. By 2013, we had established a 'Thinking Group' for teachers. This allowed us to share what we learned with Immanuel's teachers. One of the techniques we used earlier on was video to capture how these routines were playing out in our classroom. It was great to reflect on a video of my Year 12 Legal Studies class, which was doing a Chalk Talk thinking routine (Ritchhart, Church and Morrison, 2011) about whether a Constitutional Monarchy was still an appropriate system of government for Australia. This routine asks learners to consider ideas, questions or problems by writing their thoughts silently but visible to others. In this instance, it was a 10-minute silent conversation that occurred on the whiteboard. After completing the routine, the students commented:

SARAH — *I like seeing everyone's point of view. Seeing different points of view and reading it myself, imprints on my mind especially with the perspectives on the whiteboard.*
LAURA — *If you are not as confident speaking to a class, this is an easier way to express your opinion without having to talk to everyone.*
SARAH — *And it can be fun!*

AMY — *It's like a class friendly forum. It's the internet but it's friendly.*
ARJ — *It's better this way, you don't have people shout over the top, you can see clearly what people have said and you don't forget what people have said.*
HARRY — *At the start I didn't quite understand what was going on but once people started chipping in, I got an idea of what was happening, so I started writing.*

While this at the surface was a simple exercise, it reinforced to me the accessibility of this task; all were capable of contributing and responding to each other in a positive and respectful manner. Their thinking was visible, which proved to be insightful not only for the students but also for me as a teacher. I could clearly see where my students were at and where to take the next steps in learning. A revelation to me and others was how these thinking routines could be used as effective formative assessment strategies to determine next steps in teaching and learning. This experimentation with 'thinking routines' proved invaluable to me as a teacher. The learning and thinking that was happening was made visible to me.

Other teachers felt the same way. Lewis Ashton, a Year 7 teacher, shares:

'The routines are accessible for everyone—after a stimulus, e.g., video, diary entry, etc., everyone in the class can offer something to the conversation. On top of that, it allows for differentiation in terms of the deeper thinking that comes from some students in a conversation after a thinking routine.'

The beauty of these 'thinking routines' is that you can have a reception class engage in a See Think Wonder as well as a Year 12 class.

In 2015, Immanuel continued to explore these ideas. However, in any school there is often a need to refine the educational vision. With support from the University of Southern Queensland the 'Innovative Designs for Enhanced Achievement in Schools' (IDEAS) project was launched (Crowther et al., 2012). The IDEAS project began to enhance Immanuel's success by enabling the school community to clarify direction, develop a shared pedagogy and attain school alignment. Through staff workshops, parent and student surveys a direction was sought to develop four clear learning principles – connecting, creating, thinking and understanding. These were principles our teachers valued. It was what we wanted to see in our students and graduates. As most of our staff had been involved in the Creative and Critical Thinking workshops, it was pleasing to see that the importance of thinking was emphasised and the thinking that leads to understanding was valued. Our teachers could see this was important.

SERENDIPITY – CREATING CULTURES OF THINKING

In 2016, Ron Ritchhart began consultancy work with the Association of Independent Schools in South Australia in a three-year Creating Cultures of Thinking Project. This involved a group of around ten independent schools, with Immanuel being one of them, working closely with him to learn and see how this approach played out in our classrooms. This directly aligned with the College's 'Thinking' learning principle. Importantly, we had the school leadership team, including the Principal, Heads of School and the Director of Teaching and Learning, in attendance. By this time, Ritchhart had published his monumental work on classroom culture, *Creating cultures of thinking: The 8 forces we must master to truly transform our schools* (2015).

As Ritchhart (2015, p. 6) powerfully argues, 'Traditionally, policy-makers have focused on curriculum as the tool for transformation, naively assuming that teachers merely deliver curriculum to their students. Change the deliverable—Common Core, National Curriculum, International Baccalaureate Diploma—and you will have transformed education they assume. In reality, curriculum is something that is enacted with students. It plays out within the dynamics of the school and classroom culture. Thus, culture is foundational. It will determine how any curriculum comes to life.'

It was this focus on culture that became so important, a call to action. What was the culture of our classrooms? Had our teachers created a thinking culture, or were they using thinking routines as 'nice activities'? The eight cultural forces were an insightful tool for teachers to reflect on and unpack what was happening. There were so many questions –

- What were our teachers modelling?
- What were teachers prioritising in the classrooms?
- What messages did our environment send about learning?
- What were the expectations of our teachers?
- What was the language that our teachers used with the students?
- How would students perceive our interactions with them?

The great thing about culture is that it is free; it is there whether we like it or not. Our challenge was to use these cultural forces to value and promote classroom thinking. Our leaders and teachers agreed that Cultures of Thinking was not something we bought off the shelf to use as an educational 'silver bullet.'

The three-year project not only enabled us to engage in school walk-throughs at other schools but also provided important expertise in enabling us to reflect on where we were as a school. To promote the thinking or routines, we utilised video to share with staff, which was shared on the staff Learning Management System. A significant aspect of this was to hear the voices of students on these videos, with students actively reflecting on their experience of thinking routines.

A key product of the project was the prioritisation of professional development around these ideas with our staff. This involved after-school sessions as well as the development of new structures we called 'Learning Teams,' which were a were a mix of teachers from all year levels and learning areas that met about two or three times per term. Time was spent exploring and discussing with colleagues the eight cultural forces and how they played out in our classroom. We also used these teams to engage teachers in peer observations, which they did through the lens of the cultural forces. It was a collaborative effort, with everyone contributing to the collective understanding and unpacking of a Cultures of Thinking.

'AHA' MOMENTS

I have always been struck by how much Cultures of Thinking resonates with teachers who authentically seek to engage with this work. For many, it is career-changing, the 'aha' moment in their professional lives.

For Louise Cottell, Middle Years Learning Leader, it was about the importance of responding to societal and technological changes and meeting our students where they are:

> 'After twenty years of teaching, I was reflecting on how students and their lives have changed. The idea of knowing facts, which was essential in my high school education, had been quickly surpassed by access to content via the internet. Remembering and knowing wasn't enough anymore, and it didn't equip students to solve the problems facing them now or in the future. I needed to shift the focus of my teaching to being explicit about 'thinking' rather than recalling. It had become clear to me that some classes and teachers were buzzy; there was questioning, there was puzzling, there was trial and error and courage, and these were classes where students were engaged and more successful longer term. I wanted to develop this in my practice more.'

Thomas Parkin, English as an Additional Language (EAL) teacher, furthers this idea by saying:

> 'In a world where Artificial Intelligence is on the rise, it is no longer sufficient for educators to be solely the 'transmitters' of knowledge but rather understanding. The processes involved in both short-term and long-term memory are complex, but for me as a teacher, I see my value (and my role) as one that provides students plentiful opportunities to process concepts, display 'visible' thinking and to further deepen and enhance their critical and inferential logical reasoning. This is particularly important in a world where students' attention is often in a world of mass digital information.'

Similar to Louise, Tracey Corrigan, Head of English, shares:

> 'Establishing a culture of thinking facilitates a focus on growth, learning and development. It removes the focus away from content acquisition onto the importance of thinking. It also encourages a personalised approach to learning as well as a breakdown of the silo approach to teaching disciplines. In our modern world, it is becoming increasingly important for students (and teachers) to develop transferable skills. By having a shared understanding of thinking, it enhances our ability to learn and to teach.'

The 'Understanding Map' which is a visual depiction of the thinking that leads to understanding has been invaluable to develop a common language for our teachers and students (Ritchhart, Church and Morrison, 2011). As well as this, an awareness of the eight cultural forces has supported our teachers to understand the levers they have to promote, value and prioritise thinking in their classrooms (Ritchhart, 2015).

For some, such as Visual Art teacher Mel Higgins, a Culture of Thinking is about the bigger picture:

> 'It's about a mindset as a teacher, being aware of the big picture of learning that is happening in each lesson, each unit, each course and then the building upon that learning across the years. For me, it is first having a clear understanding of how I learn and how I think, and then having a wide range of resources at my disposal to provide opportunities for thinking and learning in my classroom.'

Powerfully, Thomas Parkin, EAL teacher, shares about a crucial foundational mindset that learning is a result of thinking and how it speaks to the importance of process:

'For me, the notion that 'learning' is a result of 'thinking' underpins my practice. In my classroom, it is more about the process than it is the final 'summative'. For me, teaching and learning is a process of engaging students in a range of ways, in a range of modalities, in order to challenge their thinking and to bring to the fore their own voice and perspectives while also negotiating these ideas through a pedagogical and curriculum-focused lens.'

He also touches on the idea that an authentic adoption of these ideas is a mindset change in relation to the role of the teacher:

'I also see my role as a teacher as one that seeks to challenge my students' preconceived concepts about the purpose and value of schooling, away from one that solely looks at summative or final assessments as most important, but rather the various opportunities to engage, discuss, challenge, question and reflect. If students can better understand their 'why', then the what, how, where and when will more readily follow. Modelling such 'thinking behaviours' has allowed many of my students to develop their deeper, inferential reasoning and critical thinking skills, no matter what text type or content they are engaging with. It has enhanced personal, academic and social dispositions for my students.'

IMPACT

After the three-year 'Creating Cultures of Thinking' Project, we were eager to determine its impact and gather some street data (Safir and Dugan, 2021). From 2018 to 2020, we asked our students questions around whether there had been a shift in focus on learning, understanding, deep learning and the promotion of independence. Surveys were conducted, with over 250 responses each year. The results in Figure 17.1 are percentages of the student responses.

Over this period, we could see a renewed focus on the importance of process, thinking and learning and an increased confidence in our learners. While our focus was on developing great people and 'educating for the long term,' it was interesting to note that since the emphasis to put thinking at the forefront of what we do, Immanuel achieved the

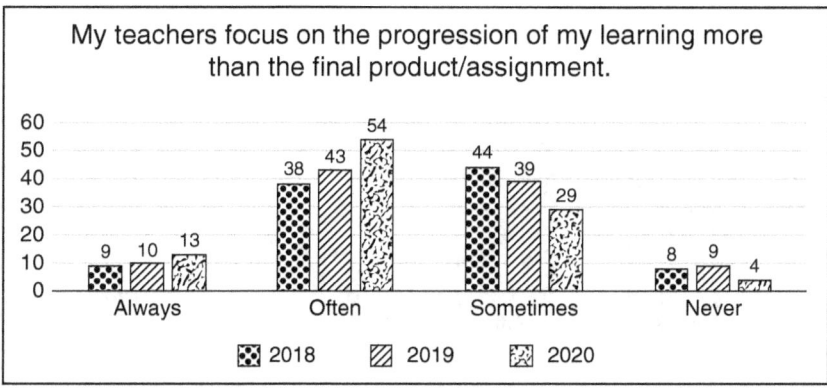

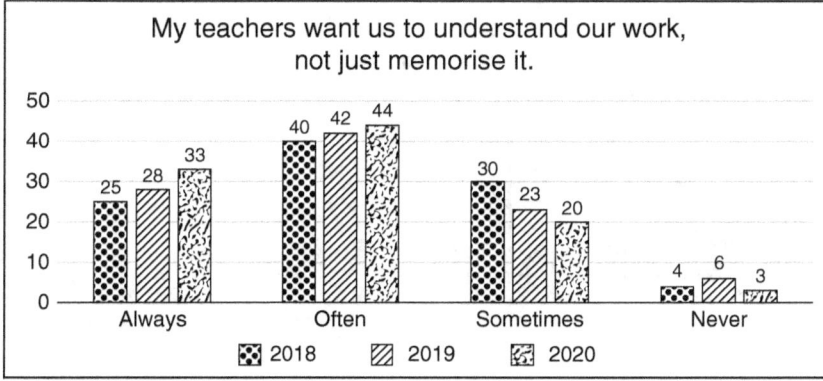

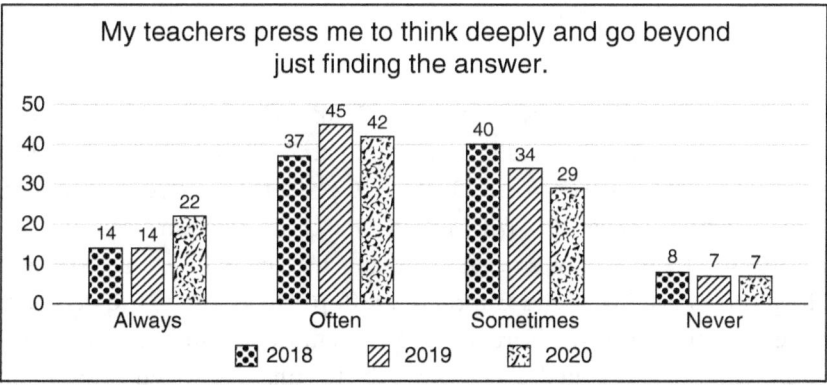

Figure 17.1 Student Survey Results From 2018 to 2020 Highlighting Shifts in Students' Perception of Their Learning Experience at Immanuel College.

(Continued)

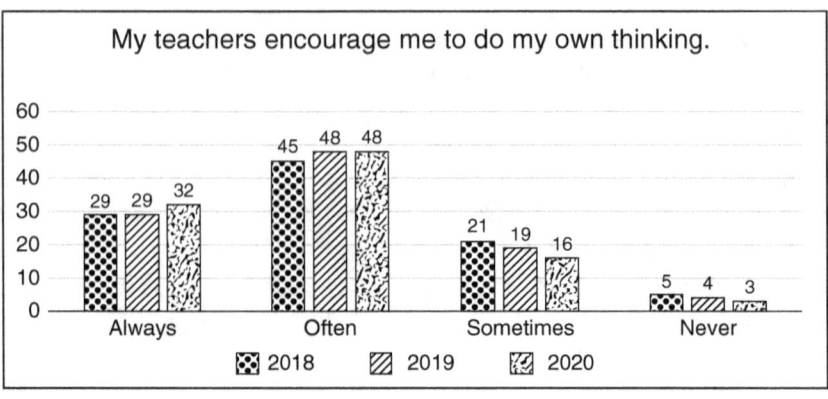

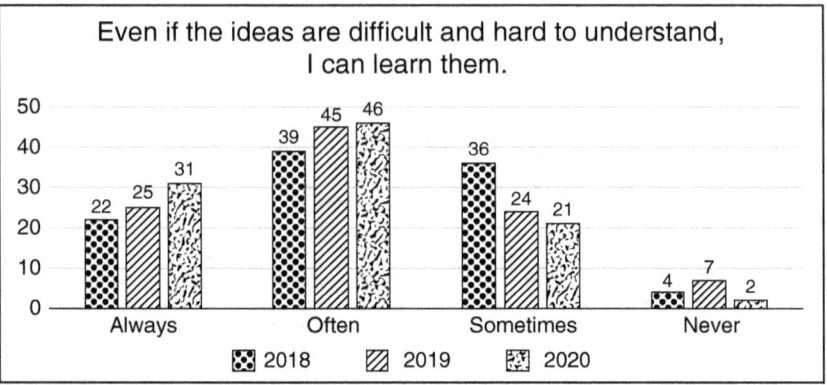

Figure 17.1 *(Continued)*

highest Australian Tertiary Admission Rank (ATAR) results in its history, with a third of its students achieving above 90 ATAR since 2018 as well as a 12% increase from 2020 to 2024 in the number of students who achieved above 70 ATAR. These data could be dismissed as non-rigorous as they did not emerge from an experimental research context. However, as Ritchhart and Church (2020, p. 16) observe, the data over time have shown how efforts to create a culture of thinking 'can in the right hands and pursued over time, greatly enhance students' performance - even in standardised tests.'

THE JOURNEY CONTINUES

One of Ritchhart's (2023) central claims which has been a guiding force for the school is that for classrooms to be cultures of thinking for students, schools must be cultures of thinking for teachers. As a result, we have prioritised Professional Learning Communities in the school as a platform for sharing and examining practice. Teaching seems to be the one profession where we often look to people outside of the profession for expertise. The old adage is everyone is an expert on schools as they have all attended one. As Horvath and Bott (2020, p. 20) argue, 'If we truly wish to advance the teaching profession, we must realign our collective focus to the expert practitioners of this field.' They go on to argue, 'the only experts in teaching are teachers themselves' (Horvath and Bott, p. 21).

Establishing a culture of thinking for teachers has enabled our teachers and leaders to take risks. As Ritchhart (2023, p. 7) argues, 'In a culture of thinking, innovation, creativity and experimentation are the norms…To build a classroom culture that encourages student risk taking, teachers need to demonstrate their own willingness to try new things.'

A culture of thinking has laid the groundwork for innovative approaches and practices at the school. In 2023, the College launched the Immanuel Discovery Centre, an innovative new building built within a garden precinct. We introduced a Year 10 program called 'The Year of Discovery.' This was a complete revamp of our current Year 10 curriculum and timetable structure, a change of which we are proud. This required risk and a letting go of older models. We were challenged by a question that David Perkins (2014) often asks, 'What's the learning that matters?' This was a key driver for change. With this question in mind and with student input, we developed over 40 new elective options. Whether it was 'How to Catch a Murderer,' a subject that fused chemistry with Legal Studies, or The Side Hustle, a subject that embraced students' entrepreneurial passions, these programs inspired our students. A program was developed that allowed teachers and students to take risks. When we look at the question of 'what's worth learning?' the question comes back to 'what thinking is happening?' The culture of thinking that prevails amongst staff has supported the innovative work that occurs in the school.

TIME FOR THINKING

Schools are complex places; in a secondary setting, students are there for a maximum of six years. Like any big organisation, we have staff who retire or leave, and staff who commence. However, a culture has been created where thinking is valued and actively promoted with staff and students. Recently, our professional learning has been centred around the Cultures of Thinking in Action mindsets and engaging staff with how these mindsets might play out in our school and context (Ritchhart, 2023).

For teachers who want to put thinking at the forefront, having time to do this is crucial as well as seeing this as part of the culture. As Louise Cottell, Middle Years Learning Leader, explains:

'The quickest strategy I would encourage others to try to develop their classroom thinking culture is to provide time to think. There is a great amount of pressure to be churning through the curriculum and completing all set tasks, but we need to stop and provide students with time to think in our classrooms. Using a timer on your phone so that you get used to the feel of what 10 seconds, 30 seconds, or a minute really feels like and then incorporating that into your classroom is a way of saying to students that you value thinking about answers as much as you value their answer.'

Mel Higgins, a Visual Art Teacher, uses time in this way:

'I have often started an art lesson with a demonstration without words. I'll purposely be very quiet. I'll have all my equipment ready to begin painting, and I'll begin. Slowly (sometimes it takes a while), the whole class becomes interested and quiet, watching me paint. I will paint something with no reference image and be indecisive at times and visibly deciding on colours to mix or where to go next, sometimes painting freely, sometimes more tentative and thoughtful. When I have painted for about 5–10 minutes, I stop and ask what students were thinking. Most think that this is what they are going to have to do, so they better take note of everything; some are thinking about how long this will go on, and some are thinking about what I'm trying to paint and how I'm thinking about it as I go.'

REMINDERS FOR THE JOURNEY

In June 2024, I was fortunate to travel with a group of nine students and two Immanuel teachers to Nyangatjatjara College, located just outside Yulara in the Northern Territory. This College provides primary and secondary education for students in the region who speak Pitjantjatjara as their first language. We stayed at the school for a week and our students spent time with the Indigenous students in attendance. The first morning, we picked up the students from the Mutitjulu community. They are the traditional owners of Uluru. A walk around Kata Tjuta awaited. It was a beautiful time together spent in a stunning and ancient backdrop. We took time to talk to the students and staff. Every night we debriefed with students and staff. One of the Nyangatjatjara teachers explained to our students the Pitjantjatjara concept of 'Ngapartji Ngapartji' meaning 'I give you something, you give me something.' It is a concept based on two-way learning (Wall, 2020). This insight guided the group thinking routines. Each night the conversations were rich. There was questioning, curiosity, listening and displays of respect. I was powerfully reminded of how enjoyable it is to participate in a culture of thinking when space and time is provided for this to occur. The 'Ngarpartji Ngarpartji' is a powerful concept reinforcing that thinking is as much a collective endeavour as an individual exercise.

Cultures of Thinking is simply an approach that has guided Immanuel to put thinking at the forefront of learning. However, Cultures of Thinking is not a program or series of lessons. It is not a 'how-to.' It is a way of recognising the different elements that make up our classrooms and how we can make purposeful decisions to promote thinking. We do this to better support young people to listen, be curious, understand different perspectives, reason with evidence, make connections and uncover complexity. I cannot think of a better way to prepare young people for a complex and changing world.

REFERENCES

Bott, D. and Horvath, J.C. (2020) *10 things schools get wrong (And how we can get them right)*. Woodridge: John Catt.

Crowther, F., Andrews, D., Morgan, A. and O'Neill, S. (2012) 'Hitting the bullseye of school improvement: the 'IDEAS' project at work in a successful school system', *Leading and Managing*, 18(2), pp. 1–33.

Harvard Project Zero. (2022) *Word – Phrase – Sentence, project zero's thinking routine toolbox.* [Online]. [Accessed 15 August 2024]. Available from: https://pz.harvard.edu/sites/default/files/Word-Phrase-Sentence.pdf

Perkins, D. (2014) *Future wise: educating our children for a changing world*. San Francisco: John Wiley & Sons.

Ritchhart, R. (2015) *Creating cultures of thinking: the 8 forces we must master to truly transform our classrooms*. San Francisco: Jossey-Bass.

Ritchhart, R. (2023) *Cultures of thinking in action: 10 mindsets to transform our teaching and students' learning*. New Jersey: Jossey-Bass.

Ritchhart, R. and Church, M. (2020) *The power of making thinking visible*. New York: Jossey Bass.

Ritchhart, R., Church, M. and Morrison, K. (2011) *Making thinking visible*. San Francisco: Jossey-Bass.

Safir, S. and Dugan, J. (2021) *Street Data: a next-generation model for equity, pedagogy, and school transformation*. San Francisco: Corwin.

Wall, M. (2020) *Lutheran Church of Australia, Ngapartji-Ngapartji – Reconciliation action plan*. [Online]. [Accessed 1 September 2024]. Available from: https://www.rap.lca.org.au/2020/11/09/engaging-in-some-cultural-awareness/

Conclusion: The Best Teachers Are Subversive
Cameron Paterson and Simon Brooks

WHAT?

We used to think that teaching was primarily about imparting knowledge and guiding students through prescribed content, with the teacher as the central authority in the classroom.

Now we think that true learning emerges when students are empowered to take ownership of their learning, actively engaging in thinking, questioning, and exploring ideas. By involving students as co-creators of their educational journey, educators can cultivate curiosity, creativity, and a sense of agency.

We used to think that educational leadership was about maintaining order, implementing solutions to problems, and ensuring compliance to established policies and practices.

Now we think that authentic educational leadership is about fostering deep shifts in teachers' beliefs, values, and mindsets. This requires leadership that builds trusting relationships, encourages vulnerability, and nurtures a culture of intellectual dialogue and exchange. True progress emerges from the collective efforts of educators and learners, rather than relying on top-down mandates.

SO WHAT?

We stand on the shoulders of giants, with much of what we deem innovative in education reform often rooted in timeless ideas. From Plato's ancient belief in a hierarchy of Bronze, Silver, and Gold people (2000) to Rousseau's progressive declaration, "Man is born free, and everywhere he is in chains" (2000), educational thought has long oscillated between tradition and change. Each generation feels their moment is unique, yet today's challenges – artificial intelligence, genetic advances, the climate crisis, and the rise of Asia – propel us into an era where change seems undeniably exponential. The certainty of the Scientific Revolution is cracking, leaving us straddling two worlds: one tethered to the past, the other to an emerging reality.

DOI: 10.4324/9781003541745-24

As Hogarth, Wilkey, and Doolah remind us in their chapter, "Curriculum didn't arrive on a boat, pedagogy didn't arrive on a boat; it was always here" (Rigney, 2015). Indigenous peoples have educated their communities for generations, equipping them with the knowledge, beliefs, and practices to thrive in complex, dynamic environments. In an era of uncertainty, Indigenous cultures offer vital insights – reconnection, resilience, and wellbeing – that may guide us through today's challenges.

History shows that revolutions, while often disruptive, are the catalyst for deep, transformative change. The abolition of slavery, civil rights movements, and women's suffrage have all reshaped society, though none without struggle. Revolutions demand a shift in mindsets, values, and beliefs – a slow and often resisted transformation of hearts and minds.

In education, we encounter similar resistance. People cling to deeply held convictions about what school should look like. Progressive approaches are often met with scepticism, and even small changes can trigger resistance from students, parents, and educators alike. Unlearning entrenched habits is painstaking work, demanding sustained effort.

Leading cultural change in schools requires patience, trust, and an understanding of context and history (Paterson, 2019). It begins with small steps, empowering teacher leaders, fostering professional learning, and cultivating collaboration. Success hinges on a genuine desire to listen, learn, and make people feel seen and heard. Valuing relationships, trusting colleagues, and ensuring an inclusive approach to change are essential.

Leadership plays a pivotal role, modelling an invitational approach to change. An invitation can be transformative: inviting colleagues into your classroom to observe and give feedback fosters a culture of vulnerability and growth. This simple act sows the seeds of meaningful change.

As the authors in this book remind us, adopting these approaches won't be easy. It can feel isolating to champion innovation in a culture steeped in conformity. Yet even without strong leadership, each of us holds the power to influence change within our sphere, through subtle shifts in our practice and by gently nudging our colleagues towards new possibilities.

Schools do not evolve unless educators challenge and question each other. Growth comes through friction and vulnerability. As Paolo Freire (2003) asserts, if the structure does not permit dialogue, it must be changed. The Italian notion of "confronto" beautifully encapsulates this spirit – engaging in passionate, even heated, intellectual exchange, yet leaving the conversation as allies, bound by shared commitment. More of this open, positive dialogue is what educators need today to foster a more resilient, connected future.

NOW WHAT?

In *Creating Cultures of Thinking*, Ron Ritchhart poses a thought-provoking question: "What do you want the children you teach to be like as adults?" (Ritchhart, 2015). It is a question which aims to shift the dial from 'how do I cover the content?' to 'what sort of people are we trying to produce?' Neil Postman (1994, p. xi) captured this sentiment powerfully writing, "Children are the living messages we send to a time we will not see". If children represent our messages to the future, we must ask ourselves: what message do we wish to send? Unfortunately, many schools still operate on a 19th century bureaucratic model, a compliance-oriented structure designed more around control than learning. Obedience and submission take precedence over thinking and creativity.

The best indicator of student learning is the task they undertake, since task predicts performance (City et al., 2009). Yet, in many schools, the task students most frequently undertake is listening to a teacher talk. There's a disconnection: what young people experience in school is increasingly out of sync with the rest of their lives. Students often pretend to listen, while teachers mistake busyness for engagement and activity for learning (Ashenden, 2024). This one-size-fits-all approach only deepens student scepticism about the relevance of schooling. As Ron Ritchhart argues, 'to create a new story of learning, we must change the role of the student and the teacher' (2023, p. 51). This book amplifies the voices of teachers and educators who are doing just this: shifting the emphasis in their schools and classrooms from teacher-centred instruction to student-centred learning, moving from control to curiosity, coverage to connection, and compliance to creativity.

As educators committed to student-centred learning, we must be wary of agendas and initiatives that risk reinforcing the traditional story of learning we aim to disrupt. In 2024, the New South Wales (NSW) Department of Education announced a deepened focus on explicit teaching, echoing similar moves in Queensland and Victoria to implement explicit instruction in reading (Hunter and Carter, 2024). There is no doubt that this vision for education is well intended, grounded in a comprehensive review of evidence-based practice, and supported by a number of publications from NSW's Centre for Education Statistics and Evaluation (CESE) and the Australian Education Research Organisation (AERO).

That said, there is a growing concern among educators about the narrow interpretation of 'evidence-based practices'. Rigid, one-size-fits-all methods, often validated solely by causal research designs like randomised controlled trials, overlook the dynamic complexities of classrooms (Brunker, 2024). Such approaches risk constraining teacher autonomy and fail to capture the nuanced, adaptive strategies that are crucial for fostering deep and lasting learning. Teaching and learning are inherently complex, and there is no single approach that works in every lesson for every school type, year level, or subject area (Brown, 2024).

If in doubt, it is vital to lean into our values and beliefs. Questions like these may help:

- Does the proposed initiative position students as empty vessels or active meaning-makers?
- Does it position teachers as information deliverers or facilitators of learning?

Such questions serve as gatekeepers to a Culture of Thinking. Ultimately, we believe that whatever we teach and however we teach it, our pedagogical choices should be guided by the principle that 'learning is a consequence of thinking' (Ritchhart, 2023).

Complex challenges require emergent practices: experimenting, prototyping, learning from mistakes, and embracing creative thinking. Dan Pink (2005) captures this shift through a vivid metaphor of human development: five figures walk in succession, representing different eras – an ape, followed by a farmer symbolising the agricultural age, an industrial worker, a knowledge worker, and finally, an artist representing today's creative age. Pink argues that we've moved from a society of farmers, to factory workers, to knowledge workers, and now, to a society of creators, empathisers, pattern recognisers, and meaning makers. In this age of information abundance, the future belongs to those who can connect the dots, recognise patterns, and weave meaning where others see none. Intelligence, in this sense, might be less about what we know and more about what we *notice*.

Cultivating Cultures of Thinking in Australian Schools shows that high levels of creativity can and do flourish in Australian classrooms. Our authors are innovative, often subversive, and creatively disrupt established norms. We offer real-world stories of teachers navigating challenges, reflecting on pivotal moments, and contextualising ideas like thinking routines and cultural forces. These narratives demonstrate how educators adapt frameworks to their unique contexts, providing practical social proof for readers to learn from and be inspired by.

This collection of essays is a heartfelt thank you to all the dedicated teachers who inspire curiosity, spark light bulb moments, and create spaces where students feel seen and valued. Teaching transcends technique. It is a profound expression of identity and integrity. Our purpose as educators goes beyond preparing students for the next test or grade-level; we're nurturing thinkers and equipping them for life.

REFERENCES

Ashenden, D. (2024) *Unbeaching the whale: Can Australia's schooling be reformed?* Melbourne: Inside Story.

Brown, J. (2024) Explicit teaching mandate – A pushback now is critical. *EduResearch Matters*. [Accessed 29 November 2024]. Available from: https://blog.aare.edu.au/explicit-teaching-mandate-a-pushback-now-is-critical/#:~:text=A%20pushback%20is%20critical%20%E2%80%93%20explicit,and%20specific%20focus%20in%20question

Brunker, N. (2024) Escape oppression now: Disrupt the dominance of evidence-based practice. *EduResearch Matters*. [Accessed 14 November 2024]. Available from: https://blog.aare.edu.au/escape-oppression-now-disrupt-the-dominance-of-evidence-based-practice/

City, E.A., Elmore, R.F., Fiarman, S.E. and Teitel, L. (2009) *Instructional rounds in education: A network approach to improving teaching and learning.* Cambridge: Harvard University Press.

Freire, P. (2003) *Pedagogy of the oppressed.* New York: The Continuum International Publishing Group.

Hunter, J.L. and Carter, D. (2024) Is there a 'right way' to teach? Recent debates suggest yes, but students and schools are much more complex. *The Conversation*. [Accessed 15 October 2024]. Available from: https://theconversation.com/is-there-a-right-way-to-teach-recent-debates-suggest-yes-but-students-and-schools-are-much-more-complex-235421

New South Wales Department of Education. (2024) *About explicit teaching.* [Accessed 13 November 2024]. Available from: https://education.nsw.gov.au/teaching-and-learning/curriculum/explicit-teaching/about-explicit-teaching

Paterson, C. (2019) *Churchill fellowship report.* NSW: Winston Churchill Trust. [Accessed 13 October 2024]. Available from: https://www.churchilltrust.com.au/fellow/cameron-paterson-nsw-2019/

Pink, D. (2005) *A whole new mind: Moving from the information age to the conceptual age.* New York: Penguin.

Plato. (2000) *The republic* ed. Translated by T. Griffith. Cambridge: Cambridge University Press.

Postman, N. (1994) *The disappearance of childhood*. New York: Vintage.

Rigney, L. (2015) *Learning to live with Aboriginal Australians*. Paper presented at the Learning to live together in culturally diverse societies conferences, University of South Australia.

Ritchhart, R. (2015) *Creating cultures of thinking: The 8 forces we must master to truly transform our schools*. San Francisco: Jossey-Bass.

Ritchhart, R. (2023) *Cultures of thinking in action: 10 mindsets to transform our teaching and students' learning*. New Jersey: Jossey-Bass.

Rousseau, J.-J. (2000) *The social contract*. Translated by G.D.H. Cole. Ware: Wordsworth Editions.

Index

Note: *Italicized* page references refer to figures and **bold** references refer to tables.

Aboriginal and Torres Strait Islander Curricula Project 62–63
Aboriginal and Torres Strait Islander Peoples 59–67
activations 147–149
active listening 16, 71, 114
activist professionalism 131
adult learner 145; about 146–157; for professional learning 145–146
adult learning 145–157; principle of 147; principles 146
affinity groups 152
'aha' moments 220–222
Alice Springs (Mparntwe) Education Declaration (Education Council) 59
ambiguity 26, 29, 171, 173
Artificial Intelligence (AI) 111, 177, 200
art of questioning 19–20
"Austin's Butterfly" (EL Education) 20
Australian Council for Educational Leaders 8
Australian Council for Educational Research (ACER) 60, 97
Australian Curriculum, Assessment and Reporting Authority 91
Australian Education Research Organisation (AERO) 232
Australian Professional Standards for Teachers 61
Australian Tertiary Admission Rank (ATAR) 18, 224

Barnes, M. 106
Barnhardt, R. 65–66
Berlyne, Daniel 26, 29
Biggs, John 75
Blum, Susan 8
Blythe, Tina 4
Boaler, Jo 105
Boles, K. 174
Bott, D. 225
Brisbane Girls Grammar School (BGGS) 204–214
Brooks, Simon 112, 118, 208
Bruner, Jerome 15, 89

Centre for Education Statistics and Evaluation (CESE) 176, 232
Centre for Leadership and Educational Equity (CLEE) 176
ChatGPT 170
Church, Mark 4, 113, 132, 136
classroom questioning 19–20
Claxton, G. 108
Cochran-Smith, Marilyn 125, 132
collaboration 90; as complex competency 97; concepts of 171; continuum 90; quality of 171
collaborative learning 88–98; challenges 97–98; and cooperative learning 90; forms of 89–90; learning to step back 88–89; pictures of practice 91–94
competition between schools 45
complexity 2, 7, 26, 29, 59, 66, 83, 106, 117, 131, 184, 186, 193, 198, 200, 227
conceptual questions 107

conceptual understanding 106–107
confusion and conflict 16–17
Connell, Raewyn 128
contact 90
content vs. thinking 184–186
contradiction 29
convergence 90
cooperation 90
cooperative learning 90
coordination 90
Corrigan, Tracey 221
Cottell, Louise 220, 226
COVID-19 pandemic 43–46, 55, 93
Creating Cultures of Thinking (Ritchhart) 74, 104, 126, 199, 206, 219, 231
'Creating Cultures of Thinking' Project 222
cross-fertilisation of ideas 204
Crowther, Frank 205–206
Culturally responsive teaching: Theory, research and practice (Gay) 58
culture of learning: benefits of cultivating 75; intentional learning within 147; over work 76, 83–84, 85
culture of thinking 3, 137–138
culture of trust 112–114
cultures of inquiry within schools/school systems 130
cultures of teaching 47
Cultures of Thinking (CoT) 1, 89, 104, 159–163; in Australian schools 131–133; challenges 1; coaching 212–213; as long-term investment 187–188; pedagogy and practice 4–5; relationship to learning and outcomes 183; training mentality 186–188; in troubled times 125–133
Cultures of Thinking in Action (Ritchhart) 108, 115, 125, 209
curiosity 24–38, 114–116; asking questions 27; authentic inquiry 27; become curator of 27–29; characteristics of 29; close looking and wondering 26–27, 29–31; communal leaning in 31;
defined 26–27; educators role 27; fostering 22; key practices for 27–37; learning opportunities around prediction/reflection 31–32; limit excessive explanation 33–34; overview 24–26; time and space for 34–37

daily structure in primary schools 52
Darling Hammond, Linda 162
Day, C. 129
deep learning 32–33, 65, 131, 188, 190, 204–205, 207, 212, 222
democratic professionalism 131
democratic teacher professionalism 129, **130**
Dewey 15
discretionary space 133
Doolah, John 230
Downes, Karen 81–82
Duckworth, E. 16

education quality in policy discourse 60–62
education renaissance: brief history of school 195–197; learning 193–194; modern tools for 192–202; as opportunity to develop collective humanity 199–202; people as product 194–195
Emilia, Reggio 95
empowering learners 9–10, 20–21
Engel, Susan 26, 38
English as an Additional Language (EAL) 221–222
English Woman's Journal 54
Erickson, H.L. 115
Erway, R. 90
evidence-based practices 132, 232
'evidence-based' Science of Learning 22
explicit, direct instruction (EDI) 192

Farrell, Janet 216, 217
Finkel, Alan 8
Finland 49–54, 60
Finnish model 52, 52

Fisher, D. 101
Foucault, M. 15
free school meals 53–54
Freire, Paolo 15, 230
French, R. 115
Frey, N. 101
Fullan, Michael 127

Gallipoli campaign 19
Gardner, Howard 205
Garmston, R.J. 150
Gay, Geneva 58
Gill, Ryan 208
Global Educational Reform Movement (GERM) 45–46, 130
global learning crises 44–46
global mindedness 149–150
Global School Meals Coalition 53
good education 45, 59–61, 62–64, 126–128
grammar of schooling 45
Gray, Peter 53
Grej of the Day (GOTD) 34–37
GROW Model 212

Hamlet (Shakespeare) 1–2
Harvard Graduate School of Education (HGSE) 208
Hattie, J. 75, 119
healthy risk-taking 112–114
Heil, Elise 22
Hermansson, Micael 34, 36
Higgins, Mel 221, 226
high-impact learning 26
Hogarth, Melitta 230
The Holocaust 113
homeschooling 18
Horvath, J.C. 225
Hughes, M. 38

I Do, We Do, You Do approach (IWY) 101–109
Immanuel College 216–227; educational journey 216; Novar Gardens campus 217

incongruity 26, 29
Indigenous educators 63
Indigenous knowledges 58–67; education quality in policy discourse 60–62; inquisitive mind 66–67; overview 58–59; paradigmatic shift 64–66; quality 59–64
Industrial Revolution 17
innovation 156–157
Innovative Designs for Enhanced Achievement in Schools (IDEAS) project 218
institutional mirroring 137
International Conference on Thinking in Melbourne 181
'In the Club, Out the Club' 107

Jenkins, Lyle 77
jigsaw groups 151
Jones, John 111

Keller, Helen 98
Kinross, Belinda 34–38
Kirkness, V.J. 65–66

Ladder of Feedback 118–119
Langton, Marcia 61
Lanning, L. A. 115
Lavié, J. M. 171
leadership 1, 9, 21, 139, 145, 147, 186, 189, 206, 230; courageous 133; teaching and education 4
Learners Think First (LTF) 102–103
learning 111; education renaissance 193–194; intention 104–105; *see also* adult learning; culture of learning; professional learning
Learning Management System 220
learning over work 74
lesson lottery 127
Levy, Josh 28–29
Li, Guofang 58
Liljedahl, P. 106
Lipman, M. 33
Little, J. W. 174

Living Historians Program 141–142, 142
Loewenstein, George 26, 28, 33–34
looping *see* teacher looping
Lotan, R. 95
Lytle, S. L. 125, 132

Main, K. 90–91, 95
Making Thinking Visible (Ritchhart, Church and Morrison) 105, 173–174
Malaguzzi 15
managerial teacher professionalism 129, **130**
Mardell, B. 82–83
marketisation of education 128
Masada College 136–143; celebration and reflection 140; culture of thinking 137–138, 141–142; empowering teachers 139–140; established models of professional learning 142–143; evolving the process 140–141; foundations of learning at 136–137; Living Historians Program 141–142, 142; navigating concerns 139–140; puzzle of practice 138; safe/supportive/thoughtful environment 136; study groups and facilitating learning 138–139; vision for future 143
Maslow, A.H. 198
Masters, G.N. 60
McTighe, J. 79, 125
meetings 170–177; clarification of norms 173–174; issues 171; methods of collaboration 175–176; purpose of collaboration 172–173; way to collaborate 174–175
Merkel, Angela 81
Merrow, John 55
messy humanity 128
mixed messages 188–190
Montessori 15
Multiplicity Lab 30
Murdoch, Kath 107, 109
mystery 29

National Aboriginal and Torres Strait Islander Curricula Project 61
National Assessment Program – Literacy and Numeracy (NAPLAN) 64–66, 192, 200, 201
National Center on Education and the Economy (NCEE) 60
Newmann, Fred 206
New Metrics Program 97
Nineteen Eighty-Four (Orwell) 28
normalising inquiry 156–157
Norms of Collaboration 150–151
Nottingham, James 105
novelty 29

open-ended problem 105–106
Organisation for Economic Co-operation and Development (OECD) 44, 48, 48–49
Orwell, George 28
Othello (Shakespeare) 80

Palmer, Parker 207
Paris Olympics 35
Parkin, Thomas 221–222
Parts, Purposes, and Complexities (PPC) 116
patterns of behaviour 5–6
patterns of interaction 5–6
patterns of thinking 5
Perkins, David 4, 103, 217, 225
Piaget 15
ping-pong style of questioning 19
Pink, Dan 232
Plato 229
play time 51–53
policy discourse: education quality in 60–62
positive school cultures 172
Post-it® 149
Postman, Neil 231
Predict Observe Explain (POE) 32
prioritisation of basic literacy and numeracy 45–46
professional autonomy 130

professionalism 125–133; framing teacher 126–129; purpose 129–131; roles of teachers **125**
professional learning 142–143; adults thrive in 146; purpose and crafting 154
Professional Learning Communities (PLCs) 159–168; action research 163–165; effective 168; effectiveness of 162–163; overview 159; peer observation 165–166; principles of cultures of thinking 159–161; reflective practices and instructional enhancement 165–166; supporting teachers 161–162; teacher reflection on 166–167
professional learning culture 136
Programme for International Student Assessment (PISA) 45, 61
Progressive Achievement Tests (PAT) 200
Project Zero 1, 3–4, 6–7, 9, 112, 136, 145, 208
protocols 139
Public Broadcasting Service (PBS) 54
punitive test-based accountability 46

Queensland Curriculum and Assessment Authority (QCAA) 207
Question Sorts thinking routine 138

Ravitch, Diane 126
Realm of Concern/Realm of Influence protocol 139
Richardson, Kevin 217
Rigney, Lester 58, 63, 66
risk-taking 137, 156–157
Ritchhart, R. 1, 4–7, 19, 74, 91, 103, 106, 108, 112, 113, 115, 125, 131, 136, 141, 145, 146–147, 156, 159, 162, 171–172, 175, 183, 199, 202, 205–206, 209, 216–217, 219, 224–225, 231

Sachs, J. 129–130, 131
Sadler, David 32

Sahlberg, P. 129
Sarason, Seymour 19
Savedge, Clare 111
schooling 5, 44–46, 49, 59, 61–62, 64–65, 76, 79, 89, 97, 123, 127–128, 130, 133, 192–193, 201
schoolishness 8
Schoolishness (Blum) 8
school-wide pedagogy 205–208
self-directed learning culture 111–120; in action 116–118; disposition of curiosity 114–116; feedback, goals, repeat 118–120; healthy risk-taking 112–114; trust 112–114
Shakespeare 1–2, 80
Shalaby, Carla 18
Sinek, Simon 80, 102, 172
Sizer, Ted 125
Skrzynecki, Peter 75, 82
Snapshot Observation Protocol 140
Socrates 15
soft skill 91
'split screen' guiding questions 108
standardisation of teaching and learning in schools 45
Start with Why (Sinek) 172
student-teacher relationships 49–51
success skills 91
supportive learning culture 137
Systematic Synthetic Phonics (SSP) 192

teacher-centred instruction 15, 193, 231
Teacher Learning Communities (TLCs) 159
teacher looping 50–51, 51
teaching 15–17, 19–20, 22
thinking 216–227; 'aha' moment 220–222; context 216–219; impact 222–224; overview 216; serendipity 219–220; time for 225–226
Thornburg, D. 96
thoughtful questioning 16
Timperley, H. 163
Tishman, Shari 4
Tizard, B. 38

training mentality 186–188
transformational learning 123, 131, 156
transforming culture and sustaining change 181–191
Troen, V. 174
Troublemakers (Shalaby) 18
Trump, Donald 81
trust culture 112–114
Tuning Protocol 139, 162, 168, 175–177
Twenge, Jean 45

Understanding Map 3, 185, 221
United Nations Educational, Scientific and Cultural Organization (UNESCO) 44–45
unlearning control 15–22; art of questioning 19–20; confusion and conflict 16–17; empowering learners 20–21; fostering cultures of thinking 22; relational connections 17–18; thinking 15–16

Vertovec, S. 58
Victorian Certificate of Education (VCE) 160, 165, 167
Vietnam War 78–79
Vygotsky, Lev 6, 15, 89

Waibel, G. 90
Warsaw Ghetto 117
Webster, Steven 78–79
wellbeing 26, 41, 76, 85, 198, 230
Wellman, B.M. 150
White monocultural teaching workforce 58
Wiggins, G. 79, 125
Wiliam, Dylan 132, 159, 162, 168
Wilkey, Justin 230
Wilson, Daniel 4
Wilson, Harriet 154
Wong, Patricia 154
work: benefits 75–77; emphasis on learning over 77–78; learning over 74; overview 73–74; playful learning mode 81–83; purpose 78–80; reflection 83–85
working agreement 151
World Bank (WB) 44
world-class education system 59–60
world-class learning system 60
World Health Organisation 43
wrong ideas 17

Zhao, Yong 8
Zorich, D. 90

For Product Safety Concerns and Information please contact our EU representative GPSR@taylorandfrancis.com
Taylor & Francis Verlag GmbH, Kaufingerstraße 24, 80331 München, Germany